NO FUTURE
— IN —
THIS COUNTRY

Davis W. Houck, General Editor

No Future in This Country

THE PROPHETIC PESSIMISM OF BISHOP HENRY McNEAL TURNER

ANDRE E. JOHNSON

University Press of Mississippi / Jackson

The University Press of Mississippi is the scholarly publishing agency of
the Mississippi Institutions of Higher Learning: Alcorn State University,
Delta State University, Jackson State University, Mississippi State University,
Mississippi University for Women, Mississippi Valley State University,
University of Mississippi, and University of Southern Mississippi.

www.upress.state.ms.us

The University Press of Mississippi is a member
of the Association of University Presses.

Copyright © 2020 by University Press of Mississippi
All rights reserved
Manufactured in the United States of America

First printing 2020
∞

Library of Congress Control Number available
ISBN 9781496830708 (hardback)
ISBN 9781496830692 (trade paperback)
ISBN 9781496830654 (epub institutional)
ISBN 9781496830661 (epub single)
ISBN 9781496830678 (pdf institutional)
ISBN 9781496830685 (pdf single)

British Library Cataloging-in-Publication Data available

CONTENTS

ACKNOWLEDGMENTS vii

INTRODUCTION
The Prophetic Pessimism of Bishop Henry McNeal Turner 3

1 "AN ABOMINABLE CONCLAVE OF NEGRO HATING DEMONS"
Turner and the *Plessy* Decision. 23

2 "NEGROES SHOULD WORSHIP A GOD WHO IS A NEGRO"
The Making of a Black Rhetorical Theologian 45

3 "AN UNHOLY WAR OF CONQUEST"
Turner and the Creation of an Antiwar Protester 67

4 "MCKINLEY, THE GOD OF FOOL NEGROES"
Turner and the Presidential Election of 1900. 87

5 "THE SALVATION OF THE NEGRO"
Turner and the Rhetoric of Emigration 115

6 "HELL IS AN IMPROVEMENT SO FAR AS THE NEGRO IS CONCERNED"
Turner and the Damning of America. 149

CONCLUSION
Reclaiming the Pessimistic Prophecy of Bishop
Henry McNeal Turner. 171

NOTES..177

INDEX..199

ACKNOWLEDGMENTS

When you finally finish writing a book, you realized just how many were a part of your journey. I first want to thank Amanda Nell Edgar, Craig Stewart, Christi Moss, and members of the #WriteOn writing group for their support, feedback, and encouragement. On days when I did not feel like writing anything at all, the writing group held me accountable and helped me find the energy to write. I would also like to thank the good people at R. P. Tracks, the place where we convene our writing group. I particularly want to thank the servers, and the many cups of coffee, other libations, and lunches they serve. They became accustomed to seeing us on Friday afternoons, and they made sure that the place was inviting and conducive to writing.

Second, I would like to thank writing group member Le'trice D. Donaldson for not only her support and encouragement but also her knowledge and scholarship of African American military history. As fate would have it, while I was working on *No Future* in our writing group, she was next to me writing about African American military members from 1870 to 1920. The conversations we had and her insights about military history and citizenship helped shape my understanding of both Turner's rhetoric and those who disagreed with him. In short, Chapter 3 of this book is much better because of her presence in our writing group.

Third, I am appreciative of the institutional support I have as well. I would like to thank the faculty, staff, and students in the Department of Communication and Film at the University of Memphis, and the faculty, staff, and students at Memphis Theological Seminary. Both institutions were supportive of this project. I also would like to thank the organizers and reviewers of the National Communication Association—especially the African American Communication and Culture and Public Address Divisions. They both continued to allow me space to present work on Turner and offered critiques that helped sharpen my arguments. I also include in my thanks the National Council of Black Studies, the Association of the Study of African American Life and History, and other conferences that allowed me to present work on Turner.

Fourth, I would like to thank the University Press of Mississippi for believing in this project. I especially appreciate Vijay Shah and Emily Bandy, who both served as editors on this project. I must also thank my copy editor Lisa Williams for her exceptional work on this project, and Lisa Corrigan, who first introduced me to the press.

Finally, I would like to thank my Gifts of Life Ministries family for allowing me to travel, write, and still serve as pastor. I am truly a blessed man of God to serve at G'Life. And, I would like to thank my wife, Lisa, who has now put up with Turner and me for over fifteen years and still can tell as many Henry McNeal Turner stories as I can.

NO FUTURE
— IN —
THIS COUNTRY

INTRODUCTION

The Prophetic Pessimism of Bishop Henry McNeal Turner

In 1902 author and lecturer D. W. Culp published *Twentieth Century Negro Literature: Or a Cyclopedia of Thought on the Vital Topics Relating to the American Negro*. Culp collected essays from one hundred African Americans addressing different topics pertinent to African Americans at the turn of the twentieth century. These women and men were leading Black intellectuals of their day. According to Culp, the purpose of the book was fivefold:

> (1) To enlighten the uninformed white people on the intellectual ability of the Negro. (2) To give to those, who are interested in the Negro race, a better idea of the extent to which he contributed to the promotion of America's civilization, and of the intellectual attainments made by him in the nineteenth century. (3) To reflect the views of the most scholarly and prominent Negroes of America on those topics, touching the Negro, that are now engaging the attention of the civilized world. (4) To point out, to the aspiring Negro youth, those men and women of their own race who, by their scholarship, by their integrity of character, and by their earnest efforts in the work of uplifting their own race, have made themselves illustrious; also, to enlighten such youth on those ethical, political, and sociological questions, touching the Negro that will sooner or later engage their attention. (5) To enlighten the Negroes on that perplexing problem, commonly called the "Race Problem" that has necessarily grown out of their contact with their ex-masters and their descendants; and also to stimulate them to make greater efforts to ascend to that plane of civilization occupied by the other enlightened peoples of the world.[1]

The book was noteworthy because, according to Culp, this was the only book that had brought together such "an array of Negro talent" writing on the multiplicity of subjects contained therein. Also, the book also offered a corrective in the interpretation and presentation of African Americans since Emancipation. Many authors used their essays as refutations of the prevailing thought and ideology of African Americans during the later nineteenth and early twentieth centuries.

Among the intellectuals Culp invited to submit an essay was Bishop Henry McNeal Turner. Culp asked him and three other prominent African Americans to address the question "Will it be possible for the Negro to attain, in this country, unto the American type of civilization?" The three other invited essayists took on more conservative to moderate tones in answering the question. Professor R. S. Lovinggood, a professor of Greek and Latin at Wiley University in Marshall, Texas, for example, suggested that it would be possible for African Americans to succeed in America and thus attain the American type of civilization. One of the reasons for this hope was Lovinggood's belief that African Americans had that "docility, that perseverance, that endurance, long-suffering patience, and that kindness which rob(s) the pangs of the hatred of the white man of much of their deadly poison." He further believed that African Americans thrived on persecution and despite what whites would do to them, Blacks would "never lose faith." "Individuals," he suggested, may lose hope, but the race will "never lose" hope.[2]

Bishop J. W. Hood of the African Methodist Episcopal Church Zion (AMEZ) offered an elaborate refutation of the belief that Africans did not contribute anything to civilization. After examining the biblical record and that of ancient Egypt, Bishop Hood summed up his answer:

> If the descendants of the accursed son of Ham could establish and maintain for five hundred years a republic which was never disturbed by sedition nor tyranny, and enjoyed a civilization in some respects better than the boasted American civilization, there is no reason why any other branch of Ham's family may not attain to the highest and best civilization.[3]

Bishop L. H. Holsey, of the Colored (now Christian) Methodist Episcopal Church (CME), took a more critical approach to the question. He started his essay by acknowledging it would be hard for African Americans to attain the American type of civilization because of the oppression faced by African Americans by the nation. "In this country," he noted, "the negro is despised and rejected, simply because he has black skin and social traits that distinguish him from other races. We cannot see, neither do we believe, that it is possible for the Negro to attain unto the American type of civilization, while he lives in the same territory and in immediate contact with the white people."[4] He closed his essay by suggesting that "no one seems to take on and absorb the American civilization more readily than the American Negro." Further, he argued that if African Americans had some of the "same advantages and was allowed to enjoy the same full and free citizenship along with his white neighbor, his advancement in civilization would be as rapid as that of the white man." "Give the Negro the white man's chance," Holsey demanded, and African Americans will "keep pace with the white man in his march toward civilization."

However, Bishop Henry McNeal Turner, senior bishop of the African Methodist Episcopal Church (AME) interrogated the merits of the question. For Turner, the question presumed America was a civilized nation at all. Moreover, if the presumption was valid, the question also assumed that African Americans had not yet attained American civilization. Therefore, in addressing the question, Turner first defined civilization. For him civilization "contemplates that fraternity, civil and political equality between man and man, that makes his rights, privileges and immunities inviolable and sacred in the eyes and hearts of his fellows, whatever may be his nationality, language, color, hair texture, or anything else that may make an external variation." He continued by noting,

> Civility comprehends harmony, system, method, complacency, urbanity, refinement, politeness, courtesy, justice, culture, general enlightenment and protection of life and person to any man, regardless of his color or nationality. It is enough for a civilized community to know that you are a human being, to pledge surety of physical and political safety to you, and this has been the sequence in all ages among civilized people. But such is not the condition of things as they apply to this country, I mean the United States.[5]

While acknowledging that the United States had "almost every form of government, necessary to regulate the affairs of a civilized country," he lamented that "we are often confronted through the public press with reports of the most barbarous and cruel outrages, that can be perpetrated upon human beings, known in the history of the world. Further, Turner wrote that "no savage nation can exceed the atrocities which are often heralded through the country and accepted by many as an incidental consequence. Men, he continued, "are hung, shot and burnt by bands of murderers who are almost invariably represented as the most influential and respectable citizens in the community, while the evidences of guilt of what is charged against the victims, who are so inhumanly outraged, are never established by proof in any court, and all we can learn about the guilt and horrible deeds charged upon the murdered victims comes from the mouth of the bloody-handed wretches who perpetrate the murders, yet they are not known according to published accounts."[6]

For Turner, "judges surrounded with court officers are powerless before these bloody mobs," and sheriffs are as "helpless as newborn babes." While admitting that some of the victims of lynching may have been guilty of some "blood-curdling crime," Turner placed the presumed guilt of the victims within the context of civilization.

> Civilization presurmises legal adjudication and the intervention of that judicial authority which civilized legislation produces. And when properly administered the accused is innocent till he gets a fair trial; no verdict of guilt from a drunken lawless mob should be accepted by a civilized country; and when they do accept it they become a barbarous people. And a barbarous people make a barbarous nation. Civilization knows no marauders, mobs or lynchers[,] and anyone adjudged guilty by a drunken band of freebooters is not guilty in the eyes of a civilized people. For the ruthless and violent perpetrators of lawless deeds, especially when they are incarnate, are murderers to all intents and purposes, and popular approval does not diminish the magnitude of the crime. Millions may say, "Well done," but God, reason, and civilization stamp them as culprits.[7]

Turner "confessed" that the United States had the "highest form of civilized institutions" of any country, and enough Bibles "to build a pyramid that would almost reach to heaven." However, while the United States had according to Turner, "all the forms and paraphernalia of civilization," he argued that "no one can say, who has any respect for truth, that the United States is a civilized nation, especially if we will take the daily papers and inspect them for a few moments, and see the deeds of horror that the ruling powers of the nation say 'well done.'"[8] While admitting that many would not and have not participated in these "violent and gory outrages" on people of African descent, he reminded his audience that physically not participating "is no virtue that calls for admiration."[9] For Turner, silence was betrayal.

> As long as they keep silent and fail to lift up their voices in protestation and declaim against it, their very silence is a world-wide acquiescence. It is practically saying, well done. There are millions of people in the country who could not stand to kill a brute, such is their nervous sensitiveness, and I have heard of

persons who would not kill a snake or a bug. But they are guilty of everything the drunken mobs do, as long as they hold their silence. Men may be ever so free from the perpetration of bloody deeds, personally, but their failure to object to any outrageous crime makes them particeps criminis.[10]

Near the close of the essay, Turner reminded his audience of the "robbery on public highways" that allows public transportation companies to place African Americans in "Jim Crow cars" and charge them the same amount as those in "rolling palaces with every comfort that it is possible for man to enjoy." "This is simple robbery on the public highways," he argued, and the "nine United States judges have approved of this robbery and said, "well done," by their verdict."[11]

Then Turner turned back to the question of the essay. "Such being the barbarous condition of the United States," he surmised, "and the low order of civilization which controls its institutions where right and justice should sit enthroned, I see nothing for the Negro to attain unto in this country."

Further he wrote that he did not see anything for African Americans to aspire after. He could return to Africa, he lamented, "especially to Liberia where a Negro government is already in existence, and learn the elements of civilization in fact; for human life is there sacred, and no man is deprived of it or any other thing that involves his manhood, without due process of law. So, my decision is that there is nothing in the United States for the Negro to learn or try to attain to."[12]

Turner's belief that African Americans had nothing to learn or try to attain in America had not always been a part of his thinking or rhetoric. Born "free" in Newberry Courthouse, South Carolina, on February 1, 1834, Turner was an autodidact who always aspired to be more. Early in his life, he had a dream in which he saw himself speaking to thousands of people and helping members of his race. His rhetorical training started at the feet of his grandmother, who taught him the art of storytelling, and the itinerant preachers who use to travel around preaching the word of God. As a child, Turner used to mimic the preachers that he heard, while his friends served as ecstatic congregants in his backyard church. When friends were not available, animals served as Turner's auditors.

Turner's father died early in his childhood, and when his mother remarried, the family moved to Abbeville, South Carolina. There Turner started to work for a group of attorneys who noticed his quick wit, sharp mind, and astounding memory. They took it upon themselves to further his educational pursuits by teaching him the classics, sciences, and even theology. He had always wanted a formal education, but the state of South Carolina did not allow African Americans to attend school or for others to teach them how to read and write. Turner would later call this moment an answer to his prayers.

Turner accepted his call to preach at the age of nineteen, in the Methodist Episcopal Church. Three years later he married Eliza Ann Peacher of Columbia, South Carolina. She would be instrumental in providing support in his early career, when Turner served as an itinerant preacher for the denomination. However, despite addressing both Black and white audiences, and his success on the revival circuit, Turner quickly became disillusioned with the Methodist Church, because, though licensed to preach, he could never be ordained or become a bishop. During a fortuitous trip to New Orleans, Turner met Willis H. Revels, who would introduce him to the African Methodist Episcopal Church (AME). Turner would later join the church and find himself assigned to churches in Baltimore and Washington, DC.

It was in the latter that Turner's public career took off. He served there not only as pastor of Israel AME Church but also as a regular correspondent for the *Christian Recorder* newspaper. Several newspapers featured his sermons, and he hosted many senators and members of Congress in his church. He had also become a supporter of the Union in the Civil War. Many of his sermons aimed at getting members of his church to support in some way the Union cause. Turner also led efforts to recruit members for the First Regiment, United States Colored Troops. For his hard work and support of the cause, President Lincoln commissioned him chaplain of the group, making him the first commissioned African American chaplain of any branch of the military.[13]

After the war and Union victory, Turner returned South and involved himself in the politics of Reconstruction. He struck an optimistic tone as he began his work in the South. He argued "let bygones be bygones" and called for Blacks and whites to work together to rebuild the South. Turner saw a multiracial democracy on the horizon, and for it to work, whites would have to allow Blacks to thrive in their freedom, while Blacks could not hold the past against whites. However, Turner's optimism would shatter after he and others were kicked out of the Georgia legislature after winning elections, leading him eventually to become pessimistic about the future of Blacks in America.

Turner's treatment of the question, his skepticism of America's being a civilized nation, the description of the abuses faced by African Americans, his use of language that was meant to shock and provoke, and his overall tone and dismissive nature toward the goodness of America, provide an example of a writer adopting a prophetic persona and using prophetic rhetoric. Once primarily only the purview of religious studies scholars, since the publication of James Darsey's seminal text *The Prophetic Tradition and Radical Rhetoric in America*, literary and rhetorical critics have found prophecy and the prophetic tradition worthy of study.[14] However, as Anthony J. Stone and I argue, "much of the study of prophetic rhetoric negates the contributions of African-American scholars and those who study African-American prophetic rhetoric." It is this lack of attention by scholars, we contend, that "lead[s] many to understand prophetic rhetoric only from a white European framework that understands the people as the New Israel and grounded in the ideals of freedom, individualism, and "called people of God." Further, we surmise that it is this "oversight that impedes scholars from seeing that the African-American version of prophetic rhetoric is profoundly different."[15]

Moreover, despite Kristen Lynn Majocha's contention that "we do not know how to uncover prophetic rhetoric," or "how to test for prophetic rhetoric,"[16] I have defined the genre as "discourse grounded in the sacred and rooted in a community experience that offers a critique of existing communities and traditions by charging and challenging society to live up to the ideals espoused while offering celebration and hope for a brighter future." It is a rhetoric "characterized by a steadfast refusal to adapt itself to the perspectives of its audience" and a rhetoric that dedicates itself to the rights of individuals. Located on the margins of society, it intends to lift the people to an ethical conception of whatever the people deem as sacred by adopting, at times, a controversial style of speaking.[17]

I further maintained that, traditionally, critics studying prophetic rhetoric tend to situate the discourse within two primary traditions.[18] The first one is apocalyptic prophecy. Barry Brummett offers a working definition of apocalyptic rhetoric by calling it a "mode of thought and discourse that empowers its audience to live in a time of disorientation and disorder by revealing to them a fundamental plan within the cosmos." Further he writes that apocalyptic rhetoric is "discourse that restores order through structures of time and history by revealing the present to be a pivotal moment in time."[19] In addition, apocalyptic rhetoric "assumes a position of knowing visions, dreams, or meditations that the prophet/speaker shares with the audience. It is a secret or divine revelation revealed only to the prophet, and it becomes the speaker's job to disclose the previously hidden."[20]

The second type is the jeremiad. The term *jeremiad*, "meaning a lamentation or doleful complaint," derives from the Old Testament prophet Jeremiah, who warned of Israel's fall and the destruction of Jerusalem. The fall came because of the people's failure to keep the Mosaic covenant. However, even though Jeremiah denounced Israel's wickedness and prophesied destruction in the short term, he always looked for the day when the nation would repent and be restored.[21]

The jeremiad became part of the American rhetorical tradition around the seventeenth century among the New England Puritans as a way to express their self-identity as a chosen people. Believing that they had a divine plan to "flee from corrupt European religious and social establishment," the Puritans, as many would later call them, felt the need to establish a "holy society" in the wilderness of America,[22] and once they settled in America, they started to reshape the jeremiad.[23] Drawing from the biblical story of the Exodus, the Puritans saw themselves as the New Israel, leaving the bondage of Europe to come into a new world they believed to be the Promised Land. They felt sure of themselves, because in being the New Israel, the Puritans believed themselves to be the "chosen ones" God called and ordained to be an instrument of God's will. With the chosen people leading the way, America was to become the "city on a hill," whose light shone for all to see.

When the Puritans fell short of their call and ideal, typically the ministers in the community called the people to task. According to Howard-Pitney,

> As Puritan society fell short of its goal of civic perfection, the jeremiad became a ubiquitous ritual of self-reproach and exhortation. Puritan ministers deplored a long list of perceived social failings, denounced the people for their sins and social misconduct, and warned of worse tribulations and divine punishments to come if they did not strictly observe once more the terms of their covenant with God.[24]

The terms of the promise spelled out unambiguously were: "God has called us to be a peculiar and special people. We are the New Israel and America is the new Promised Land. We must remember this and act accordingly. When we forget this, God's judgment will come upon us."

Not only did the jeremiad come with "self-reproach and exhortation" when things went wrong, but it also had what Bercovitch calls an "unshakable optimism." In short, the Puritans believed that when turmoil and trouble came upon them, it was indeed God's punishment for sin, *but that the punishment was a "corrective" and not for "destruction."* In other words, God maybe was angry with them, but God had not replaced them with anyone else. As Bercovitch noted, "Here, as nowhere else, [God's] vengeance was a sign of love, a father's rod used to improve the errant child. In short, their punishments confirmed the promise."[25]

In his 1902 essay, Turner's use of prophetic rhetoric, however, was not an example of the aforementioned types. He grounded his use of prophetic rhetoric within the African American prophetic tradition. Unlike the prophetic rhetoric of the jeremiad, the African American Prophetic Tradition

(AAPT) has its origins not in freedom, but in slavery. Birthed from slavery and shaped in Jim and Jane Crow America, the African American version of the prophetic tradition has been the primary vehicle that has comforted and given voice to many African Americans. Through struggle and sacrifice, this tradition has expressed Black people's call for unity and cooperation as well as the community's anger and frustrations. It has been both hopeful and pessimistic. It has celebrated the beauty and myth of American exceptionalism and its special place in the world, while at the same time damning it to hell for not living up to the ideals America espouses. It is a tradition that celebrates both the Creator or the Divine's hand in history—offering hallelujahs for deliverance from slavery and Jim and Jane Crow, while at the same time asking, "Where in the hell is God"—during tough and trying times. It is a tradition that develops a theological outlook quite different at times from orthodoxy—one that finds God again very close, but so far away.[26]

The tradition, moreover, does not reside exclusively in either the apocalyptic or the jeremiad forms of prophetic discourse. Though African Americans have used both types of prophetic speech, the contextual restraints and rhetorical exigencies have not always allowed for an apocalyptic or a jeremiadic appeal. For many African Americans, the jeremiad at times posed a significant problem. Inherent in the jeremiad is that its proponents never question the foundational premise of its belief—or, in prophetic terms, it never questions the *sacred*. People primarily using the jeremiad never once questioned their faith in America's promise and destiny. They never questioned their belief that they were the New Israel or chosen people or that America was indeed the Promised Land. Therefore, whenever calamity happened, the Puritans may have believed it was because they had sinned and gotten away from the covenant, but belief in the covenant never faltered. When calamity came, many Puritans interpreted the disaster or judgment as God showing God's love as loving parents would do from time to time. Once the people start living up to what the people hold as the *sacred*, then the calamity will cease, and God will "heal the land." However, many African Americans did not have confidence or think that "the covenant" would work for them. Therefore, if African Americans adopted a prophetic persona to appeal to their audiences, they had to find other traditions or draw from other traditions.

Until recently, scholars have not examined the African American prophetic tradition thoroughly. Earlier works, such as Glaude's *Exodus! Religion, Race and the Nation in Early Nineteenth-Century America* (2000), Haywood's *Prophesying Daughters: Black Women Preachers and the Word, 1823–1913,* Chappell's *Stone of Hope: Prophetic Religion and the Death of Jim Crow* (2004), Blum's *W. E. B. Du Bois: American Prophet* (2007), Shulman's *American*

Prophecy: Race and Redemption in American Political Culture (2008), and Newman's *Freedom's Prophet: Bishop Richard Allen, the AME Church, and the Black Founding Fathers*, (2008) drew from prophecy as "a unifying idea" or as an important thread in the text, but none of those works explicitly examine prophetic rhetoric of African Americans or the African American prophetic tradition.[27]

However, two recent books focus explicitly on the African American prophetic tradition. The first is Christopher Hobson's *The Mount of Vision: African American Prophetic Tradition: 1800–1950* (2012). Drawing from the books in the Protestant Bible, Hobson argued that there are four traditions within African American prophecy. First is the Exodus-Deuteronomy tradition in which the prophet centers on a "key event in African Americans' own salvational history with God signifying both the end of slavery as a specific event and a pattern of saving acts in history.[28]

Second is the Isaiah-Ezekiel tradition. Hobson argued that this tradition "emphasizes that the community can, with God's help win restoration after suffering through a series of events in which its own efforts and God's instrumentality achieve reform in the United States' overall life."[29] The third tradition, the Jeremiah tradition, is similar to the jeremiad in that the prophet believes that the community has turned away from the covenant and needs to turn back; and the fourth, the Daniel-Revelation tradition, is similar to the apocalyptic tradition in that the prophet believes that God is ushering in a "new day." a "new kingdom," or a "new way."[30]

The second work is my *The Forgotten Prophet: Bishop Henry McNeal Turner and the African American Prophetic Tradition* (2012). In *Forgotten Prophet*, I examined Turner's public career from 1866–1895 and placed Turner within the African American prophetic tradition. In reviewing four speech texts, I attempted to show Turner's rhetorical trajectory from one of an optimistic prophet at the end of the Civil War to one of a pessimistic prophet months before the *Plessy* decision that officially instituted separate but equal laws across the country.

In the *Forgotten Prophet*, I demonstrated how Turner's prophetic persona shifted throughout his career. During the Civil War, for instance, Turner, like many African Americans during that time believed the Civil War served two purposes—first, to free the enslaved, and second, as divine retribution for the sin of slavery. The war for Turner was an apocalyptic moment that shifted policy in America, and after the war he argued that all Americans should celebrate emancipation.

After emancipation, I argued, Turner adopted a covenantal/universal prophetic persona. In other words, Turner saw himself as a prophet to both

Blacks and whites, and as a conduit that could bring people together under a common cause. Turner saw this because, for him, emancipation was a new day or a new era for both Blacks and whites to work together and help America to become the place where anyone could enjoy freedom and justice.

With much of his oratory, Turner's hope arose from his belief in America's divine mission. This mission, suppressed during the days of slavery, found a new life after emancipation, and Turner argued that America could live up to its promise of equality. It was within this divine mission that both Blacks and whites could work together, and Turner challenged both parties to do so.

Armed with this belief in America, Turner moved to Georgia and began his work in building the AME Church and eventually involving himself in the politics of Reconstruction. However, after getting elected to the state legislature, white representatives shook Turner's belief in the American covenant at its foundation by voting to expel the African American representatives because white representatives felt that Black ones were inferior. Soon after this, Turner's prophetic persona shifted from a covenantal prophet to a representative prophet who represented the interest of African Americans.

Turner would ground his rhetoric no longer in the sacredness and divine mission of America, but rather in the sacredness and sacred character of God. Throughout the rest of his career, Turner would expand his conception and interpretation of God to demonstrate that God worked in the lives of the people Turner claimed to represent. The other noticeable change in Turner's prophetic rhetoric during this period was his conception of encouragement and hope. After his expulsion from the Georgia House of Representatives, Turner no longer saw the day where Blacks and whites would work together in unity, but now he promoted a vision where God would serve as judge of the injustices that happened to African Americans at the hands of unjust white people.

As time went on, however, Turner's prophetic persona would shift yet again. While he still operated as a representative prophet on behalf of African Americans, Turner adopted a pragmatic prophetic persona as he turned his attention to a "plan of action" rather than calling his audience to celebrate or aim for some covenant. Frustrated by society's dealings with African Americans and annoyed by African American responses to unjust treatment, Turner began to promote emigration as the answer to problems facing African Americans. For Turner, America was in an apostate condition that only God could cure. Therefore, in the meantime, African Americans should do all in their power to "seek other quarters."[31]

When he saw that African Americans were not willing or could not afford to participate in the immigration to Africa, Turner adopted a pessimistic prophetic persona. At this time in his life, Turner had no confidence in American institutions or that the American people would live up to the promises in their sacred documents. Turner's position limited his rhetorical options, but by adopting a pessimistic prophetic voice, Turner found space for his oratory, which reflected itself within the lament tradition of prophecy.

As I noted in *The Forgotten Prophet*, Turner's pessimism continued throughout the rest of his life. As Turner's cynicism grew, he also became bitter and more forceful in his attacks against society and other African Americans who found hope in anti-emigration policies such as integration and accommodation. However, it was within the lament tradition that Turner could still find relevance as an orator by offering critiques not only of society but also of Black leadership.

By this time, Turner's representative persona shifted from African Americans in general to primarily southern Blacks—the ones who faced most of the oppression and the ones more open to emigration. Turner's constant call for emigration would have sounded very hopeful to many people of the South who had nothing to lose, but also just as hopeful were the continuous reminders of injustice that affected southern Blacks because, through Turner's oratory, southern Blacks felt heard as well.

Rhetorical History

Readers should see *No Future in This Country* as a sequel of sorts to *The Forgotten Prophet*. In *No Future* I pick up where I left off in *The Forgotten Prophet* and examine Turner's public career from 1896 to his death in 1915. During this time in his life, Turner had given up hope that America would treat African Americans justly. Moreover, he also reasoned that there was no appeal to consciousness or appeal to American ideals that one could make to change society's attitude toward African Americans. As a result, his rhetoric throughout this period took on a bitter tone, and one way he communicated it was through the prophetic rhetorical tradition.

However, instead of showing a rhetorical trajectory of how Turner moved from an optimistic prophet to a pessimistic one, in *No Future* I offer a rhetorical history of Turner's prophetic rhetoric by examining exclusively his use of prophetic pessimism. I use the term *rhetorical history* as David Zaresky uses it when he argues that rhetorical history is both the "historical study of rhetorical events and the study from a rhetorical perspective of historical forces, trends, processes, and events."[32]

In *No Future*, my aim is to examine "historical events and processes from a rhetorical perspective."[33] I do this by forgrounding Turner's prophetic rhetoric in response to historical events. I examine not only Turner's response to the event in the moment of the crisis but also the rhetorical context that leads Turner to respond the way that he did. Moreover, since speech is not done in isolation, each chapter offers not only Turner's public responses but other African Americans' as well. In so doing, I am also attempting to draw attention to the "controversies among ideas and values." I argue that studying history from a rhetorical perspective helps us see that history is both dialectical and rhetorical. It is dialectical, as Zarefsky has argued, because it is "constituted through a series of relationships between seeming opposites,"[34] in the case of Turner, for example, between emigration or remaining in America. It is rhetorical because it is "public discourse that keeps these opposites in public tension." Studying the public career of Turner (1896–1915) from a rhetorical perspective not only highlights Turner and his career but also highlights the times in which Turner produced his rhetoric and, hopefully, offers a history that produces what Kathleen J. Turner called "rhetorical" and "historical" knowledge.[35]

Pessimistic Prophecy

In *The Forgotten Prophet*, I note four types of prophetic rhetoric found primarily, but not exclusively, in the AAPT. The first is celebratory prophecy. I define this as prophecy typically grounded in a sacred covenant that calls the people to celebrate an event that leads the people to celebrate the sacred (covenant).[36] The second type of prophecy used by African Americans is a *prophetic disputation* or *disputation prophecy*. Disputation occurs when the speaker offers a "quotation of the people's opinion" within the speech context and offers a refutation.[37] The third type of prophecy used by African Americans is what I call mission-oriented prophecy. A mission-oriented prophecy is a constitutive rhetoric that calls a people to participate in a divine mission by reconstituting the people from their perceived identities.[38] However, it is the fourth type of prophecy I mention—pessimistic prophecy or the prophetic lament—on which this book focuses.

In the *Forgotten Prophet*, I wrote that "while on the surface a pessimistic prophecy is in contradiction to my earlier definition of prophetic rhetoric's hope and encouragement, the pessimistic prophecy is both pessimistic and hopeful at the same time." Further, I wrote:

> For many black orators, finding the racism too entrenched and the American covenant ideals not realistic for black Americans to [attain], they become wailing and moaning prophets within what I call the *lament tradition of* prophecy. In this tradition, the prophet's primary function is to speak out on behalf of others and to chronicle their pain and suffering as well as her or his own. By speaking, the prophet offers hope and encouragement to others by acknowledging their sufferings and letting them know that they are not alone.[39]

It is important to note here that the "one practicing lamentation understands that nothing will change about her or his situation"; the goal is "simply *to speak and to get the audience to hear,* thus becoming a record chronicling the pains and sufferings of the people the prophet claims to represent."[40]

Drawing from the work of Cornel West, I located this type of prophecy in the frustration of the prophet to fight and resist racism and racist practices. However, this aggressive pessimism, as West has called it, has a way of "awakening a new zeal" and "restores for African Americans the courage to renew their struggle to appropriate the hegemonic traditions and to resist those societal forms that simply do not make sense to them, namely, those that exclude them, that predict and label them, and that sonorously silence them."[41] In short, aggressive pessimism helps speakers deal with those insurmountable obstacles placed in front of them, thereby becoming a coping strategy that staves off communal nihilism and self-destruction.[42]

I further argued that later in his life Turner engaged in this type of prophecy. Typically, it has a three-part rhetorical structure.

> First, the speaker often recalls past events to lay claim on the present conditions of the people the prophet represents. Second, within this framework, the speaker then chronicles the sufferings of the people, offering the prophetic lament. Finally, the prophet encourages the people that while nothing will change in the present, the people are not alone—the prophet hears and will represent the voice of the voiceless [, . . .] reminding others that not all is well.[43]

On the surface, prophetic pessimism closely aligns itself with what some scholars call Afro-pessimism. According to Afro-pessimists, "Afro-pessimism is a lens of interpretation that accounts for civil society's dependence on antiblack violence—a regime of violence that positions black people as internal enemies of civil society." They critique other critical theorists who presume that all sentient beings are human beings.[44]

Moreover, Afro-pessimists argue that "critical theory's lumping of blacks into the category of the human (so that black suffering is theorized as homologous to the suffering of, say, Native Americans or workers or nonblack queers, or nonblack women) is critical theory's besetting hobble—a hobble subtending another false assumption: that all sentient beings possess the discursive capacity to transform limitless space into nameable place and endless duration into recognized and incorporated events." For Afro-pessimists, this optimism is a non-starter. They "interrogate this optimism by arguing that the black (or slave) is an unspoken and/or unthought sentience for whom the transformative powers of discursive capacity are foreclosed." In short, for Black people, attempts to find space for voice and agency, to find recognition and inclusion in society will only result in more death.[45]

The person who many suggest fits this description is Ta-Nehisi Coates. His book *Between the World and Me* reads like one long ode to Afro-pessimistic thought. For Coates, racism and white supremacy is a permanent thing in America, and the destruction of the Black body is part of the American heritage. This line of thought echoes what Afro-pessimists argue when they call for us to move away from an understanding of a simple Black/white binary and to reframe racist ideology as Black/non-Black binary, "in order to deemphasize the status of whiteness and to center analysis, rather, on the anti-Black foundations of race and modern society."[46]

Much of Turner's work would also echo these sentiments. As I discuss throughout the book, Turner was becoming more and more aware of how racism functioned in America. It led him to argue that for at least Black folks in America, there was no hope of achieving any notable and positive status, because not only would white people not allow it but anti-Black ideology shaped the American ethos. However, he differed from Afro-pessimists in that he had hope that African Americans would use their agency to recognize and realize this precarious situation in which they found themselves, and that if they would act in their own interest with their own agency, they could at least break the ideological anti-Blackness that African Americans themselves carried. Therefore, Turner's hope was not that white supremacy would go away or that somehow America would destroy white supremacy. Indeed, Turner concluded that America would not and could not do so. Turner's hope was that African Americans would no longer believe and act upon the things that whiteness said about them and, in so doing, would start to believe that they could do something as bold as emigrating to Africa.

Moreover, Turner was a person of faith. From 1895 until his death, he was the senior bishop of the African Methodist Episcopal Church. Being a bishop carried its own set of rhetorical expectancies. Therefore, how did Turner, who did not believe the "hope" many of his contemporaries were proclaiming, still find relevance to speak to and about situations important to the African American community? Turner turned to prophetic rhetoric grounded in the lament tradition of prophecy.

What I argue in *No Future* is that Turner's primary focus for the last twenty years of his life was chronicling the sufferings of poor African Americans whom many believed others had forgotten. Turner rejected covenantal (jeremiad) rhetoric because he did not believe African Americans would ever be a part of the covenant. While he believed that God would eventually judge America for its indifference toward Blacks, Turner rejected apocalyptic rhetoric because he also felt that judgment was not coming soon. Therefore, it was in the lament tradition of prophecy that Turner found a space to voice his pessimistic prophecy.

At this time in his life, Turner had no confidence in American institutions or that the American people would live up to the promises outlined in their sacred documents. While he argued that emigration was the only way for African Americans to retain their "personhood" status, he also would come to believe that African Americans would never immigrate to Africa. He argued that many African Americans were so oppressed, so stripped of agency, surrounded by continued negative assessments of their personhood, that belief in emigration was not possible. Turner's position limited his rhetorical options, but by adopting a pessimistic prophetic voice that bore witness to the atrocities African Americans faced, Turner found space for his oratory.

Thus, I argue that Turner became a "*wailing and moaning prophet* whose primary function was to speak out on behalf of others and to chronicle their pain and suffering."[47] Turner's lamentations, however, were different. First, Turner's lamentations were not private, but public. Second, instead of directly addressing God, Turner's lamentations addressed the public. Therefore, Turner practiced a *public lamentation to* all who heard (or read) his words that they might understand his frustration and pain but also know and understand something about the pain and frustration of the people he claimed to represent. Consistent with the lament tradition, Turner did not expect anything—racism, lynching, and all the other problems African Americans faced—to change. His goal was simply *to speak and to get his audience to hear*. Thus, unlike with many of his contemporaries such as Frederick Douglass, Booker T. Washington, and Benjamin Tanner, Turner's prophecy became a record of the pain and suffering of Blacks, and it gave a voice to those not able to speak publicly for themselves.

Invective and Agitative Rhetoric

As part of the pessimistic prophetic tradition, Turner's use of invective and agitative rhetoric is important to note as well. According to Kofi Agyekum, an invective "is an abusive or insulting word or expression with a violent censure or reproach on the addressee." They are more "emotionally oriented and considered inappropriate and embarrassing, and intended to offend the addressee(s) or targeted group. Invectives," he continues, "are of various types depending on the degree to which the targeted person may be aggrieved by the expression." However, Agyekum also notes that incentives "tarnish and curb co-operation between people. It is the antagonistic nature of the verbal expressions and their effects that are considered as verbal taboos." Further, he writes,

> Such words are considered more offensive when used in public. The type of people present at the time and the overall social context may influence the gravity of the offence and the emotional pain it carries. An invective expression indicates that some characteristic features of the target deviate from the social norm either physically, mentally, politically, religiously, or socially. The abuser tries to draw the attention of the target to the deviation from the norm and in so doing exaggerates it.[48]

This type of rhetoric is in line with Mary McEdwards's notion of agitative rhetoric.[49] For McEdwards, agitative rhetoric "evokes extreme movement away from the status quo—usually a complete reversal of existing conditions or situations." Further, she adds that for these speakers to achieve their goals of "extreme action," they "succeed only when using language that is also extreme. It is the speaker's choice of the abrasive word instead of the bland one, his deliberate selection of the derogatory metaphor rather than the complimentary, his use of jabbing, pounding simple sentences in place of complex syntax that marks his rhetoric as agitative rather than informative or gently persuasive."[50] While McEdwards sees a distinction between invective and agitative rhetoric,[51] her agitator closely resembles invective.

> The agitator must use the jagged word, the snarling word, the insulting word; he cannot clothe his ideas in euphemistic cotton wool to spare our sensibilities. These sensibilities are precisely what the agitator must rake raw, for to agitate, one must irritate and infuriate. When we try to suppress the man using the caustic metaphor, the savage adjective, that agitative rhetoric, we end by suppressing our own abilities to come nearer our ideal society.[52]

Turner's pessimism and rhetorical laments caused him to lose much of his support. After the death of Frederick Douglass in 1895, many thought Turner was poised to take Douglass's leadership mantle. However, Turner's prophetic call kept that from happening. His strong positions against the Supreme Court, his ever-changing and at times radical theology, his antiwar position, his public support for the Democratic nominee William Jennings Bryan, his consistent push for emigration and his damning of America, were just too much. Add to this his invectives aimed at African American leaders and the constant infighting with other bishops and leaders of his church, and one begins to understand why many had disdain and utter contempt for Turner.

However, as I argue in this book, Turner's laments and prophetic pessimism are all the more relevant to study because they differ from much of African American rhetoric during this period. Regardless of whether they were assimilationist/integrationist responses or ones of accommodation, these responses had embedded within them one similar feature—*a hope for a bright and glorious future for Blacks in America*. This bright future found resonance in the oft-promoted successes, grounded in a rhetoric of what historian Ibram X. Kendi calls "uplift suasion,"[53] gained by Blacks since emancipation—successes that included property ownership, educational achievements, numbers of businesses opened and maintained, and the religious advancement of African Americans. This is not to say that African American assimilationist/integrationist and accommodationist leaders did not mention the struggles and suffering that took place within the African American community—they were just not the focus of much of their rhetoric.

Turner, on the other hand, not only highlighted the pain and suffering of African Americans but also made it the focus of his rhetoric. This focus fit within the lament tradition of prophecy—a tradition that could house Turner's bitterness and anger both with the system that would not allow Blacks to take part and with what he argued to be the apathetic nature of many Black leaders. At the same time, it gave Turner a voice as a pessimistic prophetic who declared, "There is no manhood future in the United States for the Negro."[54]

In addition, Turner's prophetic pessimism allowed him to become more philosophical that led him to offer deep and penetrating analyses of the current situations facing African Americans. For example, while many scholars recognize Du Bois as the father of Black identity studies because of his oft-cited "double consciousness" phrase,[55] Turner first saw how a flawed construction of identity would be detrimental to African Americans. Grounded in his prophetic pessimism, Turner saw what social scientists and cultural critics would acknowledge in the twentieth century—that segregation had an injurious effect upon African Americans.

In chapter 1, "'An Abominable Conclave of Negro-Hating Demons': Turner and the *Plessy* Decision," I examine the infamous *Plessy v. Ferguson* decision. I offer a rhetorical analysis of Turner's editorials and interviews about the decision, and I situate that analysis in a historical overview of Turner's relationship with the Supreme Court. In chapter 2, "'Negroes Should Worship a God Who Is a Negro': The Making of a Black Rhetorical Theologian," I examine the rhetorical trajectory of Turner's theology. By offering a close reading of Turner's editorial "God Is a Negro," I argue that Turner offers an example of what I call rhetorical theology—a theology that is contextual and relational, and one that challenges what it means to talk about God and, moreover, who can talk about God. Additionally, I suggest that Turner is a forerunner to what theologians would later call Black Theology.

In chapter 3, "'An Unholy War of Conquest': Turner and the Creation of an Antiwar Protester," I examine Turner's shift from being prowar during the American Civil War to antiwar during the Spanish-American and Cuban wars. By offering a rhetorical analysis on speeches and writings about the war, I argue that Turner not only opposed the war and thought it was an unholy and unjust war, but he also helped establish the foundation of antiwar rhetoric within the African American rhetorical tradition.

In chapter 4, "'McKinley, the God of Fool Negroes': Turner and the Presidential Election of 1900," I offer first a rhetorical history of Turner's political career leading up to the 1900 campaign. Second, I then offer a rhetorical analysis of speeches and writings from Turner as he campaigned for the Democratic nominee, William Jennings Bryan. Though Bryan lost to William McKinley in a landslide, Turner argued that his support for Bryan was in protest of the Republican Party abandoning the principles of liberty and justice for all.

In chapter 5, "'The Salvation of the Negro': Turner and the Rhetoric of Emigration," I examine the arguments that Turner makes in favor of emigration. Though he knew he was fighting a losing cause, it is out of these arguments that Turner helps to lay the foundation of the Black radical tradition. In chapter 6, "'Hell Is an Improvement So Far As the Negro Is Concerned': Turner and the Damning of America," I examine Turner's prophetic ire against America and how the country deals with race. I offer rhetorical analysis of speeches in which he condemns America, calls the flag a "contemptible rag," and suggests that African Americans have nothing to obtain if they remain in the country.

Finally, in the concluding chapter, after offering a review of the previous chapters, I turn my attention to the movements in the twentieth century that Turner foreshadowed. I close the chapter by offering some lessons that modern-day readers could learn from Turner.

1

"AN ABOMINABLE CONCLAVE OF NEGRO HATING DEMONS"
Turner and the *Plessy* Decision

In 1890 the state of Louisiana passed the Separate Car Act, which legally separated common carriers based solely on race. Refusing to sit in the "colored section," on June 7, 1892, thirty-year-old Homer Plessy intentionally sat in the "white section" of the train, and though light enough to pass for white, he purposely identified himself as Black. Railroad officials of the East Louisiana Railroad Company had Plessy arrested for illegally sitting in the white area. Unknown at the time to the officials, Plessy was part of a plan to challenge the constitutionality of Louisiana's Separate Car Act, believing the law violated the Constitution.

Opponents of the law had reason to hope that the courts would overturn the law. First, they hired Albion Tourgee to serve as lead attorney for the plaintiff. Tourgee, a popular white lawyer from upstate New York, had been a staunch defender of the rights of African Americans since the end of the Civil War. After the war, he moved to North Carolina, where he served as a judge; after his time there, he returned to New York, where he continued to fight against discrimination.

Second, Plessy was of "mixed blood" and could easily had passed for white. It was only after Plessy self-identified as "colored" that officials arrested him for breaking the law. Tourgee saw him as the "perfect victim" in this case, because he could also argue the arbitrary nature of how states decided who was and who was not colored. Finally, the case landed in the court of John Howard Ferguson, a native of Massachusetts, who had recently ruled in a prior case that having separate cars based on color was unconstitutional. However, there was a difference in that case and the *Plessy* case. The former was focused on interstate trains, and the latter on intrastate trains.

Since Plessy was traveling in an intrastate train, Ferguson ruled that the state had the authority to regulate railroad companies within their states, and he upheld the arrest of Plessy and found him guilty of breaking the statue. The case would move through the court system, finally arriving at the United States Supreme Court as *Plessy v. Ferguson*.

On May 18, 1896, in a 7–1 ruling, the Supreme Court upheld in the *Plessy* decision the constitutionality of separate but equal railroad accommodations. According to legal scholar Thomas Ross, the court engaged in a "legal rhetoric of race" that embodied two central themes: "white innocence" and "black abstraction." For Ross, "white innocence is the insistence on the innocence or absence of responsibility of the contemporary white person." Calling "white innocence" a rhetorically constructed myth, Ross argued that judges of the nineteenth century "advanced this idea of white innocence in various ways." In combining notions of originalism and judicial helplessness, "the rhetoric of white innocence," wrote Ross, "permitted white magicians to pretend for themselves, and for their white contemporaries, that the horrific circumstances of the blacks were, after all, not the white person's fault."[1]

"Black abstraction," Ross noted, "is the rhetorical depiction of the black person in an abstract context, outside of any real and rich social context." According to Ross, "Black abstraction pervaded the rhetoric of race in the nineteenth century." In writing about the rhetoric of Black abstraction in the *Plessy* case, Ross noted that the "assertion that a law that segregates by race does not connote racial inferiority makes sense only in the abstract context created in *Plessy v. Ferguson*. By not placing the Black person in the real social context of the late nineteenth century, Justice Brown was able to say with a straight face that any racial stigma flowing from de jure segregation simply must be self-imposed." Further, Ross wrote,

> Black abstraction and white innocence worked together in the legal rhetoric to obscure the degradation of blacks and to absolve the contemporary whites of responsibility for any images of degradation that might have passed through the filter of black abstraction. Thus, these rhetorical themes made the choices of the nineteenth-century judges intellectually coherent

and smoothed over the conflict between the reality of subjugation and the abstract principles of freedom and equality.[2]

A cursory examination of legal and political rhetoric during the nineteenth century would find a plethora of examples of Black abstraction. In short, by not placing African Americans in context or by framing ideas without ascribing to context or the contextual variances that shape the rhetoric itself, the court paved the way for states to continue to enact a series of laws that separated citizens based on race.

When the court reached its decision, many white newspapers across the country only reported the decision, without any comment at all. Many did not see it as a monumental case or were at all surprised by the decision. However, Louisiana newspapers applauded the action. One newspaper, while supporting the decision, lamented that the only dissenting opinion came from a "negrophilist and a believer in social equality."[3] And the *Louisiana Democrat* pronounced that the "Senegambian must now relinquish his ambition to ride in the railroad coaches with white people."[4]

An editorial in the *New Orleans Daily Picayune* mentioned the similarity in Louisiana's law and other states that discriminated based on race. Further, it noted,

> Equality of rights does not mean community of rights. The laws must recognize and uphold this distinction; otherwise, if all rights were common as well as equal, there would be practically no such thing as private property, private life, or social distinctions, but all would belong to everybody who might choose to use it.
>
> This would be absolute socialism, in which the individual would be extinguished in the vast mass of human beings, a condition repugnant to every principle of enlightened democracy.[5]

While white newspapers were indifferent to or supportive of the decision, this was not the case in the Black press, where the case was routinely criticized. For example, one editorial likened the decision to that of *Dred Scott*, where Chief Justice Taney declared that "black men have no rights that white men are bound to respect."[6] Other Black newspapers, while decrying and lamenting the decision, sought fit to also lift and celebrate the lone dissenter—Justice Harlan.[7]

However, the overwhelming response from the Black press to the *Plessy* decision centered on critique and an appeal to God for better days. An example of this came from the editorial pages of the *Indianapolis Freeman*. For example, it decried the decision, saying that it would have a "demoralizing effect" on African Americans. The writer proclaimed that the decision "will do much towards destroying the faith that Negroes may have in any institutions that white men control" and that "no matter what direction the Negro turns opposition stands like a stone wall." The writer concluded the editorial by appealing to God and suggesting that despite oppression and opposition, a "mighty God remains" and that God "will square up accounts or life is not worth the living." Grounded in the belief that God will "square up accounts," the writer saw the decision as a momentary setback. "Victory," the writer concluded, "somehow will be snatched from the teeth of seeming defeat. In due time, in this most unequal context the odds will be casted on the proper side."[8]

While others in their critiques attempted to balance their criticism with hopeful suggestions of brighter days to come, Bishop Henry McNeal Turner did not. By adopting a prophetic persona of the pessimistic prophet, Turner found space for his proclamations. His denunciations of the Supreme Court after the *Plessy* decision and throughout the rest of his career were at times coarse and visceral. In short, he did not mince any words when speaking about the Supreme Court.

In the rest of this chapter, I chart Turner's acrimonious "relationship" with the Supreme Court. Starting with the Civil Rights Bill of 1875, I chart how Turner's support and belief that the Supreme Court could or would do anything to promote fairness and protect the rights of African Americans eroded over time. As decision after decision nullified the spirit of the Thirteenth, Fourteenth, and Fifteenth Amendments and moved America from the progress of Reconstruction, Turner's rhetoric toward the Supreme Court and against the nation grew more bitter, his denouncements much stronger. However, first I examine the foundation that led to the creation and passing of the 1875 Civil Rights Act.

The Fight for Civil Rights

The Civil Rights Bill of 1866

Kirt Wilson has argued that while the history of the 1875 Civil Rights Act is complex, when one untangles the legislative processes that led to its passage, one then can see that the act is an "exemplar of the period's political culture." Moreover, it also "illustrates how the era's legislation became trapped between principle and the expedient demands of racial politics." According to Wilson, while the Union victory in the Civil War, the Emancipation Proclamation, and the Thirteenth Amendment led some states in the North to dismantle some of their segregation laws and policies, in the South, especially with the abolition of slavery, many states began to enact previously cultural norms into law. An example of this was the Black codes that southern states passed to restrict the freedom of African Americans after the passage of the Thirteenth Amendment.[9]

F. Michael Higginbotham argues that Black codes intended to effectively "reenslave" African Americans. He writes that "the Black Codes subjected Blacks to vagrancy and curfew laws in an attempt to reenslave them through convict labor provisions once they were convicted and sentenced to prison." Black codes made it a crime for Blacks to be unemployed, and, once convicted, many found themselves placed into the sort of "subservient labor tasks" they had done as enslaved people. Moreover, these Black codes applied to all Black people, irrespective of whether they were formerly enslaved or not, because the law focused on their "physical appearance instead of whether or not they were formerly enslaved."[10]

Seeing that southern states were not going to abide by the spirit of Reconstruction, Congress passed the 1866 Civil Rights Act.[11] Enacted on April 9, 1866, after Congress overrode a veto of the bill from President Johnson, it has the distinction of being the first federal law to define citizenship and to declare all citizens are equally protected by the law. G. Edward White argued that the text of the Civil Rights Acts of 1866 intended to use the "enforcement powers of Congress to alter the treatment of emancipated African American in former slave states." Section 1 of the act declared that all persons born in the United States were citizens of the United States without regard to any previous condition of slavery or involuntary servitude; except as a punishment for crime whereof the party shall have been duly convicted. The act also declared that citizens were able to enjoy the "full and equal benefit of all laws and proceedings for the security of person and property, as is enjoyed by white citizens."[12]

Further, White argued that the drafters of the act "employed familiar antebellum categories for describing persons." However, opponents of the act did not like its egalitarian nature and almost immediately, many southern states began to nullify the spirit of the act. According to the act, Black citizens had the same rights as white citizens in every state and territory in the United States and "overrode any black codes to the contrary." For many people in the South, making Black people citizens was a step too far.[13]

Opponents argued that Congress did not have the power to declare anyone a citizen, arguing that citizenship was a state action. They also argued that the act did not spell out the meaning of civil rights and immunities. In any case, many Americans dismissed the Civil Rights Act of 1866. States continued to deny Black people the rights and privileges that the Act aimed at protecting. African Americans had to contend with the destruction of their property and their lives.

One example of this type of violence happened less than a month from the passing of the bill. In what scholars now call the Memphis Massacre, from May 1 to 3, a white mob in Memphis, Tennessee, with the help of law enforcement, murdered forty-six Black people and injured 285 more. They also destroyed over a hundred houses, schools, churches, and other properties belonging to African Americans. The massacre was so horrific that it surprised many Americans that the state did not convict anyone in the murder of forty-six people. This led members of Congress to conduct an official investigation. In investigating the murder and mayhem that occurred during the massacre, the congressional committee concluded in its report

> Hardly any crime seems to have been omitted. There were burglary, robbery, arson, mayhem, rape, assassination, and murder, committed under circumstances of the most revolting atrocity, the details of which in every case are fully set out in the testimony. In many cases negroes were murdered, and their bodies remained on the ground for forty-eight hours and had reached stage of decomposition before they were buried; the relatives and friends of the murdered parties being afraid to appear on the street to claim the dead bodies, and the authorities permitted them to remain longer than they would have permitted the body of dead dog to remain on the street.[14]

With the testimonies of the survivors from the Memphis Massacre, Congress saw that the 1866 Civil Rights Act was not enough to ensure the life and property of African Americans. Many states circumvented the act by challenging its constitutionality. Therefore, Congress began to work on an amendment that it hoped would address any confusion about its original intent.

The Fourteenth Amendment

When Congress began to debate the passage of the Fourteenth Amendment, the Memphis Massacre and the protection of freed people were clearly on their minds. Bernice Donald wrote that the "Memphis Massacre had an impact far beyond Tennessee." She notes that "scholars have taken a variety of approaches to analyzing the potential impact of the Memphis Massacre on the congressional proposal and state ratification of the Fourteenth

Amendment." She suggested that while "some scholars believe the Massacre is probative of the original meaning of the Privileges and Immunities Clause, others have analyzed the Massacre with an eye towards understanding the Due Process and Equal Protection Clauses." In agreeing with legal scholar Kurt Lash, Donald wrote,

> The Fourteenth Amendment can be seen as the answer to a failure of the federal government to enforce the citizenship rights recently received by freedmen. Thus, the Fourteenth Amendment's passage would cure the defects that allowed the rampages in Memphis and New Orleans and other cities to occur. Lash's argument is based in the language of the Privileges and Immunities Clause—which enforces upon states the burden to give all citizens equal rights under the law.[15]

To address these issues, and building from the 1866 Civil Rights Act, Congress decided to broaden the category of national citizenship and to further limit the states' power to restrict the rights of citizens. They first extended the category of citizenship to include all people—specifically including Native Americans. Second, they made state citizenship and national citizenship equal with each other. Third, they limited states in restricting the rights of individuals; states could not "make or enforce any law which shall abridge the privileges or immunities of citizens of the United States," and states could not "deprive any person of life, liberty, or property, without due process of law; nor deny to any person within its jurisdiction the equal protection of the laws."

On June 16, 1866, just a little over a month after the Memphis Massacre, Secretary of State William Seward sent the amendment to the governors for ratification. As expected, every formerly Confederate state (except Tennessee) refused to ratify the amendment. The refusal led Congress to adopt the Reconstruction Acts of 1867 and 1868. The Reconstruction Acts placed the former Confederate states under federal military control. Legal scholar Orville Vernon Burton has reminded us that the Reconstruction Act "authorized new state constitutions, and United States military commanders took charge of registering all male voters to elect delegates to state conventions." He also argued that the "newly adopted state constitutions required by the Reconstruction Act provided for universal male suffrage. These state constitutions, adopted in 1868 and 1869, were forward-looking, providing free public-school systems, homestead protection, and married women's rights, among other provisions." These new state legislatures also did something else: they ratified the Fourteenth Amendment in 1868.[16]

The Fifteenth Amendment

While the Reconstruction Acts worked at getting African American men in the former Confederate states the right to vote, this was not the case in the rest of the nation. Burton summed up that "at the outset of the Civil War, only five states in the nation, all in New England, permitted African Americans to vote on the same basis as whites." At the time, many debated whether "suffrage was a right of citizenship."[17] Already declaring citizenship of all people born in the United States and its territories, Congress decided to extend the right of suffrage nationwide.

Ratified on February 3, 1870, the Fifteenth Amendment guaranteed that the "right of citizens of the United States to vote shall not be denied or abridged by the United States or by any State on account of race, color, or previous condition of servitude." With this addition, the Constitution took on a new look and meaning. For the first time, the Constitution defined what Burton calls the "new birth of freedom—citizenship and the right to vote." He wrote that "with citizenship secured by the Fourteenth Amendment and the right to vote secured by the Fifteenth, African-Americans could protect themselves from their former owners through the rule of law, shape those laws by standing for political office, and choose their own leaders with free debate and an honest ballot to the constitution."[18]

At least that was the hope. While Congress was passing laws and amendments aimed at assisting the formerly enslaved to navigate life after freedom, states were also responding—but in ways that increasingly became more oppressive and more violent. Turner chronicled much of this violence as he traveled throughout the South preaching and giving speeches on behalf of the Republican Party. In one letter to the *Christian Recorder*, the official organ of the African Methodist Episcopal Church, Turner wrote of the brutal beating of one of the deacons of the church. On a visit to Opelika, Alabama, Deacon Robert Alexander informed Turner that on Thursday evening four white citizens broke into his room at midnight and assaulted him by beating and stabbing him nearly to death. When Turner first saw him, he wrote that he looked like a "lump of curdled blood." When several African American women went "screaming" to the agent of the Freedmen's Bureau for help, he simply replied, "I can't do anything for you," and according to Turner, "he never got out of his bed."[19]

Turner also found himself the object of racist threats. In an editorial he published in the *Christian Recorder* on February 23, 1867, Turner, while visiting Rev. Robert Cromley in Warrentown, Georgia, learned that "several whites" had threatened Turner's life if he ever "returned to that place." Turner's life was spared only because fifteen African Americans "armed themselves to the teeth, with every conceivable weapon and remained by him till he got ready to leave."[20]

Throughout his travels, Turner had to face death threats all the time. Testifying before a congressional committee on November 3, 1871, Turner said, "[On] two or three occasions, I may say in a dozen instances, if I had not secreted myself in houses at times, in the woods at other times, in a hollow log at another time, I would have been assassinated by a band of night-prowlers, or rovers." When asked if he had seen any other evidence of night marauders injuring other African Americans, Turner replied that he had seen "scores of them." He recounted the times he had seen "men who had their backs lacerated" and men "who had bullets in them. He seen others with their "arms shot off; shot so badly that they had to be amputated," and others with their "legs shot off."[21]

Despite the violence and attempts on his life, Turner still held out hope for the Reconstruction project. When Congress passed and ratified the Fifteenth Amendment, Turner was elated. "The ratification of the Fifteenth Amendment to the Constitution," he wrote, "is the finish of our national fabric; it is the head stone of the world's asylum; the crowning event of the nineteenth century; the brightest glare of glory that overhung land or sea. Hereafter, the oppressed children of all countries can find a temple founded upon gratitude and religious equity, ample enough to accommodate them all." Further, Turner, in the grandest of eloquence proclaimed,

> This Amendment is an ensign of our citizenship, the prompter of our patriotism, the bandage that is to blindfold Justice while his sturdy hands hold the scales and weighs out impartial equity to all, regardless of popular favor or censure. It is the ascending ladder for the obscure and ignoble to rise to glory and renown, the well of living water never to run dry, the glaring pillar of fire in the night of public commotion, and the mantling pillar of cloud by day to repel the scorching rays of wicked prejudice. . . . It is a national guaranty, as fair as the moon, clear as the sun, and terrible as an army with banners . . . The Fifteenth Amendment is the shining robe covering in immaculate grandeur the nude and exposed parts of our country, which hitherto made her fragile and vulnerable before enemies.[22]

However, as Turner would soon discover, the "nude and exposed parts" of the country remained uncovered, even after passing the latest act to ensure African American civil rights, the Civil Rights Act of 1875.

Turner, Civil Rights, and the Supreme Court

On March 1, 1875, Congress passed the Civil Rights Act, which stated that all persons within the jurisdiction of the United States are entitled to public accommodations regardless of race and color or previous condition of servitude.[23] The passage of the bill was the culmination of hard work and protracted debate for both opponents and supporters.[24] For Turner, it was a momentous victory. He had labored hard for its passage. In April of 1874, when Turner believed reports that some members of Congress wanted to wait until after the fall midterms to pass the bill because they did not want "some indiscreet colored person" to "stir up an excitement" and "disgust the whites and drive them from us,"[25] Turner took to the editorial pages of the *Christian Recorder*.

He wondered, if Congress wanted to pass the bill, why wait? He reasoned that the "sooner they pass it, the better," because then "people will know it's law, and will conform to it." However, he further reasoned that "as long as it hangs in suspense, it remains an eyesore to thousands, and the same horrible anticipations and nightmares which many indulged about freedom, will be indulged in regard to the terrific consequences of civil rights. As soon as it becomes a fact, he continued, "so soon do the people forget all about it."[26]

He also argued that delaying the passage of the bill also invited opposition to the Republican Party from both Blacks and white voters.

> The delay of the Civil Rights Bill, is going to do the Republican Party more harm this fall than all their other blunders put together. Why? You ask. The answer is easy, Hundreds of white people who would vote the Republican ticket, will not least they be charged with voting for negro equality, & c. And on the other hand, hundreds of colored people will not vote at all. Because they have sworn they would never vote again, till they can vote under the aegis of Civil Rights. These rights are reasonable, humane and natural, the very instincts of our nature demand them.[27]

Turner closed his editorial by mentioning the upcoming congressional tribute to the late Charles Sumner, the Massachusetts senator who first authored the Civil Rights Act. He saw this as an opportunity to issue a warning to Congress. Wondering if Congress would actually go through the memorial service with the civil rights bill "hanging over their heads," Turner wrote, "If Sumner could shake off the cerements of the grave, and speak, his lion like voice, would utter in fearful intonation 'Mention not my name in Congress, till you pass my Civil Rights Bill.' Surely Congress will not go through the farce of memorial services with that bill hanging over their heads. If they do, they had better commemorate the death of the Republican party at the same time, for that day she will breathe her last."[28]

Not only Congress received Turner's prophetic ire, but President Grant did as well. When Turner believed that Grant began to waver on the bill's passage, he took again to the editorial pages of the *Christian Recorder*. He wrote that Grant, who at "one time desired the passage of the Civil Rights Bill" had "lost some of his ardor, and grown somewhat indifferent in regard to this all important measure." He reminded his readers that for him, "there is no party, when my rights are in jeopardy," arguing that "every man should measure his party allegiance, as that party measures out his manhood."[29]

Turner continued to argue for the passage of the bill. "Its failure is our failure," he proclaimed, and "its success is our success. Indeed, it holds in its grasp our destiny as a race. We stand or fall in that Bill." In a prophetic utterance, Turner even tied the passage of the bill to a move of God. "Should it fail, I shall regard it as the indignant proclamation of heaven, saying *arise and depart, for this is not your home. This is a White Man's Government*," Turner lamented. "But if it succeeds, then it may be interpreted as the voice of God; saying to the negro, 'Awake from your lethargy, and build schools, churches, houses, and prepare to run the race of life where you are.'" He concluded the editorial by reminding his readers, "Every man in the country who is opposed to the Civil Rights Bill, is opposed to the colored race, and if President Grant is opposed to its passage, then he is our enemy, yes, the deadly enemy of the colored race."[30]

When the act finally passed, in 1875, many African Americans initially saw this as the final piece needed to ensure equality in America. However, conservatives immediately challenged the law in court, and as time went on and the national government moved away from civil rights, African Americans began to fear the worst. That fear became reality in 1883, when the Supreme Court declared by an 8–1 margin that the Civil Rights Act of 1875 was unconstitutional. Writing for the majority and building off the logic the court rendered in the Slaughter Houses Cases in 1873,[31] Justice Bradley, adopting a narrow, literal reading of the Fourteenth Amendment, argued that since the amendment prohibited discriminatory action only by the state and not by individuals, there were limits on congressional authority.

> It does not invest Congress with power to legislate upon subjects which are within the domain of State legislation, but to provide modes of relief against State legislation, or State action, of the kind referred to. It does not authorize Congress to create a code of municipal law for the regulation of private rights,

but to provide modes of redress against the operation of State laws and the action of State officers executive or judicial when these are subversive of the fundamental rights specified in the amendment.[32]

Therefore, grounded in a states' rights argument, Bradley concluded:

And so, in the present case, until some State law has been passed, or some State action through its officers or agents has been taken, adverse to the rights of citizens sought to be protected by the Fourteenth Amendment, no legislation of the United States under said amendment, nor any proceeding under such legislation, can be called into activity, for the prohibitions of the amendment are against State laws and acts done under State authority.[33]

Justice Harlan, however, adopted a more holistic reading of the Constitution in his dissent. He reasoned that the court operated "upon grounds entirely too narrow and artificial." Further he declared, "I cannot resist the conclusion that the substance and spirit of the recent amendments of the Constitution have been sacrificed by a subtle and ingenious verbal criticism." Finally, grounded in the spirit of the law, Harlan wrote, "It is not the words of the law, but the internal sense of it that makes the law; the letter of the law is the body; the sense and reason of the law is the soul."[34]

While some African American leaders after the decision called for patience and understanding, through interviews, essays, letters to the editor, and speeches, Turner called the decision "death dealing" and argued that the bill not only "de-citizentized" African Americans but also placed them as a permanent underclass. He let known his feelings about the decision in an open letter to friend B. K. Sampson published first in the *Memphis Daily Appeal* on December 2, 1883, and then again in the *Christian Recorder* newspaper, on December 13, 1883. Suggesting that Sampson's call for Black leaders to make no immoderate remarks about the decision was not the best strategy, Turner charged, "Sir, the leaders of our people, especially the trainers of our youths, cannot by any logical deduction advise a tame submission to any such declaration in this advanced age."[35]

In his letter to Sampson, Turner argued that the decision was disastrous for African Americans because first, it "unsettled the civil status of the Negro," and second, the decision could lead to a mass exodus of African Americans. He also reasoned that since the decision removed citizenship status of African Americans from the United States, Blacks did not have to pledge allegiance to a country that could not and would not protect them and their civil rights. Turner argued that the decision rendered African Americans "uncivilized and outlawed."[36]

Turner further argued that the "decision merits no moderate talk; that it should be branded, battle-axed, sawed, cut and carved with the most bitter epithets and blistering denunciations that words can express." He proclaimed that the "nation deserves and will receive, if it lets that decision stand, the hiss of man, the curse of God and the ridicule of all ages." Noting that the times called for "fire eaters" instead of "conservatives," he argued, I think it is wrong in you, sir, to teach the young men of our race that is manly to sit still under any such diabolical decision."[37]

Turner closed his letter with a strong prophetic warning:

> Now I ask, shall we sit still and be conservative, hold our peace and submit to the degradation? I hope, sir, you will not say yes. You cannot afford to do it. No, not as a member of the Negro race. If the decision is correct, the United States constitution is a dirty rag, a cheat, a libel, and ought to be spit upon by every Negro in the land. More, if the decision is correct and is accepted by the country, then prepare to return to Africa, or get ready for examination.[38]

In a letter to the members and ministers of the Eighth Episcopal District of the AME Church in January 1884, Turner lamented that the decision by the court to declare the Civil Rights Act unconstitutional was, except to a "few simpletons, ingrates and government pap suckers," a "fearful blow; a civil shame, an inhuman outlaw, upon more than seven millions of American citizens." Turner argued that the decision was "born in the bitterness of prejudice, fostered in the venom of caste, and strengthened by the dangerous stimulants of State rights," and that the "decision hurls out fearful blows, which strike the negro through in the very armor of his citizenship."[39]

Further, Turner wrote,

> Now, before the God of nations and civilized man, we hold that the action of the Supreme Court is nothing less than a public outrage, and an invitation to murder all colored persons who possess the elements of true manhood—a decision far more abominable and more at variance with the true status of affairs than the Dred Scott decision, and as such should be singled out before heaven and earth.[40]

In a letter to the editor of the *New York Age* six years later, Turner's frustration with the court's decision went unabated. In responding to concerns from Republican leaders that Turner denounced the court in a recent interview with the paper, Turner reiterated his opposition to the court's decision in even stronger language by calling the decision of the Supreme Court the

"FIVE DEATH DEALING DECISIONS." After citing the language of the Civil Rights bill and quoting the Thirteenth and Fourteenth Amendments, Turner aimed in this editorial to highlight the hypocrisy of the decision. Turner argued that while the court could only see "Negroes in Kansas and Missouri intermingling with white persons, in hotels and inns; Negroes, in California and New York, associating, on equal terms, with Caucasians in theatres; and Negroes in the presence of those free from the taint of African blood, in the parlor-cars of Tennessee," the law must be unconstitutional. However, Turner argued that "Negroes may come as servants into all of the hotels, inns, theatres and parlor-cars, but they shall never be received as equals—as are other persons." He noted the hypocrisy of the decision in that that while Black people could enter the finest hotels or restaurants only if they were servants, "the gambler, cut-throat, thief, despoiler of happy homes, and the cowardly assassin, need only to have white faces in order to be accommodated with more celerity and respect than are our lawyers, doctors, teachers and humble preachers." He suggests that the *Dred Scott* decision was only a "mole-hill in comparison with this obstructing Rocky Mountain to the freedom of citizenship."[41]

Addressing concerns that he charged that under the decision of the "Republican Supreme Court, colored people may be turned out of hotels, cheated, abused and insulted on steamboats and railroads, without legal redress," Turner did not deny the charge, but rather believed the reporter made his comments seem too mild. "When I use the term 'cheated,'" Turner wrote, "I mean that colored persons are required to pay first-class fare and in payment therefor are given no-class treatment, or at least the kind with which no other human being, paying first-class fare, is served."[42]

After quoting parts of Justice Harlan's decision, Turner then offered a reminder of what the 1875 Civil Rights Act intended to do:

> Sane men know that the gentlemen in Congress who voted for this act of 1875, understood full well the condition of our country, as did the powers amending the Constitution abolishing slavery. The intention was to entirely free, not to partly liberate. The desire was to remove the once slave so far from his place of bondage, that he would not even remember it, if such a thing were possible. Congress stepped in and said, he shall vote, he shall serve on juries, he shall testify in court, he shall enter the professions, he shall hold offices, he shall be treated like other men, in all places the conduct of which is regulated by law, he shall in no way be reminded by partial treatment, by discrimination, that he was once a "chattel," a "thing." . . . The height of absurdity, the chief point in idiocy,

the brand of total imbecility, is to say, that the Negro shall vote a privilege into existence which one citizen may enjoy for pay, to the exclusion of another..... Are colored men to vote grants to railroads upon which they cannot receive equal accommodation? Do you know of anything more degrading to our country, more damnable?[43]

Turner's disappointment with the Supreme Court and its decision did not cease even four years later, when he published the entire decision as a pamphlet commemorating its ten-year anniversary, in 1893. Turner's reason for the publishing of the pamphlet was his belief that the "great mass of our people in this country, including black and white, appear to be so profoundly ignorant of the cruel, disgraceful and inhuman condition of things affecting the colored race."[44] Even after ten years, Turner claimed that he had met "hundreds of persons, who, in their stupid ignorance, have attempted to justify the action of the Supreme Court in fettering the arms of justice and disgracing the nation by transforming it into a savage country."
Further, he lamented:

> For that decision alone authorized and now sustains all the unjust discriminations, proscriptions and robberies perpetrated by public carriers upon millions of the nation's most loyal defenders. It fathers all the *"Jim-Crow cars"* into which colored people are huddled and compelled to pay as much as the whites, who are given the finest accommodations. It has made the ballot of the black man a parody, his citizenship a nullity and his freedom a burlesque. It has engendered the bitterest feeling between the whites and blacks, and resulted in the deaths of thousands, who would have been living and enjoying life today. And as long as the accompanying decision remains the verdict of the nation, it can never be accepted as a civil, much less a Christian, country.[45]

However, unlike in his previous letter and editorial, Turner levels a critique upon African Americans who he believed supported the decision. He argued that the "colored man or woman who can find contentment, menaced and shackled by such flagrant and stalking injustice as the Supreme Court has inflicted upon them, must be devoid of all manliness and those self-protecting instincts that prompt even animals to fight or run." At the time of this writing, Turner urged African Americans that they must "put forth endeavors for a better condition of things here or leave it and search for a land more congenial," and if a person does not, he or she is "evidently of the lowest type of human existence, and slavery would be a more befitting sphere for the exercise of his [or her] dwarfed and servile powers than freedom."[46] Three years later the court would render the *Plessy* decision, and Turner, for one, was not surprised.

Plessy v. Ferguson

Just a month before the court handed down the *Plessy* decision, the justices ruled in what would have been a "landmark case"—as far as African Americans were concerned. The case involved two Black men—John Gibson and Charles (Charley) Smith—who were on trial for murder in Washington County, Mississippi.[47] Arguing that there had never been a jury summoned that included Black men, they sought to have their case moved to federal court. The courts denied their request, and they both were subsequently found guilty. When the state courts of Mississippi denied their petitions, and after subsequent appeals failed, the Supreme Court ruled in favor of the state courts.

Justice Harlan, who would later become a hero to African Americans, delivered the opinion of the court. Harlan argued that the Supreme Court could not interfere with a constitutional law of a state where that state was not in violation of the Constitution of the United States. He further argued in his opinion that a fair reading and interpretation of the Mississippi state law in question did not violate the plaintiff's rights to a fair and impartial trial. In writing about the case, an editor of the *Chattanooga Times*, in perhaps a window on the dissent he would present publicly just a month later in the *Plessy* decision, wrote, "He [Harlan] said the court recognized that the safety of the colored race would be imperiled if any discrimination was permitted because of race, but that the record in these cases did not show any, and that therefore the only course left was to affirm the decision of the State Supreme Court."[48]

When the court publicized the decision, Turner was not surprised. In an editorial titled, "Farewell Negro," Turner wrote that despite raising and collecting a lot of money "to aid in getting this case before the Supreme Court," he had "no faith in the abominable conclave from the beginning." It was "useless to comment," because he believed that there were "no rights in this country for the black man, but to be a free slave." He noted that his "indignation" was "too intense" to comment fully at this time upon what he called a "hellish decision." He promised to do it in the future when the "excitement is not so raging."[49] Turner, however, never got a chance to write further about the *Smith* decision. He focused his attention on the other decision delivered just a little over a month after *Smith*—and it would be this decision that changed the lives of many African Americans.

Turner's Pessimistic Persona:
"An Abominable Conclave of Negro Hating Demons"

While others continued to call for calm and understanding of the *Plessy* decision, Turner continued his all-out assault. In an editorial published one month after what he called the "infamous decision,"[50] Turner did not withhold his disappointment. Turner called the court an "abominable conclave of negro hating demons" (with one exception) who "issued another decree that colored men and women must be driven into Jim Crow cars whenever it suits the whim of any white community."[51] He further noticed the unfairness of such a policy when he lamented that Blacks, though relegated to the Jim Crow car, still had to "pay as much for a seat in those hog pens as the white people pay in cars of ease and luxury."[52]

Next, Turner shifted and heaped praise on that earlier one exception—Justice John M. Harlan, whom he called the "only righteous and just man associated with that body." However, his focus on Harlan did not last long, as he turned his attention back to the other justices who had caused the court to be a "stench in the nostrils of the civilized world." Further, if what he had said earlier did not resonate with his readers, Turner wrote:

> We beg the devil's pardon, however, for comparing the members of the Supreme Court to him. For let it be said to the credit of the devil, he has never been known to so degrade himself as to be guilty of any such discrimination as the so-called Supreme Court, who is composed of some second and third handed lawyers who were too ignorant and worthless to make a decent living, until by some trick or maneuver, they succeed in beguiling the president to appoint them to a place on the Supreme bench, simply because they had a white face and not for any merit possessed, for there is not a Negro on the sugar cane farms of Louisiana or the rice-grown swamps of South Carolina who is not equal of any member of the Supreme Court, Justice Harlan excepted.[53]

He closed his editorial in disgust. "Well," he wrote, "let the black man grin and endure and possess his soul in patience and wait for a better day." He suggested that members of the Supreme Court "will all be in hell in a dozen or more years and that, furthermore, "their children's children will be ashamed to own them as their ancestors." Ending his editorial, he foresaw a day when "negro jurists will sit upon the same bench they are now disgracing and render righteous decisions."[54]

Two months after the decision, Turner decided to publish the entire opinion in his *Voice of Missions* newspaper. The headline, meant to capture the attention of his readers, read in large letters, "Sackcloth and Ashes for the Negro."[55] Following that was the phrase "The Brutal Decision of the United States Supreme Court: The Most Infamous Piece of Judicial Jugglery Known Since Time Began." Just below those headings, Turner put in capital letters "A DECISION UNKNOWN IN HELL ITSELF."

Further under the same heading Turner revisited previous language against the Supreme Court when he wrote, again in all capital letters, "THE BARBAROUS AGES REVIVED AND SURPASSED—BLACK NURSES AND DOGS CAN RIDE IN FIRST-CLASS CARS, BUT COLORED GENTLEMEN AND LADIES RULED OUT BY A BANDITTI OF TYRANTS."

"Fool Judges," Turner continued, "Distort and Debauch the United States Constitution to Further Degrade the Race that has been Loyal to the Nation in Every Struggle for Its Existence." He ended his headline by recalling, "Judge Taney's Decision is but a Bagatelle, compared to this latter day Fulmination—Justice Harlan the only Righteous Judge in the Corrupt Conclave—An angel Among Demons—Let us teach Our Children to revere His Name and Keep it in Everlasting Remembrance."

This was not the only major headline in this edition of the paper that day. Also included was a headline that focused on Justice Harlan's dissent. At the top in capital letters, it read simply, JUSTICE JOHN M. HARLAN, followed by "The Only Righteous Justice on the Supreme Bench." For Turner, Harlan spoke for "God and Humanity" in "Words that Glitter, Expressions Golden," and in "Language that will be QUOTED BY UNBORN GENERATIONS."

Turner was not finished heaping praise on Harlan. He called Justice Harlan the "Achilles of Equality" and the one man who balanced the weights of Justice and wanted his readers to "read his Immortal, God Endorsed and Mighty Defense of the Right." He closed this headline with an admonishment to his readers to "HEAR! HEAR! HEAR!"

Later, in a letter to the *Cleveland Gazette*, Turner continued to lament and excoriate the *Plessy* decision. Turner started his letter by writing, "I have absolutely no interest in the issues of the bloody, lynching nation, with its brutal Supreme Court in Washington City issuing decisions against my race which were never dreamed of in hell."[56] He implicated both political parties—Democrat and Republican—and wrote that "neither of them care anything about the Negro," because in Turner's estimation, neither party in Congress "ever open their mouths about the way [his] race is butchered, shot and burnt without law or civil rule."[57]

Turner continued his denunciation when he wrote, "This rotten country has no business being a nation anyway." He called the nation "an organized mob" and said that those who did not participate directly in "lawless murders,

Jim Crow car discriminations and every other devilment against [his] race, stand by and say 'well done' by their silence."[58]

In Turner's estimation the only people who could speak against "the 'mobocracy' of this sham nation," are the people of England. Therefore, Turner would "welcome no information unless it be concerning the reformation or extermination of this bloody-handed country—north and south alike—for one is as guilty as the other."[59]

Turner's aversion toward and disappointment with the Supreme Court continued throughout the rest of his career. He argued that the court took away the civil rights of African Americans but always believed that the "God of Nations" was on their side. Later, in an interview with the *Savannah Morning News*, which the *Voice of Missions* reprinted, Turner, in foreshadowing his break from the Republican Party, said that he had been "cooling towards the Republican party ever since the "decision of the Supreme Court said that the "Negro has no civil rights." Turner argued that since the Civil Cases in 1883, the court has been "against the Negro where the question of his political or civil rights were involved." "The Supreme Court," Turner maintained, had "de-citizentized the Negro and has nullified the amendments to the Constitution."[60]

In Turner's *Voice of the People* newspaper, he continued his critique and prophetic denunciations of the Supreme Court. In responding to white congregational minister Dr. H. S. Bradley, who earlier said that Blacks were American citizens, Turner quipped, "I wish he was correct." He reasoned that Bradley's optimism was because the "doctor had not been appraised of the fact that the Supreme Court issued a legislative decision taking away every vestige of his [African Americans'] civil rights."[61] This led Turner to surmise that the "Supreme Court of the United States is against us."[62]

In writing about the rhetoric of Malcolm X, Robert E. Terrill argued that Malcolm produced a rhetoric of oppositional prudence, "demonstrating for his audience members a prudential reasoning that invites them outside the confines of the dominant culture." "Prudence," Terrill continued, "emphasizes the inventional and individualized perception of possibilities inherent in any given situation," "directs its audience to attend in particular ways to its relationships with the other," while also preparing the audience to "function in a world in which truth is contingent, unstable and mired in temporal circumstance." For Terrill, "The concept of prudence, in other words, offers access to a point of intersection between rhetoric and the world. These texts present their audience with a modeled enactment of prudence; they invite their audiences, in effect, to deliberate and act in life in the same way that the rhetor has deliberated and acted in the rhetorical invention of the text."[63]

Terrill's use of prudence, and more specifically "oppositional prudence," clarifies Turner's pessimistic prophecy. When Turner began his prophetic denunciations against the Supreme Court, he placed himself outside of the dominant culture. While other African American leaders were trying to find understanding in the court's rulings, Turner discerned that the times had changed, and that one had to employ a new rhetoric for the times. Indeed, by 1883 the nation began to tire of civil rights, and while others saw the 1883 decision declaring the Civil Rights Act unconstitutional as an anomaly, Turner discerned that it was only the beginning.

As I attempted to show, Turner viciously and vigorously attacked the decision. However, Turner had not yet switched to a pessimistic persona. As I noted in *The Forgotten Prophet*, Turner was still very much a pragmatic prophet—looking to work with anyone who would support his vision for African Americans—especially emigration. Indeed, he used these critiques as inventional tools, to call African Americans to what I called a "messianic-oriented prophecy." Thus, his critiques of the court during this time—while many times acerbic and bitter—reflected a vision of African Americans recognizing and accepting the call to emigrate.[64]

After the *Plessy* decision, Turner was already in pessimistic mode. While he still promoted emigration as the viable option for African Americans, he knew it would not happen. Therefore, his critiques of the Supreme Court became stronger and more stringent. He discerned that the times called for an understanding that African Americans were not citizens of the United States and that if Congress could not pass a Civil Rights bill that could withstand a challenge in the Supreme Court, and if the court would not interpret the constitutional amendments in a just manner, then African Americans must govern themselves accordingly in this new world.

Turner's aversion to the Supreme Court started years before the *Plessy* decision. For Turner, the damage had already been done when the court declared constitutional the 1875 Civil Rights Act. Turner's prophecy found a home within the pessimistic tradition, and, true to the pessimistic persona, Turner did not appeal to the covenant or call for the people to keep trust and faith in the institutions (namely, the Supreme Court) of America. Turner grounded his prophecy in a belief that God would have the last word. However, in his appeal to God, he did not believe, as in apocalyptic discourse, that an end was coming soon. Turner's appeal to God was for patience and endurance for African Americans to wait for a better day.

To some this may seem to be a resignation of the passivity that many critique Black religion as having—reasoning that the faith is, as Benjamin Mays once put it, a "compensatory religion"—a religion meant to make people feel good about their own suffering.[65] However, Turner was not calling for this. His "wait for a better day" was, first, advice and counsel for the concrete and present-day reality for African Americans. There was not anything African Americans could do at the present to change this decision, and part of the pessimistic persona is the recognition of the current or "real-life situation" facing the people one claims to represent. For Turner to put a "spin" or a happy face on what he believed to be abominable would have rendered the prophet of no use.

Secondly, Turner's seeking God and asking his audience to "wait for a better day" was a call to stay active in discerning any moves of God. Indeed, Turner believed that God was still active in the lives of African Americans, and as prophet his call was to get his audience to believe this, even if they could not see it at the time. This was important in the rhetoric of Turner, because while he did see a day when Black jurists would serve on the Supreme Court, he did not say when, nor does he give any indication that it would be soon. For Turner, the prayer is for patience to endure and he stands with others who now must live under the new law.

As Turner and some others predicted, immediately after the *Plessy* decision, states started to enact separate but equal facilities in all areas of life. Turner saw these laws as meant to make African Americans feel inferior, and to mimic, as closely as possible, the days of slavery. However, as he prayed and lamented both to God and to his audience, he began to recognize something about this God he had served nearly all his life. He noticed how he and others talked about God and how God and religion framed many of the decisions politicians made into law. Who was this God that Turner and other African Americans prayed to and believed to be sovereign in the universe? Did this God have a problem with African Americans? Was this God on the side of white people? Was God punishing African Americans for some past sin?

Turner began to understand that African Americans would continue to feel undervalued and unappreciated until they at least could believe that God stood with them, that God was for them, and indeed that God looked like them. In short, God could no longer represent white; God had to represent Black. Indeed, for Turner, God had to be Black.

2

"NEGROES SHOULD WORSHIP A GOD WHO IS A NEGRO"

The Making of a Black Rhetorical Theologian

It would not take long for Turner to personally feel the effects of the *Plessy* decision. On February 21, 1897, the *New York Times* published an article with the headline "Bishop Turner Went Hungry." The subheading read, "Southern Railroads Provide No Lunches for Negroes." In this short article, the *Times* shared with readers how Turner, while traveling in the state of Georgia, found eating options nonexistent. When the train stopped at a place where passengers could get off and get something to eat, the owner of the establishment would not serve Turner. The *Times* writer noted that after the owner elected not to serve Turner, the "Bishop had no luncheon and had to go hungry."[1]

Two weeks later, the *Christian Recorder* published a story from the *New York Sun* about the incident and provided more details. In the *Recorder*'s retelling, we learn that Turner was "coming from a parochial visit in the lower part of the state and early in the morning the train stopped at Macon." According to the *Recorder*, Turner had "travelled all night and had a headache." So he decided to get a cup of coffee and a sandwich to "fortify himself for the remainder of the journey." Upon leaving the train, Turner approached the lunch counter. To his dismay, the clerk at the counter simply said that they did "not entertain niggers at that counter." After hearing that, Turner had to "swallow his mortification and humiliation and go away hungry."[2]

Not that he had not felt this rejection before. Even before the *Plessy* decision, Turner shared a story about a restaurant that he would frequently visit while traveling through Danville, Virginia. He wrote that he always felt welcomed there, but one time after he sat down to eat, some white gentlemen entered and took seats at the table. The owner of the establishment came to Turner and asked him to move, which Turner did with no problem and finished his dinner. However, when Turner returned to Danville and stopped by the restaurant, he was told by the owner that he could not serve him any longer in the establishment. Refusing the owner's offer to send his food to the car, Turner left the establishment and resumed his travels.[3]

To understand what was happening to him and many African Americans in this era of state-sponsored discrimination, Turner began to reexamine his own theology and his understanding of God. In his introduction to J. M. Conner's *Outlines of Christian Theology* book, Turner wrote that "never in the history of the Christian Church did the sacred truths of Divine revelation have to wrestle with so many insidious and ensnaring enemies, as have been projected and embellished within the last one or two decades." Undoubtedly talking about how segregation and racism were enemies of the church, Turner continued, arguing that

> Rationalistic interpretations of Biblical doctrines have been supplemented with false premises, corrupt, but garnished philosophies, and illogical conclusions have been reached and palmed off on the reading world by the glare of mere rhetoric, when, in fact, these opposing theories are nothing but the fascinations of imaginary hypothecations, which, instead of being denounced by the scholars of the Church, are too often lifted to the plane of respectability—by assuming to give them scholarly battle, when, in most instances, they should have simply hurled against them the battering-rams of denunciation. Reason is the highest faculty which God has imparted to man, and is the most powerful agent in reducing the doctrines of Christianity to their component parts; and analogical reasoning is an indispensable factor in simplifying those doctrines.[4]

However, even with reason guiding his theological vision, Turner was quick to add that "logical postulate, in all human experiences, has been sufficient to guide man as to his life and conduct." For Turner, God had placed in the hands of humans a "supernatural and sufficient revelation" of God's will that would help people "to understand and practicalize the virtues and graces which should ornament us here, and prepare us for a felicitous eternity, because this revelation is addressed to our understanding, and thereby to our hearts and consciences."[5]

It was this understanding of theology that probably led Turner in the February 1898 edition of the *Voice of Missions* newspaper, to publish his editorial "God Is a Negro." In it Turner not only offered a deep theological analysis of God-talk, language, and hermeneutics but also provided a radical version of a contextual theology that predates our modern understanding of the term. In addition, Turner's editorial offered a response to the hegemonic Christian interpretation of his day, asking African Americans to see and experience God in a new and affirming way.

In this chapter, I first offer a brief sketch of the theological thought, or more specifically, the God-talk language, of Turner.[6] I then offer a rhetorical analysis of the text and argue that Turner engaged in what some scholars call rhetorical theology. By maintaining that all theology is at its core a form of argument, rhetorical theology places emphasis on how a speaker or writer situates language in order to persuade its hearers of a certain position. In other words, when Turner spoke and wrote "God is a Negro," he was not doing systematic theology; he was engaged in a public theology, which is a rhetorical enterprise that has as its aim a persuasive function within a specific context.

On the Road to Blackness

Charting Turner's theological trajectory is not easy. As Turner biographer Stephen Angell has noted, "sources for Turner's theology are scattered."[7] There is not a collection of Turner papers or a Turner archive, and until recently, there has not been any collection of Turner writings to examine such a theology. Anyone wanting to discover the theology of Henry McNeal Turner would have to wade through many different artifacts at many different locations to get some sense of the subject.[8]

Moreover, according to Angell, Turner never wrote a theological treatise on any subject. "Unlike his AME colleagues Theophilus G. Steward, Benjamin Tanner, and James C. Embry, he [Turner] never wrote a treatise on such topics as the doctrine of God or the significance of Jesus for Christians." Many believed that he planned to write a volume of theology after the second edition of his *Methodist Polity* in 1889, but apparently it was never completed, and no drafts are extant.[9] Josephus Coan, on the other hand, argued that writing a definitive statement of his theology was of no interest to Turner. "His views were expressed," wrote Coan, "in his sermons, addresses, letters, articles and editorials. They were preached and taught from the pulpit as well as the legislative halls; through church and secular press."[10]

The closest detailed study of Turner's theology is Angell's epilogue in his *Bishop Henry McNeal Turner and the African American Religion in the South*. Angell argued that while Turner is renowned for his "God is a Negro" declaration, "there were many other significant dimensions to his theology."

> He [Turner] was also a fervent evangelical coming to terms with the new Biblical scholarship of his age; an energetic promoter of the gospel of upward mobility and self-improvement; a proud heir of African-American church traditions of spirit possession and shouting religion; a liturgical innovator who thoroughly mixed "high church" and "low church" customs; and a Christian who obviously wrestled with, but never completely resolved his feeling about, the teachings of his religion's founder, Jesus of Nazareth.[11]

We do, however, know at least one book that helped shape Turner's theology and gave it foundation. In 1884 the bishops of the AME Church placed in their catalog of studies for new ministers Samuel Wakefield's *Christian Theology*. Among the ones happy to see its insertion was Turner. Writing in the *Christian Recorder* on September 18, 1884, Turner celebrated the announcement of the book's inclusion in the catalog of studies. He lamented that the textbooks the bishops assigned prior—Watson's *Theological Institutes* and Halston's *Systematic Theology*—were "too costly and heavy" and "too cumbersome for the circuit rider to carry."[12]

In supporting Wakefield's *Christian Theology*, he noted that it was in the "reach for everyone" at a "price of $2.50." He suggested the book would be able to "answer all the demands and enable our preachers to convert the world if they will." Further, he felt so strongly about the book that he claimed he would not "admit any preacher on trial in the future, nor ordain any deacon or elder who has not studied Wakefield." He continued, "Preaching elders who expect to offer brethren for any of these positions had better arm them with Wakefield at once, otherwise I positively will not regard them, for there is no excuse; none."[13]

Assuming, then, that Wakefield's text shaped Turner's theology as well, Turner would have believed along with Wakefield that "theology was a science that examines the existence, character and attributes of God." This would also include "God's laws and government, doctrines and duties that humans need to perform." Turner would have seen theology and divinity as synonymous, both embracing the whole system of revealed religion, and both signifying learned or scientific instruction respecting God." Hence, for Turner, "a theologian, or divine, is one who is able thoroughly to explain, prove, and defend the doctrines of religion, and to teach them to others."[14]

This may help explain Turner's biblical literalism in his earlier career. In the pages of the *Christian Recorder*, Turner wrote two scathing reviews of Bishop John William Colenso's findings in his book *The Pentateuch and the Book of Joshua Critically Examined*. In the book, Bishop Colenso questioned the historicity of the first five books of the Bible. For Turner, that was a bridge too far. Turner argued that the Bible differed from all others because of its consistency. Despite Bishop Colenso's claims, Turner suggested that the Bible does not contradict itself—it is linked from "Genesis to Revelation." Turner believed that theological difference may come from differences of opinion, but these differences did not "impeach the plan of divine procedure." Believing that if one could ever "impose inconsistency upon God one would destroy one of God's essential attributes," Turner maintained that God was the same "under every dispensation," and God's word in both the Old and New Testaments bore God's image.[15]

When one writer attempted to refute the doctrine of the Trinity, Turner maintained that "God's tripersonality" is set forth in the "guide book of inspiration." He warned that a "little corruption, however minute it may be out-magnifies purity a hundred per centum wherever there is an effort to combine them." Turner added, "One thing is certain, truth and error has no connexion, good and bad no unity, friendship and hatred no alliance. No man can love and hate you at the same time."[16]

Turner's belief in the doctrine of the Trinity led to a strong dependence upon the doctrine of Divine Providence. In reflecting theologically about the Civil War, though Turner argued that the "nation is passing through a terrible revolution" and this tribulation may be in "God's providence"—working for her good," he also maintained that there was "no law in nature" that requires "some repulse to properly secure good results." He suggested that "reverses, political and moral, may sometimes be commuted for glorious ends, but to conclude these channels of indispensable necessity, is to acknowledge the existence of the devil as important as the existence of God, in the scale of physical and moral elevation."[17]

It was also his belief in Providence that led him to wrestle with the ethics of slavery and God's role in the institution.[18] The issue of slavery, more than any other subject, posed problems for Turner theologically. On the one hand, Turner and many others saw the Civil War as God's punishment upon the nation for allowing slavery. "But many of us have now concluded," wrote Turner, "that the judgment of God will never cease its plagues upon this nation, till slavery and oppression shall be foiled, and right, equity, and justice shall be seen in all its grand regalia, leading on in triumphant conquest the victories of humanity." He argued that the "institution of slavery must go" and that it would take African Americans fighting for their "God-given rights" for freedom to come.[19]

Even after emancipation, Turner argued that as it related to slavery, the Bible was misinterpreted and preachers "blasphemously" charged God with "sanctioning human slavery." In his eulogy of him, Turner celebrated his good friend United States senator from Massachusetts Charles Sumner on his fight against slavery. "From that time till the overthrow of slavery" Turner preached, "Mr. Sumner spoke to man but his blood spoke to God. Mr. Sumner marshaled the armies of the nation against the institution of slavery, but his blood marshaled the armies of heaven."[20]

While not supporting the idea of slavery and definitely not supporting how whites practiced slavery, Turner nevertheless grounded his rationale of slavery in the Providence of God and the divine mission of America.

> The early settlers of this country had run from outrage themselves and had manifested a desire to civilize the heathen and to build up an asylum for the oppressed of all nations and to enact laws, which would contemplate justice to all men. Therefore, God seeing the African stand in need of civilization sanctioned for a while the slave trade not that it was in harmony with his fundamental laws for one man to rule another, nor did God ever contemplate that the Negro was to be reduced to the status of a vassal, but as a subject of moral and intellectual culture. So God winked or lidded his eyeballs at the institution of slavery as a test of the white man's obedience, and elevation of the Negro.[21]

After becoming bishop, Turner continued to expound on slavery and God's role in the institution. One way he did this was to differentiate between what he called a "providential" and a "divine" institution. In an open letter to Benjamin Tanner, then editor of the *Christian Recorder*, Turner wrote, "I do not believe that American slavery was a divine institution, but I do believe it was a providential institution and that God intends to make it the primal factor in the civilization and Christianization of that dark continent, and that any person whomsoever opposes the return of a sufficient number of her descendants to begin the grand work, which in the near future will be consummated, is fighting the God of the universe face to face."[22]

Again, grounded in his notion of Providence, Turner argued that slavery was a providential but not divine institution. In an interview in 1883 with the *Atlanta Constitution*, he reasoned that since slavery happened, God must had allowed it to happen, and if God did it, then there must have been a reason. For Turner, that reason was so that African Americans could be "the means or instruments of redeeming Africa." Admittedly, at the time Turner did not know how God intended to use America for the purpose of redeeming Africa, because as he also noted, the time had not "fully arrived."[23] Later, in an interview with the same newspaper, Turner expounded more on his reasoning. Again he argued that "slavery was a providential institution" and that God allowed African Americans to "become slave[s] and to be thrown in contact with the whites of this progressive nation for the purpose of imbibing its civilization and Christianity and ultimately return in such sufficient numbers as to rescue the millions of our race in our fatherland from heathen darkness."[24]

His notions of Providence were truly evident in his letter to the editor responding to a previous essay titled, "The Negro Problem." The Negro question had not been a problem for him, because he had examined the issue in the "light of history and providence." In a strongly worded statement on providence, Turner wrote that "there is a God that runs this universe; nor are nations and people any exception." He argued that while "an infinite number of laws may harness up the mighty machinery, there is a God in the background nevertheless, and he rules in the armies of heaven and among the inhabitants of the earth." Further, Turner wrote:

> Slavery was a providential institution, not a divine institution; for had it been, it would have been as eternal as any attribute belonging to the godhead. One is temporary and contingent, the other immutable and eternal. God was not asleep or oblivious to passing events. When the Negro was being captured, and brought to this country and subjected to a state of unrequired servitude, He knew the horrors of their past and present condition, and foresaw the grand sequel which awaited the termination of their slave ordeal. God knew that the slave regime, although exceedingly pyrotechnical at times, was the most rapid transit from barbarism to Christian civilization for the Negro. Negro as I am, and being thoroughly acquainted with the characteristics of my race, I am frank to make this declaration, odd as it may seem to many.

Turner closed his essay by arguing that the hand of God was in the institution of slavery. While acknowledging that "slavery has been a dark providence," Turner argued that behind that providence "God hides a smiling face if men will only see their duty and adjust themselves to it."[25]

While Turner did not write a systematic theological treatise, he did write several religious and theological essays. One of the first was his "The Sabbath Historically and Scientifically Considered." In this essay Turner examined and explained the Sabbath Day and offered theological and religious understanding of the Holy Day. Turner understood the Sabbath not as a specific day, "but a consecration of one seventh of our time to rest and for religious improvement." However, this did not mean that everyone was at "liberty to make his own Sabbath," because, Turner reasoned, it was "essential to have harmony and cooperation with those [with whom] we are identified."[26]

One, then, according to Turner, should take Sabbath seriously by resting, or consequences will follow. In Turner's reasoning "the law of God is that man and laboring beast should rest on the Sabbath. The only exceptions are ministers of the Gospel, whose work-day is the Sabbath, and they are exempt from daily labor, as remuneration for Sabbath toil." He warned his readers near the end of his essay that the "least violation of his Sabbath law is invariably attended with fearful consequences. Its allotment is so highly sanctioned by our Creator, that it constitutes a part of the essential properties of our very existence. And those who ignore its claims have to atone in premature graves, or suffer the sequel of God's frowning blast."[27]

The preaching ministry also influenced Turner's theology. He focused a lot of his preaching to the Holy Ghost (Spirit). In a sermon titled "The Power of the Holy Ghost," Turner believed that the Holy Ghost was the "one thing needed for the church" and that "sacrifices and offerings" are not acceptable by God. For Turner, God required the service of one "enlightened by the Holy Ghost."[28]

On more than one occasion, he lamented the preaching that was going on in the church and called for "hot, burning exhortations."[29] He argued that the "spirit of exhortation is the spirit of the Church" and that there were "so many insipid sermons preached in our day that exhortations should be revived." His reasoning was that the exhortation was the "most effective way to call sinners" and that "systematic sermons are not in harmony with the Bible nor the ways of God." Turner further argued, "Pulpit eloquence and flowery diction that does not involve the salvation of souls, is simple both, a sounding brass and a tinkling symbol [sic]."[30] This is why he personally had no use for written (read) sermons. According to Turner,

> The soul has as much for it as it has for written sermons, which have done more to blight the power of the pulpit than anything else conceivable. I do not refer to special occasions, when some doctrinal subject is being treated. But what does a man look like standing in the pulpit, calling upon sinners to come to God, with his eyes upon a sheet of paper, and his head hanging down as though he was afraid to face the people? He is relying about as much upon the aid of the Holy Spirit as he is upon a petrified fossil. Moreover, it is all intellect and no soul, and no man can preach effectively through intellect alone. I repeat, it is time to revive exhortational [sic] service in our Church, and the sooner the better for thousands, if not millions.[31]

For Turner, there was a difference between "simply delivering "fine addresses" or "speeches over the Bible" and "Bible preaching." "How often," he wrote, "do we hear an address from the pulpit which has no more preach in it than there is a bray of an ass? Preaching will move people sooner or later; mere speeches, never."

Turner argued that anyone "God ever called to preach can take the Bible and hymn book alone, with the Holy Spirit and alarm the nation." He suggested that the reason why African Americans did not "turn out" great evangelists on the scale of Moody, Jones, and Small was because many of "our scholars were too high strung and timid." Further, Turner wrote,

> True we have men of great revival power, such as Grant of Texas, but I need not mention names; but where is the minister who is making it a specialty? Think of it, and tremble for our condition as a race. Not a great colored revival preacher in the United States. Several on a small scale, I admit. Ministers often are relating their great triumphs to me, speaking about having a dozen or two converts, or possibly a hundred. But a man that God called to preach who cannot count his converts by the thousands, has nothing to congratulate himself over, unless his minister life had been of brief duration.[32]

While Turner was a proponent of education, he did not believe it was a substitute for the Spirit of God. In a letter to ministers of his district in 1884, he wrote, "I care not what reputation a minister has for learning, he will never be regarded by me as a great minister unless he exhibits great interest in the salvation of souls." He believed in "divine call to the ministry," and he also believed that "God never calls a man who he knows has no elements of success in him."[33]

Turner's theology of preaching extended to women as well. On November 30, 1885, Turner ordained Sarah A. Hughes of Raleigh, North Carolina, with deacon's orders. As reported in the *New York Times*, she was a "well-educated, bright mulatto who could preach."[34] She had already filled several appointments as pastor in her area and had the support of the churches she served. When she came around the altar to have the bishop ordain her, "the entire congregation, both white and colored," looked on with intense interest. Finally, after the bishop "halted for some minutes and looked up," apparently, as the *New York Times* said, in "deep thought," he placed his hands on her head and said, "Take thou authority to execute the office of a deacon in the church of God, in the name of the Father, the Son, and Holy Ghost." After he presented her with a Bible, she rose as having the distinction of becoming the first ordained woman in the AME Church. However, her ordination did not last long, as the other bishops of the church rescinded the ordination and forbade Turner ever to ordain another woman. It would take another seventy-three years for the church to ordain another women—Rebecca Glover, in 1948. This time, the bishops did not rescind the ordination, opening up a pathway for bishops to ordain women as local elders in 1956 and iterant orders in 1960.[35]

Turner's theological leanings led him to exchange with people of different faith traditions as well. On one trip to Massachusetts, Turner spoke at a camp meeting of the Spiritualists. They impressed Turner with their séances, spiritual manifestations, and materializations, and though they disagreed with him on the doctrine of Hell, they did cheer him on other subjects and enjoyed his nearly ninety-minute speech. However, what impressed Turner the most was that at the conclusion of his speech, many white women and men came up to shake his hand, while others brought him messages from his deceased wife and mother and other deceased ministers that Turner had known. Turner did not know what to make of all of this, but he reasoned, "I do not know what to do with those spiritualists, so I leave them in God's hands and wish them well. I must say, however, before leaving them that I never saw a people so free from prejudice in my life. They appear to have no conception of a man's color."[36]

At another Spiritualist campground meeting in Lake Pleasant, Massachusetts, Turner spoke twice to mainly white audiences numbering in the thousands. Turner filled his speeches with theological affirmations such as his belief in the "triune God, Father, Son, and Holy Ghost, in heaven and hell, in a resurrection from the dead, and in a judgment day." He also told his audiences that he affirmed all the articles of faith in Methodism, and though they disagreed on some points, Turner wrote that his remarks "met either the approval or sympathy of nearly everyone present, and I was literally lionized."[37]

What really impressed Turner was how the people—especially the "ladies"—treated him after the service. Many of them "pressed forward" for an introduction and openly "locked arms with him." Taken aback by the kindness shown from the Spiritualists, in his second address Turner asked if they knew he was "Negro" because he was not used to "such adulations from white people."

It was his dealings with the Spiritualists that helped Turner appreciate Henry Theodore (H. T.) Johnson's book *Divine Logos, or the Wonderful Word of John*. Published in 1890, the book is a "theological treatise on the Gospel of John that focuses on Jesus' person, claims and character." Turner saw the publication of the book as an "answer to [his] prayers" that "God would raise up men" in his church that could "handle the Scriptures in the light of modern exegesis and orthodox theology." He thus considered himself "at the feet of Prof. Johnson in the publication of his book of the "Gospel of St. John."[38] Turner, in his review of the book, was impressed at the "extensive knowledge" that Johnson displayed in his "critical" handling of the scriptures grounded in sound "theistic argument." He likened Johnson's handling of scripture to that of a modern-day "Origen or an Augustine." Eschewing the mistakes that ministers of his age fall victim to, Turner suggested, "Prof. Johnson sets forth doctrine as a truth held for its practical value and a dogma held merely for its place in a creed." With his interest in the practical value of the faith and religion, along with a concern for the contextual realties that lay before him, Turner begin to reexamine his theological positions and sought to discover a faith that would be indeed relevant to his church and to African Americans in general.

The Creation of Turner's Black Rhetorical Theology

Following the practical value of the faith from H. T. Johnson and his own wrestling with scripture, Turner, on August 15, 1893, delivered a speech at the World's Fair in Chicago titled, "The African as a Tradesman and Mechanic."[39] Turner's aims were to demonstrate that African Americans were indeed successful in both mechanics and trade. However, Turner did not confine himself to his titled topic. In the speech Turner early on addressed the contested humanity of Africans. Drawing upon his "forty years of reading" and his visits to the African continent, Turner declared first that the "African was a human being, possessing the traits and habitudes peculiar to mankind—talking, singing, thinking and acting like a man with special peculiarities"; thus, the "Negro is a man to all intents and purposes." However, Turner took it further. Not only were Black people human, just like other humans, he also argued that as "revolting as the theory may appear to some present, I believe that all humanity started black—that black was the original color of mankind."[40]

Grounded in both the Bible and the science of his day, Turner declared that "God dug this world out of blackness" and "darkness was upon the face of the great deep." He also drew upon the latest scientific discoveries of his day by citing both geology claims and fossil records. Declared Turner,

> So, as I see it, instead of black being an abnormal color, an execrated color, a color to be despised and made the badge of degradation and infamy, to the extent that it involves the humanity of those who are black, if it is any color at all, it is the primordial, most ancient and original color of mankind. I have

reached this conclusion after years of meditation, with such lights as revelation affords to my understanding, aided by the stylus of geology and the archaeological collections found in the British Museum. Yet my interpretations may be greatly at fault and my conclusions wholly absurd, but scientific analyses undoubtedly make black the base of all color, and the black man is, therefore, a primitive man.[41]

Turner proclaimed that the "black man" was an "indispensable necessity to the growth, process, and civilization of the world." Turner argued that without Black people humankind would be "incomplete" and "nature would have a vacuum and the world would be unfinished." Even Christianity, argued Turner, needed Black people, because while whites gave it "system, logic, and abstractions," Black people gave it "feeling, sanctified emotion, heartthrobs and ecstasy." He closed his speech by declaring,

> Thus, God and nature need the black man, for without him there would be an aching void in earth and heaven. The universe would be in want of a balance wheel and the God of eternity would again have to light the forges of creation and perform another day's work before the morning stars would sing together and the sons of God shout for joy.[42]

According to the *Galveston Daily News*, early in Turner's speech there were "looks of amazement" and "shudders" from the crowd. However, as Turner continued, many in the crowd began to smile and appreciate his address. When he finished, Turner received thunderous applause from the audience. Many in the audience celebrated Turner's theological interpretations that gave way to a reclaiming of agency for many African Americans who lived daily with feelings of unworthiness and oppression. After his speech, Mrs. Maggie Porter, an original Fisk Jubilee singer, entertained the crowd with a couple of songs, and soon thereafter, not able to keep quiet any longer, Bishop Stevenson of South Carolina stood up and, raising his right hand, proclaimed, "Bishop Turner is right!"[43]

Others, however, had other opinions. The *Savannah Courier* dismissed Turner's lecture by noting that even if "Adam was black" and that the "Ethiopians were the most ancient and illustrious people," it did not "change the state of the colored man at the present day with relation to the white man." The *Sea Coast Echo* in Bay St. Louis, Mississippi, also dismissed Turner. Quoting the *Albany News*, they reasoned that Adam and Eve could not have been Black, because "they were banished from Eden for eating an apple" and not for "stealing chickens and watermelons."[44]

The *Grenada Sentinel* wrote that if Adam and Eve were Black, and that white people were a result of evolutionary change as Turner charged, it was then "thankful to evolutionary change." The paper based its reasoning not in its own racist beliefs, but in what it argued was African Americans' hatred of themselves. "We have never yet seen," they wrote, "a black man that was proud of his color, but we have been approached by quite a number of enquiring colored citizens and asked seriously why is it that their skin was black and ours white?" While admitting that they did not know, the writer immediately shifted to a color-blind solution to the problem by declaring that only if (presumably) Black folks would follow the footsteps of Christ, our Savior, colors, races, classes, and caste will disappear beyond this stage of existence.[45]

It was not only the newspaper that took issue with Turner's notion that Adam and Eve were Black; the esteemed Frederick Douglass also disagreed. In an interview published in the *Omaha Daily Bee*, the reporter asked Douglass what he thought about the theory. Douglass responded,

> I differ with Bishop Turner on the subject. Adam was not a black man, according to my notion of thinking. The word Adam means "red," and I don't think the name fitted his complexion if he was a man of ebony hue. Adam was evidently a red man—not an Indian but inclined to be a human being of reddish tendencies in complexion, or in hair. The name given him must have been a euphonious one. Bishop Turner is a great and good man, but I think he errs in his theory in differing with the best and oldest philosophers of these times as well as those of ancient periods.[46]

Two years later, on October 27, 1895, Turner delivered the keynote sermonic address at the first gathering of the newly formed National Baptist Convention. Turner, who by this time was senior bishop of the AME Church, enjoyed a great relationship with Baptists. He had preached and lectured in many Baptist churches throughout his career, and the notoriety that Turner would bring to the first convention of Black Baptists helped establish the National Baptist Convention. Turner filled the sermon with critiques of the status quo and the racism that continued unabated. He also offered "sweeping denunciations" of whites for the "wrongs of lynching." That, however, did not cause the greatest stir. It was in this sermon that Turner, building on his argument that Adam and Eve were Black, that he declared, "I worship a Negro God. I believe God is a Negro. Negroes should worship a God who is a Negro."

While his speech at the World's Fair received great applause and recognition, his sermon at the Baptist Convention did not receive the same attention or affirmation. Many in the audience on that day, while celebrating his denunciations of lynching and current conditions of Black people, were uncomfortable with Turner declaring that God was a Negro. One Black man, who identified himself as not being a "race man," declared, "If I should get to heaven and find only Negroes there, I think I would want to take my hat and walk out!" Yet another approached Turner after he finished his sermon and asked if Turner was afraid that God would curse him for calling God a Negro. Turner mused later in an editorial in the *Voice of Missions* newspaper, "Had [I] called him a buckra, or said that God was white or that God resembled a white man, that ministerial coon would have shouted." Turner continued:

> No race that does not believe that they bear the likeness and similitude of God will never amount to anything. . . . The American Africans believe they resemble the devil, and hence the contempt they have for themselves and each other. . . . The bulk of the American Negroes believe they are made like the devil, look like the devil, and the bulk of them act like the devil. . . . It is as much impossible to develop a race of symmetrical and common-sense Negroes in this country who are worshipping white gods all the time, as it is to build a railroad to the moon.[47]

Henry Lyman Morehouse, at the time field secretary of the American Baptist Convention and namesake of Morehouse College, speaking about Turner's sermon, lamented, "My soul was pained, inexpressibly pained and I know many of you were pained also." He continued:

> Brethren, must every race on this planet have a God of its own color—a white God for the white man, a black God for the black man, a red God for the Indian, a yellow God for the Chinese? Talk of this sort of the race spirit beside itself—the race spirit gone mad. Talk of this sort is almost blasphemous. As we all know, our God is not a God of any nationality, or any race, but of the whole human family; and as to color—God is a Spirit to be worshipped by renewed spirits in whatever colored bodies for a time they tabernacle on earth.[48]

Morehouse's colorblind approach to and about God carried the day. The delegates of the convention unanimously adopted a vote of thanks to Morehouse for his speech and continued after the speech to give praise and admiration. This celebration led Morehouse to conclude that the "Baptist leaders of our colored brethren have no sympathy with such ultra-utterances as those of Bishop Turner."[49]

Three years later, after continuous attacks on his newfound theological belief, Turner finally addressed his critics in an editorial simply titled "God Is a Negro."[50]

God Is a Negro

After setting the occasion for the editorial, Turner started his defense by arguing that African Americans have just as much "right biblically and otherwise to believe that God is a Negro" as white people do to believe that "God is a fine-looking, symmetrical and ornamented white man." Then Turner shifted back to addressing African Americans, calling them "fools," because, according to Turner, most of them also believe "God is a white-skinned, blue-eyed, straight-haired, projecting-nosed compressed-lipped and finely robed white gentleman sitting upon a throne somewhere in the heavens."

Turner's opening salvo does two things. First, it prepares his audience that a defense is coming. Turner argues that he could defend his position "biblically and otherwise" that God is a Negro. Furthermore, African Americans have the same rights equal to whites who suggest that God is a "fine-looking, symmetrical and ornamented white man." For Turner, the right to believe and see God as one chooses was of the utmost importance—especially at a time when Blacks did not have or were losing rights. Second, Turner's opening acknowledges that God is a human construction—"that if whites can believe that God is white, blacks have just as much right to believe otherwise." He makes this clear next when he writes

> Every race of people since time began who have attempted to describe their God by words, or by painting, or by carvings, or by any other form or figure have conveyed the idea that the God who made them and shaped their destinies was symbolized in themselves, and why should not the Negro believe that he resembles God as much as other people? We do not believe that there is any hope for a race of people who do not believe that they look like God.[51]

Here Turner notes that "human agency that is in play when talking about God." God-talk for humans is necessary because humans have always symbolized the God who made humans and "shaped their destinies." For Turner, since others (whites) do this already, why not African Americans? The God who made them should look like them, because there is no "hope for a race of people who do not believe that they look like God."[52]

Turner's God-talk also opens a contextual understanding about God and how people in different contexts relate to God. Turner not only invites his African American audience to "see themselves in God" but also pushes against a "universal conception of the Deity." For Turner, God is not white, and just because many people, including many African Americans, see this as a universal understanding of God does not make them right. Turner argues that humans, through language, "determine and decide what God looks like." For Turner, the framing and construction of God and God talk is of the utmost importance, because the discourse derived from an understanding of God shapes the destiny of a people. Turner adds to this line of thought when he continues, "Demented though we be, whenever we reach the conclusion that God or even that Jesus Christ, while in the flesh, was a white man, we shall hang our gospel trumpet upon the willow and cease to preach."[53]

Turner's belief in a personal God led him to declare, "God is a Negro." Turner argued, "Blackness is much older than whiteness, for black was here before white, if the Hebrew word coshach, or chasack, has any meaning." While he did not "believe in the eternity of matter," he did argue that "chaos floated in infinite darkness or blackness, millions, billions, quintillions and eons of years before God said, 'Let there be light.'" Furthermore, Turner reasoned that "during that time God had no material light Himself and was shrouded in darkness."[54]

Drawing from the biblical narrative found in the book of Genesis, Turner offered a reinterpretation of the "origins of creation." According to the biblical account, "In the beginning God created the heaven and the earth, and the earth was a formless void and darkness covered the face of the deep while a wind from God swept over the face of the waters."[55] Therefore, in Turner's view, creation did not start when God said, "Let there be light"; creation started when God first created—and that creation was in darkness, and that "blackness" lasted a long time.[56]

In Turner's reading of creation as found in the book of Genesis, "blackness is much older than whiteness and if there is any hierarchy in the cosmos; blackness should predominate." While he could have continued that line of thinking, he did not. This would have a been a good place to proclaim Blackness over whiteness, but Turner offered that while he was not a "stickler as to God's color," he certainly protested, "against God being a white man or against God being white at all." A critical reading of Turner's nuance—when he protests God "being a white man or against God being white at all"—is the "possibility that God could be something other than male."[57]

As discussed more in chapter 4, Turner argues that this belief in a white God is more reason for African Americans to support emigration. "For as long as we remain among whites," declares Turner, "the Negro will believe that the devil is black and that the Negro favors the devil and that God is white and the Negro bears no resemblance to Him." He argues that this type of thinking is itself "contemptuous and degrading." It would lead to many Black people "trying to get white and the other half will spend their days trying to be white men's scullions in order to please the whites; and the time they should be giving to the study of such things [as] will dignify and make our race great will be devoted to studying about how unfortunate they are in not being white."[58]

Grounded in his appeal for emigration, Turner argues that if Black people "remain among white people, blacks will have an inferiority complex about themselves." Not only will Black people "believe the devil is black and God is white," it will also begin to shape how "they act and relate with each other as well as with larger society." The appeal to be white and to aspire to whiteness was problematic because instead of aspiring to greatness in their own bodies, African Americans would lament how "unfortunate they are at not being white."[59]

Turner attempts to demonstrate the "pathological dangers for Black people in viewing God from within the prism of White supremacy." Framing God as white inevitably leads to feeling of inferiority. Racist ideology purposely frames "God as White" and "beholden to White interest," while at the same time "declaring that the devil and all manner of evil are Black." Turner understood how God-talk as constructed in a racist framework could be degrading to people who felt as if God did not bear any resemblance to them at all. Turner wanted to refute this line of thinking, so he concluded his remarks by repeating "God is a Negro."[60]

After the publication of "God Is a Negro," unlike some of the respondents to the sermon two years earlier, many in the Black community supported Turner's claims. The editor of the *Richmond Planet* had "no condemnation for Bishop Turner." The newspaper suggested to its readers that Turner "has a way of saying things which will make you pause and gaze on him with amazement." In addition, it stated that his "earnest countenance, the sincerity of his utterances and boundless depth of his race love cause you to respect and admire him."[61]

Another person offering support of Turner's declaration that "God is a Negro," was A. D. (Adolphus) Griffith, theologian and editor of the *New Age* in Portland, Oregon. Quoted in the *Daily Capital Journal* of Salem, Oregon, Griffith, while claiming to have "never given a thought" about the color of God, reasoned that Turner's assertion should be "just as potent as the assertion of the white man that God is white." Further, he noted that "no one knows the color of God" and that the "only reason that American people believe that God is a white man with blue eyes and straight hair is because a white man says so."[62]

Even some Black Baptists came around to Turner's position. In an essay from the Negro Baptist Publishing House published in the *Richmond Planet* on February 12, 1898, Rev. B. F. Graham remembered "sensational enunciation" that sprang from Turner's lips that day when Turner expressed his belief that "God was a Negro." Graham, in his understanding of who and how interpretation develops, seemly echoed Turner's arguments when he wrote, "find a white child or a black child for that matter that hasn't by reason of the white man's faithful picturing of the Deity, in the mind's eye a large, grand gray-haired old gentleman (white of course) as the portrait of the Father." He argued that religious literature coming from our "white brethren" show a "spirit of discrimination" and called for Black Baptists to produce their own religious material.[63]

Turner's Rhetorical Theology

Religious scholars and theologians have recently begun to examine the role rhetoric plays in theology. David Cunningham, in his book *Faithful Persuasion*, claims that "Christian theology is best understood as persuasive argument," and that "theologians are involved in debates, disputes and arguments."[64] Theologians, he argues, "are always seeking to persuade others—and to persuade themselves—of a particular understanding of the Christian faith."[65] Therefore, the "goal of Christian theology for Cunningham is 'faithful persuasion,' a theology that speaks in ways faithful to the God of Jesus Christ and persuasive to the world that God has always loved."[66]

In do no harm, theologian Stephen Ray notes rhetoric's role in constructing theology and doctrine in his book *Do No Harm*. He does this by offering a "rhetorical analysis of several doctrines of sin that looks specifically at the multiple ways these doctrines employ destructively stereotypic language and images in their accounts of sin in its social dimension."[67] Grounded in a metaphorical and somewhat critical rhetorical analysis, Ray warns theologians to "watch their mouths" because the way they talk about sin can be harmful.[68] Drawing from the work of literary critic Steven Mailloux, Dan Compier offers a methodological approach to theology. His notion of "rhetorical theology" grounds itself in a rhetorical hermeneutic. In this way, Compier can analyze theological texts by placing them within their historical context.[69]

However, while these and other works that bridge rhetoric and theology are helpful, they really do not define what rhetorical theology is. Cunningham in a later work offers a working definition of what he means by rhetorical theology when he suggests that it is theology that is concerned about the "practical implications of doctrine."[70] For Cunningham, a rhetorical theology does not "inquire to the truth of a doctrine in a purely abstract sense, instead attention is given to contexts and outcomes."[71]

Building upon Cunningham's definition, I have argued that "rhetorical theology is attentive to the ways an audience, within a particular context, is persuaded or moved to act." I suggest that this "invariably leads the critic to ask, "What rhetorical strategies and personas did the theologian use to produce the document?" and "How did the critic invite the audience to participate in the theological position that was presented?" For me, these and other questions "frame the discussion of rhetorical theology."[72]

Moreover, I suggested that "rhetorical theology maintains that all theology is at its core a form of argument—argument that seeks to persuade its hearers to a certain position." Furthermore, "Rhetorical theology focuses less on theory and focuses more on method and practice. While it maintains that theory be can derived from method, for the critic, she or he comes to the rhetorical task seeking guidance and understanding from the text, rather than imposing theoretical concepts upon the text."[73]

However, rhetorical theology also has a commitment to the practice of rhetoric. I have argued that "rhetorical theology understands that rhetoric is a contextual art—meaning that rhetoric finds its home within a particular situation and context."

> Rhetoric at its best is not a list of theoretical concepts in search for the perfect text that demonstrates rhetoric's vitality. Rather, rhetoric is a study of the rhetorical situations that gave rise to the response and an examination of how the speaker/writer invited the audience to respond. It is not, then, a study on how audiences actually responded, but only on how the speaker invited the audience to respond.

Rhetorical criticism at its best is a study of the language that came from a particular context in which a speaker/writer felt a need to respond.

Here I argue that an understanding of rhetorical theology helps us to understanding Turner's *God is a Negro* rhetoric. First, if rhetorical theology concerns itself with "the practical implications of doctrines, then Turner engages in a discursive analysis of the nature of God."

> By calling "God a Negro," Turner means not to engage in a systematic treatment of the Godhead or extrapolate a theoretical concept of God's nature. Turner responds to the contextual reality facing him and other African Americans during his time—how do black people authentically serve a God in which they cannot see themselves favoring? Image is important and how one constructs God will have an impact on how a person sees herself or himself.[74]

Second, I argue that Turner "offers an understanding of a "rhetorically constructed God." Turner, by "challenging racialized notions of God," not only did he note that "ideas, conceptions, and reality of God are not fixed, but these very ideas come from people using language (rhetoric) to describe and construct their own visions and ideas of God. Furthermore,

> Turner's "God Is a Negro" text is Turner's attempt to engage in the public discourse on the very nature of God. In taking this presumptuous stand, Turner invited his audience to see God differently, to challenge preconceived notions of God, and to live out a new reality that saw God not only loving them but also helping his African American audience understand that they too bear the image of God.[75]

In short, what Turner invited his audience to see was that "language we use to talk about God is at best problematic and at worse deceitful and racist." In addition, "understanding this rhetorically constructed God offers adherents a site of liberation, because they too are not only invited to offer different visions of God, but now they also have a moral obligation to since it is tied to their own freedom and liberation." Turner's understanding of God that God not only *loves you* but *stands with* and *for you* because you too bear the image of God, is essential and important for people of faith—especially ones that are told daily that God does not.[76]

It was an understanding of God from this hermeneutical framework that led Bishop Alfred R. Tucker—bishop of the Church of England in Eastern Equatorial Africa—to agree with Turner's assumptions. In an article published in the *Voice of Missions*, the writer praises Tucker's missionary efforts at attaining "African race identity." The writer wrote that Tucker "desired for his African converts, an African God, an African Almighty and an African All-Sufficient." Turner would have been quite pleased.

After the publication of Turner's "God Is a Negro" editorial, Turner prepared for his trip to South Africa. The preparation had to have taken a toll on him, because at the same time, he was still grieving the death of his second wife, Martha, who died on January 10, 1898, at the age of forty-seven. In the same edition of the *Voice of Missions* that "God Is a Negro" appeared, Turner wrote a touching and moving eulogy celebrating the life and memory of his wife, Martha Turner. Turner wrote about the "life she lived," the "heavenly songs she delighted to sing," and the "comprehensive and earnest prayers she so frequently offered the Father of Mercies around the family altar" that helped her to prepare for a death that she talked about frequently.[77]

Despite his grief, Turner departed for South Africa on February 6, 1898. While in South Africa, however, America was about to start participating in death on a massive scale. Not since the Civil War would Americans participate in a war with so many deaths. As one who served the Union in the Civil War, Turner was sought after on his return to America for his opinion on this new war—a war fought not for emancipation, but under the guise of imperialism. Reflecting on his own war experience and the current plight of Blacks in America, Turner did share his opinions on this new war—and many did not like what he had to say.

3

"AN UNHOLY WAR OF CONQUEST"
Turner and the Creation of an Antiwar Protester

On April 25, 1898, the United States declared war on Spain behind the mysterious explosion of the US battleship *Maine* two months earlier. By the end of the year, the war would be over, and Spain would lose control over Cuba, Puerto Rico, the Philippines, and Guam. Due to the Teller Amendment,[1] America could not annex Cuba, which led many Cubans to believe they were going to become an independent country. However, as the Cuban Constitutional Convention found out in 1901, America would not leave the island until it adopted the Platt amendment. According to historian Howard Zinn, the Platt amendment, named after Connecticut's Republican senator Orville Hitchcock Platt, gave America "the right to intervene for the preservation of Cuban independence, the maintenance of a government adequate for the protection of life, property, and individual liberty."[2] After the convention rejected the amendment several times, and after continued pressure by the United States and its interests, three months later, the convention finally adopted the amendment.

While the Platt amendment protected Cuba from becoming an outright colony of the United States, the war did lead to a number of "direct annexations by the United States." While America annexed Puerto Rico, the Hawaii Islands, Wake Island, and Guam with seemingly no problem, there was some debate about whether or not to annex the Philippines. After praying to God for "light and guidance," President McKinley decided that he could not "give them back to Spain," because for him, that would have been "cowardly and dishonorable." Neither could he give them to France or Germany, because they were America's "commercial rivals in the Orient. Nor could he just allow them to govern themselves as God told him, "they were unfit for self-government—and they would soon have anarchy and misrule." So the only thing left to do according to McKinley was to "take them all and to educate the Filipinos, and uplift and civilize and Christianize them, and by God's grace do the very best we could by them." After coming to his decision, he went to bed and slept soundly.[3]

This did not sit well with the people of the Philippines. In February of 1899, they fought back, as they did with Spain. Emilio Aguinaldo, who had fought with the United States against Spain, had now become the leader of the Filipino resistance. He tried to negotiate with the United States to established Filipino independence within a US protectorate, but America rejected his offer. The resistance lasted three years before America finally crushed the opposition. It took over seventy thousand troops and thousands of battle casualties. Zinn called it a "harsh war"; many Filipinos died not only from war casualties but also from disease.[4]

In this chapter I examine Turner's war rhetoric. I examine his rhetoric during the Civil War and contrast it with his rhetoric during the Spanish-American war. Grounded in his prophetic pessimism, not only does Turner's rhetoric shift, but in his critiques of the government and his outright denunciations of African Americans who support the war, I argue that Turner creates his own antiwar rhetoric that anticipates contemporary antiwar rhetoric.

Turner's Civil War Rhetoric

At the eve of the Civil War, Turner was not a supporter. Writing in his journal, Turner noted that while he had planned to hear soon that the nation would be at war, he thought the idea was insane. In writing about the people who talked about going to war, Turner argued that they had not considered the cost and had not considered "what they (were) going to do and where they will end this painful conflict." He thought the idea was a "wicked" one and that the proponents of war forgot there was a hell and a God. His prayer leading up to the war was "God help the people to think before they are beyond the reach of thought."[5]

However, by the time he came to Washington, DC, to serve Israel AME Church, his position on the war had changed. While Turner did support the war effort, he did not withhold any critique of the administration's action when he felt it was needed. In one editorial he likened the war to the Egyptian plagues found in the Bible's book of Exodus and argued that Pharaoh was Abraham Lincoln and not Jefferson Davis. Moreover, in what would have been a surprise for many, Turner, instead of seeing America as Israel, saw America as Egypt. Turner grounded his jeremiad in an argument that accused Lincoln as "unwilling to comply with a dispensation of liberation." In short, for Turner, since Lincoln had not done anything about slavery up until this time, a series of plagues began—starting with Fort Sumter.[6]

When Confederates started to gain victories over the Union, Turner saw it as an act of God. He believed that "God's plan of teaching her [Union] sense [was] through Southern victories." After those victories, "there [was] an appeal to negro sympathy, from parties in high position, but so soon as the tide turns, so soon [was] he discarded." Turner wrote that he had heard a rumor that the government was contemplating using African Americans in the war effort but also offered a warning. He suggested that they would "have a hard time raising Negro regiments to place in the front of the battle or anywhere else, unless freedom, eternal freedom, is guaranteed to them, their children, and their brethren."[7]

After receiving word that Lincoln finally signed the Emancipation Proclamation, to go into effect January 1, 1863, Turner stepped up his efforts to persuade African Americans to support the war effort. In his editorial titled "Call to Action," Turner wrote eloquently:

> The time has arrived in the history of the American African, when grave and solemn responsibilities stare him in the face. The proclamation of President Lincoln, promising in the short space of a hundred days, to liberate thousands, and hundreds of thousands of human beings, born under, and held in subjection to the most cruel vassalage that ever stained a nation's garment, has opened up a new series of obligations, consequences, and results, never known to our honored sires, nor actually met with through the long chain of a glorious ancestry. We live in one of the most eventful periods of the world's revolution—a period, virtually speaking, that "kings and prophets waited for, but never saw."[8]

For Turner, the proclamation from Lincoln "banished the fog, and silenced the doubt." Up until the signing of the proclamation, many African Americans wondered just where Lincoln stood on emancipation. Afterward, Turner could write:

> All can now see that the stern intention of the Presidential policy is, to wage the war in favor of freedom, till the last groan of the anguished heart slave shall

be hushed in the ears of nature's God. This definition of the policy bids us rise, and for ourselves think, act, and do. We have stood still and seen the salvation of God, while we besought him with teary eyes and bleeding hearts; but the stand still day bid us adieu Sept. 22, 1862. A new era, a new dispensation of things, is now upon us, *to action, to action*, is the cry. We must now begin to think, to plan, and to legislate for ourselves.[9]

Not only did Turner write appeals for the columns of the *Christian Recorder* newspaper, he also proclaimed his support of the war effort from the pulpit of Israel AME Church. In a sermon published in the *Christian Recorder* by Thomas H. C. Hinton titled, "The Colored Men and the Draft," Turner admonished his congregation for its lackluster effort in supporting the war. Using as his text Psalms 85:8, "I will hear what God the Lord will speak; for he will speak peace unto his people, and to his saints; but let them not turn again to folly," Turner called for his audience to hear from the Lord.[10]

In this sermon, Turner contextualized the text—reminding his audience that the words from Psalms 85 came after a seventy-year captivity in Babylon. It was after their time in captivity that the people were "willing to hear what God would speak to them." Connecting their sorrow with his own congregation, Turner noted that they too "had suffered years of captivity with all its degradation, toil, and woe, and they were thus sufficiently humiliated to become willing to listen to God's voice." For Turner, in order to hear the voice of God, one sometimes had to go through some suffering. When this happens, Turner advised, "turn to God and hear what he [has] to say, and perfect peace will come."[11]

Turner suggested in the sermon that just like the children of Israel, America was going through an affliction. However, instead of a seeing this as punishment from God, Turner saw this as positive, because God designed these afflictions to "humble our pride and work for our highest good." Moreover, if that was the case for individuals, he reasoned, it was also the case for nations. This is why Turner then could adopt the prophetic persona and call the nation to repentance:

> This great and mighty nation has been full of wickedness. We are being punished. Bloodshed and all the horrors and devastations of war are abroad in the land. It is estimated that over 300,000 souls have gone down to dust during the war. Yet we have not reformed. We are not humbled. Our churches, both white and colored, are even more indifferent than ever amid this dire affliction, while thousands are going down in the grave and to eternal death. What is the matter? The voice of God has not been listened to. All our sorrows are the fruit of

sin. We must repent. Individuals cannot be saved without repentance. Nations must repent. The high and mighty as well as the poorest must get down in the dust of humility and repentance before God, or they cannot be saved. We are all disposed to find fault with others, and blame them for our troubles. We are constantly pulling the mote out of our brother's eye.[12]

However, Turner also argued that African Americans were part of the problem. Therefore, he called upon his congregation to "love our enemies," because there was too much "hatred in this land." Moreover, he connected God's deliverance to how African Americans forgave their oppressors. "God will never deliver us while we cherish such hellish feelings. Look at this nation, we are hating each other." While he did see that the "dominant, or white race," was hating African Americans, he also noticed how African Americans felt about white Americans.

And we, in turn, have the same revengeful feeling toward the white race. Think you, my brethren, we can ever obtain the favor of God, with the blessings of peace as a nation, while he witnesses such murder in our hearts, as many of us now cherish? We have got to put away these abominations. It is the cause of our troubles. We have been cherishing the feeling of hatred, until we have gone to butchering each other by the thousands. We must love our enemies and pray for them which despitefully use and persecute us.[13]

By arguing that both whites and Blacks were culpable for the judgment that fell upon them, Turner turned to offer a solution for his audience. For African Americans, it was to support the war effort and especially the draft that was now commencing.

The war has gone on for nearly three years, and our people have been enjoying it. Many have forgotten the church of God, and gone away to mix in sin, swearing, and breaking God's holy day. We, as colored people, have been praying for the dawn of this very day. We have even been shouting the year of jubilee, when liberty has been proclaimed to the captive. Just as our prayers are being answered, just as victory is dawning, just as God is about to deliver us, we hear the hoarse voice of murmuring and complaint. You are just like the people of Israel, who, though delivered by the wonderful power of God from Egyptian bondage, murmured at God and his servant Moses.[14]

According to Turner, for African Americans, it was now their turn to join the battle for freedom. "In all parts of this afflicted country families have been broken—fathers, husbands, and sons have been stricken down, and mourning and desolation have gone into thousands of families," he proclaimed, "but our race has been free from these afflictions."[15]

Moreover, it frustrated Turner that some African Americans would complain about the draft and blamed Turner as the prime mover in this effort. Turner, however, distanced himself from that, even though he was indeed one of the people who lobbied for African Americans to serve in the Union forces. He declared that all African Americans should "be in favor of the war until our race is free." Turner believed that if African Americans would do this, "God shall be honored, and the rebellion put down." He warned them not to "grumble," and if they did, he argued, they "insult[ed] God and put an everlasting stain on [their] posterity." Turner closed his sermon with a strong admonition to trust God.

> God will surely speak peace when His work, which this affliction is designed to produce, is accomplished. Then the millennium will dawn. Our race, that has been afflicted and downtrodden, shall then stand still and see the salvation of the Lord. For our little privations now, remember that thousands of our race will be free and enjoy their God-given rights. God is already doing more for us than we deserve. Instead, then, of fault-finding, go to Him with hearts of humility and gratitude. Praise Him for what He has done, and give your lives to His service.[16]

Turner's promotion of the war effort during the Civil War did not go unnoticed. The president awarded him a commission, and he became the first African American commissioned chaplain in the Armed Forces.

Turner's writings while a chaplain and his chronicling of the war effort from his vantage point became must-reads for the *Christian Recorder*'s audience. While much of his writing centered on reports from the battlefield of the heroics from his First Regiment, United States Colored Troops, Turner did make time for other topics as well. Whether it was eulogizing former mentors, admonishing readers to write to their loved ones, calling for a merger of the AME and AME Zion Church, commenting on electoral politics, or writing on the religious habits of both Union and Confederate soldiers, Turner quickly developed his public persona as one who could write on and discuss many different topics.

In discussing his writing style and rhetoric, Jean Lee Cole suggests that "Turner's boisterous, and at times bombastic, diction and syntax leap off the page. He is a lover of syllables and lists, of hyperbole and excess; his sentences spill over the rules of grammar. He respects few rules of literary decorum." Moreover, she adds:

> As he came to be seen as a personage in his own right, the columns become more journal than journalism, more exhortation than reportage. Throughout, Turner exhibits a sheer love of language, as well as a deep concern for the future of black America. His columns are an assertion of a distinctly black notion of free selfhood, rooted in black oral and sermonic traditions, that form a counterpoint to the more genteel, sentimental mode that dominated African American writing of the time.[17]

Turner's service and participation in the Civil War continued to help shape his persona after the end of the war. Turner was quick to remind people of his service when attacked. When Turner accepted an honorary vice president position with the American Colonization Society, many in the African American community criticized him. He, in turn, reminded his critics of his service in the Civil War.

> I am also called a cur in your paper, and requested to stick my tail between my legs because a set of uncharitable and narrow-hearted men, too narrow to help their running brethren who are trying to escape further persecution, saw fit in their senseless babble to denounce me and the Colonization society. What does their denunciation amount to more than the bray of an ass? I am willing for such a herd to denounce me the remainder of their earthly existence, unless I do something worse than talk and write about Africa. Why did they not denounce me when I was traveling, speaking, and raising ten thousand soldiers in the late war, to go and fight to release them from the slave pen?[18]

After the war, Turner wanted to make sure that people did not forget African American soldiers' contribution to the war effort. In writing in defense of the 1875 Civil Rights Bill, he reminded his readers that "the blood of the negro has had to mingle with the white man's blood, in every war, this country has had; and in the last war, the demon of secession and division, withstood the world, till the negro with his blood and prowess helped subdue him on the field of battle." He warned that the United States may have to call upon African Americans" in another distressful hour again" but wondered "does anyone suppose, that the Negro would heed the cry? Does anyone suppose that he would rush to arms, and pour out his blood like water again to save a country, which had repeatedly broken faith with him?"[19]

Turner's rhetorical questions aside, when America called upon African Americans to serve in the next war, they readily and wholeheartedly served.

African American Support for the Spanish-American War

When America embarked on these wars, many African Americans relished an opportunity to serve.[20] One such person was George T. Robinson. Writing for the *National Baptist Magazine*, Robinson described how he felt when the war first started.: "When I had learned the true condition of the patriotic, struggling Cubans for liberty, I had a yearning to strike a blow for their deliverance; especially did I feel it my Christian duty when the noncombatants, including women and children, were hurdled [*sic*] in the Cuban cities to die of starvation." Noting that casualty count of the destruction of the *Maine* included twenty-two African Americans, Robinson wrote that after the government called for volunteers, "[My] love for suffering humanity, as well as my patriotism, was aroused. . . . My opportunity had come, and July 18, 1898, I left Nashville for Camp Thomas, Ky., reaching there on the 19th, as happy as a boy who dons pants for the first time."[21]

Much of the support for the war effort came from the Black press, and while many editorials conditioned Black support with Black officer enlistment and leadership, many editors appealed to African Americans' notions of citizenship. In short, they argued that since African Americans too were citizens of the country, they should take part in whatever course of action their leadership decided to take.

For example, the editors of the *Cleveland Gazette*, while acknowledging the "injustice done to the Afro-American," nevertheless called upon Black people to support and serve in the war effort. "Let us not stand upon the asking, but show ourselves ready to maintain intact the government from which we derive our hopes for life, liberty, and happiness." Other editors noted the similarities between Cubans and African Americans in justifying their support for war. "War with Spain means a good deal; we understand that a great amount of people in Cuba are Negroes, then we hope to see this government stand by them and protect them from all hazards." In one editorial, titled "Negro's Duty to Support the Government," the writer admonished, "[W]hile we may differ regarding the justness of the cause of war, when the majority decides for it, then it is the duty of every citizen to lay aside all personal feeling and enter heartily into the country's cause and [do] all in our power for the success of our cause."[22]

Another appeal used to persuade African Americans to support the war effort was that by demonstrating courage on the battlefield overseas, things would get better for African Americans at home. An editorial in the *Iowa State Bystander* supported this line of thinking: "[I]n many respects we think that the present war will help the colored man in America. . . . his loyalty will establish a friendlier feeling in the South between the two races, his bravery and patriotism in the hour of need may serve as a lesson to their southern brothers as to what loyalty, true and equal manhood is."[23]

Yet another appeal used by the Black press was to promote expansion and imperialism. Some editors argued that expansion would offer African Americans more opportunities than they had in the United States. An example of this line of thinking came from the *St. Joseph (Missouri) Radical*: "[We] believe in imperial America. Negro editors should encourage the expansion idea, since it means the opening up of avenues for employment of members of the race. Every negro should be thinking along this line." In yet another editorial that supported expansion as granting opportunities for African Americans, the editor of the *Coffeyville American* wrote, "Of all men the negro should favor territorial expansion. The retention of Uncle Sam's newly-acquired possessions furnishes a brighter outlook for the negro climatically, industrially and socially than any other class of American citizens." In anticipating the invasion of the Philippines, the editor of the *Wisconsin Weekly Advocate* wrote, "[W]e predict that once the Philippines are part of the United States that here will be found a field where the negro can easily carve out a home for himself which will yield him a handsome return for his labors."[24]

Many Black newspapers also appealed to African Americans' sense of patriotism and love of country. In yet another editorial from the *Iowa State Bystander*, the editors wrote, "[T]he love of our country, its flag, and its laws should enthuse and stimulate each of us to that higher degree of patriotism. . . . Our forefathers labored, tilled, fought, bled, and died to perpetuate this country and leave a heritage to us. Let us be men and show loyalty and we shall be rewarded."[25]

Orator and writer Nannie H. Burroughs, who would later help found and become the first president of the Women's Convention of the National Baptist Convention, echoed the aforementioned sentiments in a speech titled, "Should the Negro Take Part in the Spanish-American Trouble?" Quoted in the *Washington Bee*, Burroughs, speaking before the Congressional Lyceum, said that the "Negro is a citizen and as such, notwithstanding the fact that in certain sections of the country he was lynched and denied the exercise of the rights to which he is enitled, he could not justly sulk in his tent when his country called him to duty."[26]

Lawyer Thomas L. Jones, delivering an address before the Varick Lyceum in Washington, DC, offered his support of the war. As quoted by the *Washington Bee* newspaper, Jones closed his oration on a hopeful and upbeat note.

> The Spanish-American war will mark a new era for the negro in our national history. It is his opportunity, he who advises him otherwise is a traitor to the Negroes['] best interest. Let there be no backward step. This is a fight for humanity and for liberty and as Americans, let there be no division among us, and when the war is over, Cuba is saved, the wrongs perpetrated among us avenged and our national honor vindicated, all of the sister nations of the earth shall applaud your deed and the American people will be compelled to accord you that honor and distinction which shall be due to all of her loyal sons whose sacrifices and valor brought victory and triumph to the nation.[27]

However, there was no bigger supporter of the Spanish-American War than Henry Hugh Proctor, the first African American pastor of First Congregational Church in Atlanta. As pastors did during the Civil War, Proctor preached sermons to his congregation encouraging them to support the war effort. He preached one such sermon on Sunday evening, May 1, 1898, at his church, for the Colored Military Companies of Atlanta. Using as his text Mark 12:17, "Render to Caesar the things that are Caesar's," Proctor delivered a detailed exhortation as to why African Americans should support the war. He started the sermon reminding the congregation how the people of Cuba "have been trying to throw off the Spanish yoke" for nearly a century. While there had been three military attempts to accomplish this purpose, Proctor reminded them that the United States had remained neutral and continued to debate the "Cuban question." "While our sympathies were with the struggling Cubans," said Proctor, he argued that the United States could not "break faith with Spain."[28]

When, however, America decided to "break faith with Spain" and declare war, Proctor argued that Americans should support the effort. He proclaimed,

> In the judgment of the President the Congress and the American people, the time has come when our obligations to Spain have been superseded by our duties to the struggling people of Cuba. Accordingly war has been declared, and war actually exists between the Republic of the United States and the Kingdom of Spain. Already the fleets are lining up and the sounds of the guns of war are resounding in our ears. Our land is trembling under the feet of our soldiery rushing to the defense of our eastern coast. The conflict between democracy and aristocracy is on.[29]

Next, Proctor moved to the reason why he and indeed all Christians should support the war. He argued that this was a Christian war and that while "war is a terrible thing," sometimes it often "requires war to bring peace." Further, Proctor saw the war effort as not one of passions—greed or vengeance—but one of compassion. "It [the war]," said Proctor, "finds Christian justification on grounds of humanity." Quoting Matthew 15:32, where Jesus said, "I have compassion on the multitude," Proctor offered a defense of his position.

> The state of things that exists in Cuba is terrible. The island is laid waste, homes are desolate, the people are starving, multitudes are dying. And this almost in sight of our shores. This state of things has become a stench in the nostrils of the American people. This destruction is intolerable and in the spirit of Christ they rise up in just indignation and declare their compassion for the multitudes of Cuba. "I have compassion on the multitude." It is not a war of passion against the Spaniard, but of compassion for the Cuban. Are we not our brother's keeper?[30]

Proctor then got to the main point of his sermon—"what attitude should colored citizens sustain toward the government in this crisis?" In wrestling with this question, he told his audience that he wanted to "discuss this in the light of Christian principle, with the hope of promoting clear thinking and right action." Then, reminding his congregation of Jesus' words "render unto Caesar things that are Caesar's," he charged them to be loyal. In fact, Proctor suggested that it was Jesus himself saying, "Be loyal." To solidify his argument, he further surmised that there was a principle and almost a parallel. Noting that Jesus lived under oppression from the Roman government during his time, he likened that to African Americans living under oppression during his day. "It can hardly be said that we as a race enjoy full political rights. We are in partial political suppression. We suffer wrongs. Yet does not Jesus say to us as to his fellow citizen of Judea, 'Render unto Caesar the things that are Caesar's'? Be loyal."[31]

This line of thinking led Proctor to state plainly his position:

> In answering the question, what attitude the Negro should take in this crisis, I say it should be that of loyalty to the Stars and Stripes. They should exercise the spirit of loyalty at all times and under all circumstances, and when their services are solicited on the same basis as others, they should go to the front and fight for the flag like men. The country could not ask more; they could not do less.[32]

While some like Proctor argued that African Americans should support the war effort, others did not. One of them was Bishop Henry McNeal Turner.

Turner would take Proctor and others to task as being naive in believing that America would appreciate the bravery that many Black soldiers exhibited. But many of the arguments from preachers and editors must have sounded familiar, because they were some of the same arguments Turner made during the Civil War to get African Americans to support that war effort.

Turner and the Spanish-American War

There was much debate of whether or not to engage in war with Spain prior to the official start of the Spanish-American War. As early as 1896, Turner wrote an editorial on his position. He suggested that the United States would get a "good flogging" if the country went to war with Spain. While he did argue that Spain was no match for the United States, his reasoning for an American defeat lay in his belief that other countries in Europe would come to Spain's aid. He suggested that many men in countries such as Portugal, France, England, and portions of Germany were "just waiting on something to do." "They will rush to the aid of Spain from every European country like grasshoppers," he wrote, "and they will be glad of the opportunity." Further, he argued that the rich men of the continent will make sure that they fund the war effort by pouring "billions of dollars into the coffers of Spain."[33]

In responding to the suggestion that African Americans sympathized with the "Cuban rebels because "they were Negroes," Turner retorted that "Spain knew no Negro" and "Spain knew no color," and as such, Turner argued, the "Negro phase is out of the question." He based his argument on how well officials in Madrid treated him after the death of Secretary of State Walter Q. Gresham. According to Turner, when the queen rode out, he rode in the second carriage in the royal procession. However, his stronger argument against African American sympathy for the Cuban rebels was his belief that if America saw Cubans as they did African Americans, the country would have no interest in helping Cuba at all. "If the United States saw nothing in the Cuban rebels but aid for Cuban Negroes," Turner wrote, "everybody with any sense would know at once that this country would be but little concerned." Further, he surmised that America "would be too glad of an opportunity to rush there and help put down the Negro" and hoped that African Americans would not allow themselves to "be beguiled by such sophistry." He closed the editorial warning that if the United States got into war with Spain, he would "stump the country against black men taking up a gun."[34]

When talk of war in Cuba started, Turner wondered why some African Americans were more concerned about the happenings in Cuba than in their own state. Especially troubling for Turner was how some African American preachers would lift up in prayer Spain's oppression of Cuba at the expense of not saying anything about the oppression African Americans suffered under the American government. He called them "fool Negroes" who were "mourning, sighing and shedding crocodile tears over the conditions of Cubans." One example was a preacher in the Alabama conference. Wrote Turner:

> At one of our Alabama conferences a preacher of some parts became so affected about the oppressed Cubans that he prayed for the Lord to deliver them from the cruel Spanish, when right at his door whole states are disenfranchising the Negro, lynching him and filling penitentiaries with our race, and making them the victims of every form of injustice, but not a word did the prayer say in behalf of his own race beyond "God bless our people in all parts of the country.[35]

Next, he mentioned how South Carolina had already disfranchised over 140,000 in their state alone, and not a "prayer is offered for a thing so insignificant as that." Mississippi, he wrote, "did the same thing a year ago and no general protest has even been heard by the race." He further lamented, "What time has the American Negro to talk about Cuba or bewail the fate of Cubans when they have degradation and political, civil, and we fear physical death all around and among them at home?"[36]

However, Turner saved much of his venom for his next editorial. After returning from Africa, Turner set his sights on the Cuban crisis by focusing his attention not on the war itself, but on how the military treated African American soldiers. For Turner, African Americans were not treated equally. They were made the "butt of ridicule," their "faults were magnified" and "still the bone of contention." Further, he wrote they were "being snubbed while even defending the stars and stripes. This is not news to us, however, we knew it would be the case before we returned to the country or before we heard a word uttered. We do not see what the Negro is so anxious to fight for anyway, he has no country here and never will have."[37]

Turner then shifted to the hypocrisy in the justification of war with Spain. While noting that many supported the war with Spain as a humanitarian effort to stop Spain's cruel and brutal treatment of the Cubans, Turner responded, "[P]physician heal thyself very appropriately comes in here." Turner then argued,

> Enough men have been lynched to death to reach a mile high if laid one upon another and enough women and children to form the head and foot slab if they could be arranged to stand upon the head of each other. The United States

puts more people to death without law than all the other nations of the earth combined. So our humanitarianism is too ridiculous to be made a count in the argument of justification.[38]

Turner added that the "Negro will be exterminated soon enough at best without being over anxious to die in the defense of a country that is decimating his numbers daily."[39]

A part of Turner's argument against the Spanish-American War was his attitude toward Spain. Turner visited Spain and by all accounts had a wonderful time there. "We have been through the very heart of Spain," he wrote in one editorial. "We have ridden in the Royal Procession in the third carriage from her Majesty the Queen."[40] For Turner, Spain had "kinder people" and was "far ahead of the dominant class of the United States in the principles of humanity when involving race and color."[41]

In another editorial, he noted that in Spain "a man is a man in her domain." On visits to Spain, Turner had seen "black men and black women enjoying every privilege that was being enjoyed by people of any other color." He wrote on how he stopped at some of the "finest hotels" to dine and marveled at the "respect and honor" that the owners showed toward him. He even noticed that some Americans were there and how they "exhibited their disapproval" because he was seated at a table in the midst of them. These encounters led Turner to argue that Spain was a "far better friend to our race than the United States will ever be."[42]

In yet another editorial on the war in Cuba, Turner lamented the amount of money that the United States had "thrown away" with this "hypocritical war." Again he noted the hypocrisy of people who would lift America's humanity and "overflowing sympathy" for the Cuban people and their suffering at the hands of Spain, but not for African Americans suffering at the hands of the United States. Turner lamented how men were "killed for asking for a glass of soda water and lynched upon being a suspicioned of burning a barn not valued at ten dollars" and how a mob lynched another man "upon the charge of stealing a couple of biscuits." When these and other atrocities happened, Turner noted that nothing was done, nor was "any attempt made to do anything with these infamous demons who perpetrate these hellish outrages." He concluded by writing that the United States is the "most infernalized nation this side of the gulf of Damnation itself."[43]

When America found itself in the Philippines, Turner's critiques became sharper and harsher. Not only did the American government find itself in the line of Turner's fire, African American leaders, ministers, and soldiers themselves were not exempt from Turner's prophetic denunciations. Turner argued that the Filipinos were the ones fighting for freedom and that African Americans had no business going to war to fight against people with whom they had so much in common. He did not like that African Americans, who knew something about fighting for freedom, would help deny the people of Philippines their freedom. Earlier in his career, Turner actively recruited African Americans to serve in the Civil War. By 1899 and with the start of war in the Philippines, Turner thought that African Americans should not enter the army at all.

In his editorial "The Negro Should Not Enter the Army," Turner started by charging the AME ministers, whom he called the "most progressive, enlightened, and racial" of all Black ministers, to start telling "young men" of the race to "stay out of the United States Army." Then he punctuated his opening with his reason: "If this is a white man's government, and we grant that it is, let him take care of it."[44]

He further accentuated his reason when he wrote:

> The Negro has no flag to defend. There is not a star in the flag of this nation, out of the forty odd, that the colored race can claim, nor is there any symbol signalized in the colors of the flag that he can presume to call his, unless it would be the stripes, and the stripes are now too good for him. He is only regarded as entitled to powder and lead and the burning fagots. He has no civil, social, political, judicial or existing rights any longer. He may exist, be or live till the lynchers say he must die, and when they get ready to demand his life, the nation, from President McKinley down, down and down to the most contemptible white riff-raff, says well done![45]

For Turner, African Americans who enlisted were "abused, misrepresented and vilified when they passed through the country." Further, Turner wrote,

> If they came out of the cars and walked about the depot, they were charged with trying to kill men, women and children, and fire the cities and villages. If they sat in the cars and failed to get out, the newspapers branded them with cowardice, and said they were afraid, they knew what would follow, while one town would telegraph to the next that Negro soldiers would pass through. "Have your armed police at the railroad station, armed to the teeth and ready to shoot them down upon the slightest provocation." Yet the same towns and villages were ready to supply them with all the rot-gut whiskey they were able to purchase, to transform them into maniacs and human devils, if these soldiers were low enough to drink the infernal drug.[46]

Now Turner is able to ask rhetorically, "What does the Negro want to enlist, lay his life upon the altar of the nation and die for? What is to be gained? Where is the credit? Who will accord it to him? In what particular will the race be benefited?" These questions invited his audience to think critically and reflectively on the situation. If whites were not respecting Blacks who served, then why would it be any different for ones who did not serve?[47]

Turner then shares a story with his audience:

A Cuban from Havana who was compelled to ride with us in a jim-crow car a week ago, and who was as mad as vengeance at this restriction of his manhood, told us that the diabolical prejudice of the United States was being exhibited there, and his curse-words were sulphuric vengeance itself. He said "This valuing a man by his color was unknown in Cuba until the scoundrels and villains of this country went there." He showed us papers which represented him as a great business man, dealing in the finest tobacco and cigars, yet he was compelled to ride in the jim-crow car or be mobbed at every station, and this Cuban was not a black man.[48]

It did not make any sense to Turner for African Americans to fight in this or any war. "If you got any life to throw away," he urged, "throw it away for a better purpose, in a nobler act, in doing something that will perpetuate your memory." Then, upon remembering his own service in the military, he placed it in perspective.

While we are the first Africanite Chaplain in the history of the nation, and have once been proud of the flag of this nation as it waved and flaunted in the air, as a Negro we regard it a worthless rag. It is the symbol of liberty, of manhood sovereignty and of national independence to the white man, we grant, and he should justly be proud of it, but to the colored man, that has any sense, any honor, and is not a scullionized fool, it is a miserable dirty rag.[49]

In closing, Turner again not only urged AME ministers but all Black ministers to "fight the enlistment of colored men in the United States Army."

The Negro minister of the gospel who would encourage enlistment in the United States army, in the conditions things are now, encourages murder and the shedding of innocent blood for nothing, as the foolish young men do not know what steps they are taking. Moreover, the bulk of the white people do not want colored soldiers. Our own governor disapproves of it. The majority of the white press is against it. They regard the black soldiers as monstrosities, and we regard them monstrosities also. Again we say to the colored men, stay out of the United States army. Take no oath to protect any flag that offers no protection to its sable defenders. If we had the voice of seven thunders, we would sound a protest against Negro enlistment till the very ground shook below our feet.[50]

Later, in an editorial titled, "Shoot the Fool Negroes," Turner showed no patience for those who enlisted in the army. The editorial starts with three short sentence fragments for effect: "This ungrateful country." "This land of lynchers." "This nation of color prejudice." A contrasting elongated sentence ramps up his attack:

This white man's heaven and black man's hell, it appears, proposes to raise Negro regiments to go ten thousand miles to the Philippine Islands to murder and slaughter those innocents heroes, those brave defenders of liberty, that cluster of swarthy skin men, who are trying to keep out of the clutches of this color poison and venomous nation, which proposes to subjugate them and establish Jim Crow cars and rob them of their civil and political rights and entail upon them the curse of American hate because of their swarthy complexion.[51]

Turner also targeted his condemnation and disgust toward African American participation in the war effort; he called the ones who elected to serve "scullionized Negroes" not "fit to brush the dust from the feet of the Filipino." He also criticized "government pap suckers" who help promote the recruitment of African Americans to "go there and shoot down these men [Filipinos]" who were "struggling to make conditions better for themselves and their children." He prayed that every African American that went to war in the Philippines would meet the "frown of God."[52]

Anticipating that some would argue that his comments might appear too strong or that he went too far, he softened them by reminding his readers that he was no "advocate of murder or tragic death." Turner argued that he would not "pray for the ships that bear them to sink in the ocean," and further he noted that he would not ask that the "fool scullionized coons who go there be shot to death." While celebrating his magnanimity, that his "heart is not so cruel as to want to take the life of any man," however, he did pray that the "Filipinos will shoot the hats off their heads, the epaulets from their shoulders, the bars and stripes from their arms and perforate their coats and pants with bullets." He further maintained that the Negro had not more business there "than the Angel Gabriel has in the penitentiary. If African Americans returned from war, Turner wrote, "they will be hated, cursed and denounced for their bravery." Finally, Turner closed the editorial by summing up his feelings about African Americans serving in the army; he called them "contemptible fools."[53]

Recovering from a mild stroke that left him partially paralyzed and "nearly speechless," Turner was able to continue his criticism and disdain toward African Americans serving in combat. In an editorial titled, "The Philippine Insurrection," Turner felt called to enter his "solemn protest against the unholy war of conquest" that was, in his estimation, "the crime of the century." Turner saw the Filipinos as a "feeble band of sable patriots" that were "not white" and "on their native soil surrounded by their homes and graves of their sires." For Turner, the Filipinos maintained a "heroic . . . struggle for their God-given rights and liberties." He further charged the McKinley administration with "recognizing human slavery" in parts of the Philippine Islands and was disappointed that "colored soldiers" from America were "executing his diabolical will."[54] Turner also noted that the McKinley policy would tax the people of the Philippines and Puerto Rico but would not give them any type of representation in Congress. He likened that policy to being "taxed without representation," the very outrage, he reminded his readers, "that gave birth to the American revolution."[55]

However, what pained Turner was African American participation in the war. In what would be his strongest condemnation of both the war and African American soldiers, Turner wrote:

> I boil over with disgust when I remember that colored men from this country that I am personally acquainted with are there fighting to subjugate a people of their own color and bring them to such a degraded state. I can scarcely keep from saying that I hope the Filipinos will wipe such soldiers from the face of the earth. I have as much sympathy for them as I have for thieves, rogues, cut throats and lynchers. Those black American soldiers have nothing to fight for, to say the least, and to go there and shoot down innocent men and take the country away from them, that God gave them, is too much for me to think about.[56]

In his study of Daniel Webster's antiwar rhetoric, Craig Smith suggested that "anti-war rhetoric often raises the issues of racism and moral superiority," especially in cases where antiwar rhetors charge that a nation is engaging in imperialistic behavior. Typically, Smith wrote, when "imperialism has been justified on the ground that the colonized are inferior persons who need to be helped to the fruits of a better government," the antiwar rhetor must respond in one of three ways. First, the rhetor must "demonstrate that those colonized do not need the fruits of one's culture"; second, that it is not in the best interest of the country to intervene; and third, that the colonized culture is so inferior that it would lead to an "entrapment in a quagmire."[57]

An examination of Turner's antiwar rhetoric, however, does not reveal this strategy. Turner focuses primarily on two issues. For both wars Turner argued that America should not get involved, and the reasoning was different in both conflicts. First, when America debated getting involved in Cuba, Turner argued that American involvement would lead to defeat. He suggested that a war with Spain would be a war not only with that country but with many other European countries. He believed that America was going to get what it justly needed, a "good flogging."

The reason he predicted defeat for America lay partially in his belief that America was a corrupt nation. Long gone was his belief that America was the land of freedom, justice, and equality, as he had felt right after the Civil War. For Turner, God judged America for the sin of slavery, and after emancipation America was on the right path to do right by African Americans and all of its citizens.

Now Turner saw America as a country of "bloody lynchers" that practiced "colorphobia." In rejecting arguments that Cuban rebels "were principally negroes" and that alone should garner African American support, Turner responded that Spain was in a better moral position than the United States as it related to the race question. Turner drew heavily from his own experiences traveling through Spain to conclude that it treated African Americans much better than America did. Furthermore, he argued that the Spanish were far ahead of the dominant class of the United States.

Turner's critiques of the war, however, were not limited to America. He also targeted his venom toward Black ministers, whom he found overly sympathetic toward the Cuban plight but not toward African Americans suffering in America. Turner had a hard time understanding why some Black ministers could pray for the Lord to "deliver the Cubans" from the "cruel Spanish" when they would not pray for the oppression that was happening "right at his door." Again, he reasoned that Spain was not the oppressor that the national media had made it out to be. Moreover, based on his experience, there was not a "kinder people than the Spanish."[58]

When the war in the Philippines commenced, Turner's antiwar rhetoric took a harsher tone and focused more on African American involvement. First he called for African Americans not to enter the army, since it was a "white man's government." Turner argued, "[L]et him take care of it." Second, unlike with the resistance in Cuba, Turner identified with the Filipinos and saw them as identifying better with African Americans. Moreover, he saw them as "sable patriots" and as people who wanted only to defend their country from invasion. Finally, Turner also directed much of his criticism during this period toward Black soldiers. He was angry that Black men would volunteer and practically "beg" to shoot and kill people who had not done anything other than to stand against invasion.

Despite Turner's impassioned rhetoric, the war continued, and African Americans continued to serve. However, as the Philippine campaign went on, African American sentiment began to shift. Despite the efforts of Booker T. Washington to promote the war effort throughout the McKinley administration, many Black newspapers that favored the war with Spain, and ones that first supported the Philippine insurrection, now began to oppose the war, citing many of the reasons Turner did. The *Coffeyville American* wondered why McKinley had "liberated some of the oppressed colonies of another nation." The editor of the *Herald* in Brunswick, Georgia, refused to greet President McKinley when he passed through. The *Progress* in Omaha, Nebraska, called the war an "unrighteous cause," and the *Salt Lake City Broad Ax* called it "inhuman, blood-thirsty, and wrong." Even the *Iowa State Bystander* switched positions when it wrote that "a nation that cannot or will not protect its citizens in a time of peace has no right to ask its citizens to protect it in a time of war." As the war went on, many began to see the war as Turner did, and while not as critical as Turner, Black newspaper editors saw the war as immoral, unjust, and simply not right.[59]

Their opposition to the administration's war effort did not stop many of these same newspapers from endorsing McKinley in the 1900 presidential election. Many African American newspaper editors argued that while they opposed the war effort, and while McKinley had not done nearly enough in the way of anti-lynching legislation for African Americans, he still would be a better choice than any Democrat. Much of this, of course, had to do with the fact that McKinley was a Republican, and since emancipation African Americans were solidly Republican in their political makeup. To support the Democratic nominee for president and to do it so publicly as to "take to the stump" would have been anathema to African Americans. Therefore, the overwhelming majority of African Americans supported McKinley in the 1900 presidential election. One that did not was Henry McNeal Turner, and while many eventually came to his side on the war question, many did not for his unwavering support of the Democratic nominee—William Jennings Bryan.

4

"MCKINLEY, THE GOD OF FOOL NEGROES"
Turner and the Presidential Election of 1900

Turner began 1900 recovering from a stroke. In December of 1899, while presiding over the Georgia Conference at Savannah, Turner fell ill with a stroke and with a bout of paralysis that stayed with him for the rest of his life. To make matters even worse, on his way back to Atlanta, the railroad company would not allow him to ride in a sleeper car, because of strict segregation laws in the state of Georgia. According to the newspaper account, "officials of this Georgia railroad told this almost helpless sick man that the rules of the road would not allow him a berth in the sleeping car." The newspaper account, however, said also that Turner "acted like a true Christian gentleman," and "without murmur or complaint he was carried in his helplessness into the ill-ventilated crowded common car."[1]

Due to his illness, Turner did not attend the Emancipation Day celebration held January 1, 1900. Sponsored by several fraternal/benevolent societies in the area, the group held the event at Shiloh AME Church in Atlanta. Rev. J. S. Flipper, pastor of St. Paul AME Church in Atlanta, delivered the oration after an excellent introduction by the pastor of Shiloh, Rev. L. A. Towns. The Atlanta Dixie Band provided the music for the occasion, and Capt. M. H. Bentley "delivered a pointed speech" on behalf of "old ex-slave citizens." Later in the program, upon the suggestion of Capt. Bentley, the lodge members introduced the following resolution:

> In consideration of the great usefulness of Rt. Rev. H. M. Turner, DD, LLD, presiding Bishop of the 6th Episcopal District comprising the states of Georgia and Alabama, and whereas, we, the great empire state of the South, in due recognition of this day set apart forever by us as a day of joy and gladness. And whereas, in the wise providence of God one of the great pioneers of Georgia and leaders of the Negro race has been taken away from us and confined to his room, and, whereas he, the Rt. Rev. H. M. Turner was stricken with a partial stroke of paralysis whilst engaged in holding the Georgia Conference at Savannah, and, whereas the stroke is continued and we are deprived of his presence and his counseling words on such an important occasion; we do condole with him in these hours of his confinement; therefore be it resolved, that we extend to him our sympathies in order to cherish him and let him know that he is still in the minds and hearts of his fellow laborers and countrymen. Be it further resolved that we pledge ourselves that we pray for him continually, and if in the providence of God he is restored to health again, that he will continue his daring fight for the race, God and nations more vigorously than ever.[2]

As the year ended, however, Turner found himself at odds with many African American leaders. As his anathemas against America continued along with his strong emigrationist position and attacks against African American leaders, Turner found critics at every turn. Nevertheless, many could have forgiven him for his pessimism on the race question, social equality, and other ideological issues that African Americans discussed. However, what turned many Blacks against Turner was his support of the Democratic nominee William Jennings Bryan for president in the 1900 election. At the time, the overwhelming majority of Blacks were members of the Republican Party. By supporting and campaigning for Bryan, Turner went against tradition and paid a heavy price for his decision.

In this chapter I examine Turner's role in both electoral and organizational politics. Turner was a crucial figure in the Colored Conventions Movement. His success there led him to seek office during Reconstruction. Turner would become part of the first group of African Americans elected to the Georgia legislature. The moment, however, was short-lived, because conservative members of the house voted to expel all African Americans. After appealing to congress, the ousted members returned to their seats and began promoting many positive reforms. Near the end of Reconstruction, however, white conservatives had gained control of the state legislature. With the state now "redeemed," Turner and other Blacks started to organize outside of traditional electoral politics. By gathering in conventions, writing editorials, and protesting uncivil and unjust behavior directed toward them, African Americans, though shut out of electoral politics, did not stop politicking. What was left of the franchise, they intended to use in collective and powerful ways.

The Politician and Preacher

Turner had made a name for himself in Washington, DC, and with also serving as a chaplain in the Civil War, his foray into politics started on a high and optimistic note. In what would be his introduction to many in Georgia, Turner delivered a keynote speech before a packed house at Springfield Baptist Church on January 1, 1866, in Augusta, Georgia. Organizers called the day the First Anniversary of Freedom and celebrated the end of the Civil War and the ratification of the Thirteenth Amendment that abolished chattel slavery. Many in the audience that day sensed the mood and were ready to tackle the rebuilding project of the South through Reconstruction efforts. With celebration in the air and moving forward on the minds of his audience, Turner ended his speech by charging Blacks to seek reconciliation. "Let us love the whites, and let by-gones be by-gones, neither taunt nor insult them for past grievances, respect them; honor them; work for them; but still let us be men. Let us show them we can be a people, respectable, virtuous, honest, and industrious, and soon their prejudice will melt away, and with God for our father, we will all be brothers."[3]

It was this optimism that led Turner to get involved in the politics of Reconstruction and assist the state of Georgia in its efforts. One of the first places Turner turned his attention was the Colored Conventions Movement.[4] Started in 1830, Colored Conventions gave African Americans space and place to voice their opinions and concerns about the issues and problems many faced daily. Delegates promoted the ideas of equal treatment under the law, suffrage, temperance, education, and moral reforms. Historian Howard Bell argued that the conventions not only "mirrored progress, but influenced Negro opinion, and demonstrated to the American public that the man of color was ready to assume the full responsibilities of citizenship."[5]

Ten days after his emancipation address, Turner joined other African Americans to hold a Freedmen's Convention in Augusta, Georgia. Turner made his presence known throughout the convention, advocating for the masses of new delegates, many of whom were recently freed. When one delegate suggested that *Cushing's Manual* operate as the rules governing the convention, Turner objected, because many of the participants were not used to the formality of conventions. Turner thought that a few simple rules would suffice, and after much discussion Turner's suggestion prevailed. From this convention delegates created the Georgia Equal Rights Association, which met in April 1866. The convention's president, J. E. Bryant, named Turner as one of the editors of the association's organ the *Loyal Georgian*. Also, the convention named Turner as its delegate to congress to represent the interest of the delegation.[6]

At the Equal Rights and Education Convention in October of 1866, delegates appointed Turner to a committee responsible for conferring with the rival Union League for "uniting all the friends of equal rights in one convention." Like previous conventions, it selected Turner to serve as the official Washington delegate on behalf of African Americans in Georgia, and he recommended that the leaders of the convention publish the proceedings from the meeting.[7]

When writing weeks later in the *Recorder*, Turner praised the work of the African American delegates.

> The convention of colored men from all parts of the State, which was held here a few weeks since, did honor to our race, and exhibited a degree of progress intellectually, and highly commendable, in a people so recently freed. There was marked ability developed in their entire proceedings, the idea that colored men could not govern themselves, if permitted, is all a hoax. The addresses which they prepared and memorialized the legislature with, will stand as a monument of colored ability in Georgia for centuries.[8]

While working within the Colored Conventions Movement during this period of his career, Turner's rhetoric continued to be both hopeful and optimistic. In a speech to the Union League Association on April 29, 1867, he said that it "behooves both colors to cooperate, to join hands, and strive to the same goal." He called for a unified South and argued that the "Southern gentleman was the best and truest friend of the Negro."[9]

From his letters to the Union Republican Congressional Committee, we discover how formerly enslaved people learned and disseminated information about Reconstruction. Turner wrote that he and others would participate in "dialogues" that instructed the freed people about their rights. They would "read over the dialogues to the delegates" and comment on them at "great length so that no mistake might be entertained."[10]

While reading the dialogue, Turner would act as a freed person, and his colleague and friend Tunis Campbell would play the role of what Turner called the "true Republican." Turner would ask questions about the new Reconstruction measurers, and Campbell would answer in a "suitable voice, giving emphasis to the facts being related." "You ought to have seen the effect which it produced," remarked Turner. "When Campbell would read some of those pointed replies, the whole house would ring with shouts, and shake with the spasmodic motions and peculiar gestures of the audience." Turner suggested that this way of learning had double the effect upon uneducated masses and ordered them to be read until the people "[knew] them by heart" and could "relate them from memory." According to Turner, many of the recently emancipated people sought after the dialogues. Turner reported that while traveling, he would come up upon "25–30 people sitting under a tree reading the Reconstruction dialogues."[11]

However, this did not stop opponents of Reconstruction, and Turner wrote on some of the disappointments as well. After writing about the strife between landowners and laborers, he lamented that politically things were at a "boiling point." Writing for the *Christian Recorder* newspaper in August of 1867, Turner called the contest between the "retrogressive" and "progressive" parties "bitter." He noted how the opponents of Reconstruction were doing "all in their power to retard, if not thwart the measure." Additionally, he noted how Confederate sympathizer and future United States senator Benjamin Hill was one of its leading opponents. "The Hon. Mr. Hill," wrote Turner, "has written several very bitter articles, denouncing everybody but him and his, which from their venom and malignant epithets did much harm among the common whites. He wrote some fifteen or sixteen articles which have been copied by most of the conservative papers, notwithstanding they were devoid of reason or consistency."[12]

Turner, however, grounded in his optimism and belief in democracy, held out hope for the Reconstruction project. In an editorial in the *Recorder* published August 31, 1867, while admitting there had been a "vast amount of ignorance here among all classes, relative to the state of the country," "thanked God that all parties are to be elevated through the ordeal [Reconstruction] we are passing." Turner believed that Reconstruction in the state of Georgia was inevitable. In addition, he did not believe that a majority of whites were going to "vote to keep up civil commotion and political strife," and continue to oppose reconstruction efforts.[13]

Turner's hard work on behalf of Reconstruction efforts did not go unnoticed. When it was time to create the state constitution, Turner served as a delegate and made an impact. His hard work and dedication paid off again when the people of his district voted for him to serve as a delegate to the constitutional convention. One historian said that Turner offered "several resolutions and expressed opinions on numerous subjects." In a friendly mind-set, Turner introduced resolutions that called for a one-dollar poll tax on voting, and educational requirements for voting, and favored removing all voting restrictions on white southerners. Moreover, understanding the hardships of many southerners after the war, for those who could not pay their taxes, Turner supported measures that protected property owners from losing their land and homes.

Remembering that while growing up in South Carolina he could not attend school because the state law forbade African Americans from receiving an education, Turner also offered a resolution for the state to provide free schools for its citizens. According to one historian, in the preamble of the resolution, Turner pointed out that the "moral, intellectual and physical greatness of a nation was dependent upon the literary status of the people who support it, and that it was the duty of a democratic government to provide for the education of its citizenry, especially when the vote of the masses determines the issues, laws, and directors of the nation's destiny." When the resolution was referred to the Committee on Education, the committee refused to report or comment on it.[14]

Due to Turner's commitment and hard work on behalf of the Republican Party, in June 1868 the people of Georgia (Bibb County) elected Henry McNeal Turner to the Georgia House of Representatives.[15] Two months later, however, conservatives introduced a bill that would deny the African American members the right to serve in the legislature, because their newly adopted state constitution did not explicitly give African Americans the right to hold office.

After much debate on the measure to expel African American members, Turner addressed the body on September 3, 1868. Understanding that expulsion was a foregone conclusion, Turner proclaimed, "You may expel *us*, gentlemen, by *your* votes, today; but, while *you* do it, remember that there is a just God in heaven, whose All-seeing Eye beholds alike the acts of the oppressor and the oppressed, and who despite the machinations of the wicked, never fails to vindicate the cause of Justice, and the sanctity of His own handiwork."[16]

After the expulsion, Turner issued a call for a state convention. After listing grievances and naming the reasons for such action, Turner concluded,

> In view of this state of things, we call upon the colored men of every county in this state to send delegates to a state convention of colored citizens, to be held in the city of Macon, on the first Tuesday in October, 1868, for the purpose of taking into consideration our condition, and determining upon the best course for the future. There can be no doubt that our personal liberty is in as great danger as our civil and political rights. The same power which would override the constitution in one thing will do it in another. It is, therefore, a solemn duty

which every colored man owes to himself, his family, and his country, to maintain his manhood and his right of citizenship."[17]

By all accounts the convention was a success. In attendance were 136 delegates representing eighty-two counties. It aimed to "inform the freedmen of their political standing, and advise them in regards to the fall elections." The convention named Turner as its president, which allowed him to deliver the keynote address. According to Sanford, in the speech Turner "acknowledged the honor of his office, and criticized the Legislature as being illegal and revolutionary." Throughout the meeting, the convention established committees on "resolutions, finance, murders, and outrages, on memorializing Congress, and on address(ing) to the people of Georgia."[18]

Two months later, in December 1868, Turner testified before a congressional hearing on the Reconstruction efforts in the state of Georgia. He acknowledged that he was not only a member of that convention but also served as president. When George Boutwell of Massachusetts asked, "Did the convention represent the Negro population of the State pretty extensively?" Turner responded,

> Very extensively. There were not members from all the counties. The poverty of our people was so great that in some instances two counties joined together and sent one man to represent them both. One hundred and eighty delegates were present from all parts of the State. What is known in Georgia as "the negro belt" was well represented; I mean the middle and southern parts of the State. Several of our delegates had to walk 50 or 60 miles; and one man, I think, walked 105 miles to get to the convention, owing to the fact that neither he nor his constituents were able to pay his fare there by railroad.[19]

Turner further noted that the convention appointed a select committee on "murder and outrages" in which every member submitted a report. "A synopsis of the report was made by the committee," Turner continued, "which I would be glad to place in the hands of this committee if they will allow me." Turner added, "If I had known that I would be called upon by the committee to make a statement in regard to the condition of the colored people, being president of the Civil Rights Association, and receiving letters and reports from all parts of the state, I could have laid before you an immense mass of documents on that subject."[20]

While still expelled from the legislature, African Americans continued to fight for their civil and political rights. Led by Turner, African American lobbying efforts paid off. On December 22, 1869, Congress passed the "Georgia

Bill," which placed the state under military jurisdiction of the Reconstruction Acts of 1867 and required the adoption of the Fifteenth Amendment as a condition for admission back into the Union. Under this bill of reorganization, the General Assembly met on January 10, 1870. This time the entire body was present—including the expelled African Americans.

The victory was short-lived. After the state's ratifying the Fifteenth Amendment and earning a place back in the Union in July 1870, conservatives planned their "redemption" of the state. In December 1870, Turner survived reelection, but Democrats regained control of both state houses. In January of 1871, Turner called for African Americans to hold another state convention in Atlanta, starting February 1, 1871, to address the results of recent elections in which Democrats took control of the Georgia statehouse. "Whatever is done," wrote Turner, in the pages of the *Recorder*, "must, in order to be effective, be the work of mature deliberation, where all the statesmanship, experience, and intellectual sagacity in our possession can be brought into requisition." Turner also was not opposed to others outside of Georgia coming to the Convention.

> Representative Colored gentlemen from other States, who may design to visit us, may expect the courteous usual from those whose interest and destiny are identical. The people are requested to send the most intelligent men in their counties as Delegates, and supply them with means to meet their board and traveling expenses, and to furnish them with all the documentary information possible relative to the late Election, School Organization, Labor Movements, Administration of Justice, Emigration Feeling, Acquisition of Property, and the general condition of our people, etc. Delegates are expected to remain at least three days in session, or till their work is completed.[21]

Apparently, due to the issues and concerns that the convention attempted to address, there was a need for "more practical understanding and mutual cooperation." Delegates concluded that a "more thorough union of effort, action, and organization" was needed to address what were the beginning stages of dismantling hard-fought Reconstruction victories. Therefore, on February 3, 1871, the convention adopted a preamble and resolution that authorized Turner, as the president of the Georgia State Convention, to issue a call in its name "to be held at such time and place as he and those whom he may advise, shall determine best." Despite their best efforts to rally support, the elections of 1872 told a different story. This time Democrats won in larger margins, effectively ending Reconstruction in that state. Turner turned his attention to the church and started serving as pastor of St. Philip AME Church in Savannah, Georgia.[22]

Post-Reconstruction Politics

Turner attended the 1876 Republican National Convention in hopes of reigniting the spirit of the earlier radicalism of the party. Many still appreciated the hard work he did to establish the Republican Party in the state of Georgia and offered him a speaking spot at the convention. He was to second the presidential nomination of James G. Blaine—a United States senator and former House Speaker from Maine. In his speech Turner extolled the virtues of Blaine. "For twenty-five years," Turner said, "he had been in its front, and today he stands the champion of Republican principles." For Turner, Blaine originated the "spirit of the fourteenth amendment," had stood by Lincoln during the "great struggle this country was passing through for freedom and justice and equality to all mankind," and had helped "chase out of this nation a set of insurgents who lifted impious hands against that flag that still floats over us."[23]

Turner also supported Blaine because he felt he was a representative of "Young America." Turner reminded his audience that Blaine was no "dead fossil" and that he was "not tied on to any old constitutional barriers that shut out a parcel, a class of God's humanity and tie him to a set of principles that are antiquated." He closed his speech by reminding his audience that after the Democrats won the previous election, it was Blaine on the floor of Congress who "shook aloft the banner of the Republican Party, united the party and defied the Democracy of this nation and breathed again the spirit of activity and hope into this prostrate Republican Party."[24]

However, despite optimism and high hopes for radical change during Reconstruction, the 1876 elections told a different story. First, Turner's candidate lost the nomination to Rutherford B. Hayes. Second, in the general election, Hayes and his vice-presidential candidate, William Wheeler of New York, lost the popular vote to the Democrats Samuel J. Tilden and Thomas H. Hendricks. Through an informal agreement, however, and with the majority Democratic Congress at the time, the twenty "disputed" electoral votes all went to Hayes, in effect giving him the election. This deal came with a cost. To receive the votes, Hayes promised to pull the remaining troops out from the South, effectively ending Reconstruction throughout the South.

With troops pulled out of the remaining southern states, the politics of redemption could go on unabated. Seeing how white conservatives regained electoral power through violence and intimidation tactics, Turner, in a letter to the *Recorder* published December 14, 1876, criticized the government, and especially those in the North, as not doing enough to protect the lives, property, and franchise of African Americans. For Turner, the nation was bound by every consideration to secure citizens "protection of life and person." Instead, African Americans were hurled into a "vortex of a new revolution," which would have "taxed the skill and energies of the most enlightened people on earth." Accordingly, for Turner, "the meanness of this nation towards the negro, will never be known until it is read in the glare of eternity." Further, he declared:

> When they say, "we have done everything we could for the colored people of the South" they utter a thousand falsehoods in one breath; and there is not a negro whose blood has been shed, that does not crimson the garments of every white man in the North. The best that can be said for this country is that it is a nation of murderers. The North has been killing Southern negroes as virtually as the Ku-klux and White Leagues have, and every white statesman, orator minister of the Gospel, merchant, doctor, and private citizen in this whole nation, who has not fought these massacres (for holding your mouth is no excuse) and the injustice perpetrated to blacks, the nation's wards are guilty before God. And if they ever get to heaven at all, they will have to swim there through the blood of forty-six thousand negroes, which it is reported in Washington have been killed since January 1866.[25]

He closed his letter with:

> These words may startle somebody. . . . My pen trembles with indignation as it traces lines of this paper, and I am only one out of ten hundred thousands of colored men whose hearts are galled and whose ire is inflamed. . . . It requires no renown sage to see that God is now lashing this nation upon its back and in my imagination I can hear it as literally crying; "Oh pray massa!" as ever I heard the slave men of the South. May God slash this nation; may it writhe; may it groan and sigh; and may it bleed and die, or else learn wisdom; learn humanity black or white, brown or red.[26]

As the politics of Reconstruction gave way to the politics of redemption, Turner's political options began to recede. No longer able to participate in state electoral politics, his frustration with the national Republican Party became evident in his writings. Two months before his own election as bishop in the AME Church, Turner, in a letter to the *Christian Recorder* published March 25, 1880, wrote that he had "thought it prudent to keep out of the Presidential agitation for the reason that I am down upon the whole nation." Claiming that the nation has treated his race with the "kindness that a hungry snake treats a helpless frog," Turner wrote that he was as "near a rebel to this Government as any Negro ever got to be." Frustrated by how society treated

African Americans and seeing how the race "has been treated with so much treachery, vile contempt, and diabolical meanness," Turner lamented that he wished he would have never been born, so that he would not have to witness "deviltry perpetrated upon my people by a so-called civilized country."[27]

In the 1884 presidential election, Turner preferred atheist Robert G. Ingersoll for president. In an interview published in the *GRIT* newspaper on February 24, 1884, when asked, "Would you vote for a man who did not believe as you do" regarding "religious conviction," Turner responded, "I detest Col. Ingersoll's atheism as much as any man. But he is as good, if not better, than a man who believes in God and daily blasphemes his name. Yes, he is better than a God-believing blasphemer. While I detest and regret the atheism of Mr. Ingersoll, he is a better man than half the so-called white Christians in the nation."[28]

Ingersoll did not run for office, but Democratic nominee Grover Cleveland did—and won. Turner saw this as a rebuke from God against the Republican Party. Writing in the *AME Journal Review* in January 1885, Turner summed up the defeat of the Republican Party:

> The defeat of the Republican Party in the late election is due to its treachery towards the Negro. It was formed in the Providence of God to free the Negro and to saturate the institutions of the Nation with equal and exact justice to all men; and the moment it sanctioned discrimination, proscription and injustice, and sought to rear up a Solid North against a Solid South, thus leaving the race exposed to the fury of their enemies, then Providence injects another course of events. He permits treacherous white Republicans to lead the party to destruction; that was exhibiting such blatant-faced treachery towards black Republicans. Thus it was not a Democratic victory as such, but the Democrats have been resurrected by the aid of treacherous Republicans to serve the purpose of a scourge upon a treacherous party.[29]

By 1890 Turner had officially left the Republican Party but had interest in supporting the Federal Elections bill that year. Introduced in Congress by Republicans Henry Cabot Lodge, in the House, and George Frisbie Hoar in the Senate, the bill sought to establish federal oversight over federal elections. Arguably, this was a measure that would have protected the vote of African Americans. Turner, in a letter to the *Christian Recorder* published August 28, 1890, wrote in support of the measure:

> I left the Republican Party after I saw it did not intend to remedy that hell-born decision which the Supreme Court of the United States issued, taking away our

civil rights. But when the pending bill was offered and passed the Lower House, I said thank God for that little. The Negro is not entirely forgotten after all. If the bill passes he may be a small factor yet, and in process of time recover his civil rights. Weak as the bill is, it is better than nothing. It would be a menace in our favor at least. But it seems that the bill is to be defeated by democrats, Negro hating republicans and a herd of Negro monstrosities, who want nothing but the smiles of some white man, whose curs they are. There are a set of brainless, low babblers belonging to our race who desire nothing but the degradation of themselves and our people.[30]

To Turner's disappointment, but not surprise, while the bill passed the House, it failed to gain support in the Senate.

Turner supported the presidency of Republican President Benjamin Harrison. In a letter published September 11, 1890, in the *Christian Recorder*, Turner criticized African Americans who "castigated" Harrison and his administration. Turner called Harrison the "most impartial President that has been in the White House since the death of Mr. Lincoln." Further, Harrison appointed "more colored men in office since Grant, Hayes, Garfield, Arthur and Cleveland all put together," and more importantly, "his appointments in the aggregate have been more honorable. He has appointed colored men where he knew they had to superintend white men and women. Nor has he hesitated or staggered to do so." He closed his letter:

> In conclusion, President Harrison is entitled to the respect and gratitude of our race, and the colored people of this country owe it to their manhood and honor to uphold his hand and show their gratitude by working for his re-election; otherwise, we are a set of ingrates. And all that I have said in regard to President Harrison may be said in the main of his cabinet, for this is practically a Negro administration, and we are blind if we cannot see it. While my position as a Bishop presumably puts me out of politics, I am strongly inclined to seek membership in the next national republican nomination convention, just for the purpose of trying to renominate Harrison for the presidency.[31]

In the 1890s Turner turned his attention away from electoral politics and focused on his emigration campaign. As I discuss more in chapter 5, Turner called for a national convention to address the issue of emigration. However, that did not stop reporters from asking Turner about his political positions. When asked by one in 1894 who would be the next president, Turner replied, "Oh, my God, you have got me now. I do not care who since he is not a friend of my race." He did, however, mention that the person African Americans would support would be "Justice Harlan, of the Supreme Court, whether he was nominated by the Democratic or Republican party."[32]

Nor did his turn away from electoral politics insulate him from controversy. In March of 1897, an article appeared in the *New York Times* with the headline: "'Negroes, Get Guns!' A Colored Bishop Advises Men of His Race to Resist Lynching, and Prays That Their Aim May Be Good." The *Times* reprinted the article from Turner's *Voice of Missions* newspaper.[33] In it Turner offered commentary on the lynching of John Johnson and Archibald Jointry.[34] For Turner, to make matters worse, the lynching took place in New Orleans and only a few miles away from a meeting of the AME bishops. "Let every Negro in this country with a spark of manhood in him supply his house with one, two, or three guns or with a seven or a sixteen shooter," Turner advised, and "keep them loaded and ready for immediate use and when his domicile is invaded by bloody lynchers or any mob by day or night, Sabbath or weekday, turn loose your missiles of death and blow your fiendish invaders into a thousand giblets." Turner closed his editorial with, "Again, we say, get guns, Negroes, get guns, and may God give you good aim when you shoot."[35]

Despite squarely placing his editorial within a self-defense framework, many opponents and some supporters of Turner's denounced he comments and called them ill-advised. The *Roanoke Times*, citing the Republican-leaning *New York Mail and Express* wrote, "Two wrongs never make a right . . . to urge the people to rise in armed revolt against lynchers is both unwise and un-Christian. Bishop Turner is a bad adviser when he incites his followers to trample upon the law and justice to avenge the wrongs of their race."[36]

Other newspapers blamed the lynching on the victims. For instance, the *Abbeville Press and Banner* wrote, "If Bishop Turner had advised his young men to restrain themselves, to observe the laws of the church and the statues of the state, he might stop lynching. . . . If Bishop Turner would save the young men of his race from being lynched, he must teach them to respect the laws of God and man." The *Wilmington Semi-weekly Messenger*, in an editorial titled "The Worst Possible Advice," advised Turner "and his brethren in the ministry [to] induce their race to cease to rob and assault helpless whites and learn to be more moral and law-abiding, and there will be no use of shotguns and shooters for either race. Lynchings will cease when murders and rapes cease."[37]

The Black press was also critical of Turner's editorial. The *Salt Lake City Broad Ax* questioned Turner's "belief in the Bible" and his loyalty to the teachings of Jesus. In a column it stated, "It does seem so very strange to hear a minister of the gospel advising the people to not only violate the laws of the land but also to set aside the commandments of the Bible and the teachings of the One who is encircled in the hearts of hundreds of millions of His humble followers. . . . When a preacher gets up and utters such sentiments as these, he should be condemned by all honest men." It is worth noting that the editorial condemning Turner's call for self-defense appeared next to a story of how presumably Bible-believing Christian lynchers took William Clement from a jail cell to lynch him. After fighting off the men, he escaped the lynching, but not the six bullets that they found in him the next day. Still alive, he was taken by the sheriff back to jail for trial.[38]

Even fellow bishop and friend W. J. Gaines publicly rebuked Turner. Gaines wrote that while he was "as empathetic in [his] condemnation of the lawless and godless crime of lynching as Bishop Turner" was, Turner was "entirely too radical." He too adopted a victim-blaming approach when he wrote that "the best remedy for our evils is education and Christianity. The crimes for which lynching is the punishment are committed by the most ignorant of our race. It will take time to educate them." Bishop Gaines closed by challenging African Americans not to "indulge in extravagances such as that to which Bishop Turner is giving expression."[39] However, for Bishop Gaines and other Black leaders, Turner had only started such extravagances.

The effects of a stroke limited Bishop Turner's activity in the early part of 1900. However, feeling better by May of that year, Turner attended the General Conference of the AME Church. After the conference, in June, African American leaders met in Philadelphia with plans to start a National Negro Party. According to reports the plan was to "organize the party in every state of the Union and nominate candidates for state and congressional offices." Speaking to reporters after the meeting, H. C. C. Astwood said that the platform "[would] insist upon the observance of the constitution of the United States, the civil and political rights of every citizen without race color or condition." The party would further support the "opposition of monopolies, trusts and rings and the duty of the government to control all public conveyance such as railroads, etc., and all telegraph and telephone operations, so as not to burden the people with unnecessary taxation."[40]

One leader absent from the meeting was Turner. When told about the effort, he expressed doubt that any "practical results" could come from the initiative, because African Americans made up such a small part of the electorate. He said that he would be in favor, however, of a political party if it intended to "secure an appropriation" that would enable African Americans to "move to a place where they can be by themselves." He took "no stock" in any movement that did not contemplate the "separation of the races." Further, he argued that for the African American to "reach the highest development of which he is capable, the Negro should be by himself where he would not occupy a secondary potion."[41]

Two months later, after taking some time off from his work, on August 16, 1900, Turner married Harriet A. Wayman, the widow of Bishop A. W. Wayman of the AME Church and good friend of Turner, in Baltimore. It had been two and a half years since the death of Turner's second wife, Martha, who died January 10, 1898. Turner's first wife, Eliza, had died on July 19, 1889. According to reports it was the third marriage for Wayman as well. Wayman was a "woman of culture, having received a classical and musical education." While married to Bishop Wayman, she served as his administrative secretary. The couple honeymooned in Asbury Park, New Jersey, spending time with Turner's son before returning to the bishop's home in Atlanta. Two weeks after his wedding, the *New York Times* in the August 31, 1900, edition announced to the world that not only did Bishop Turner support Bryan in the upcoming election, he was also going to vigorously campaign—or "stump"—for him. Any rest or time with his newly wedded wife would simply have to wait.[42]

Turner and the 1900 Presidential Campaign

While it was no secret that Turner was frustrated with the McKinley administration and preferred his Democratic challenger William Jennings Bryan, still feeling the effects of his earlier stroke, Turner promised not to campaign or stump for Bryan. In an editorial published in his *Voice of Missions* newspaper in July, Turner refuted charges that since he supported Bryan, that meant he supported the Democratic Party and switched his affiliation. He also noted that in his "paralyzed condition" (effects from an earlier stroke) he could not make speeches or take the stump in the interest of the Democratic Party. However, Turner still did not hide his feelings on which candidate he supported. "If Bryan is elected," reasoned Turner, "lynching will stop, or be greatly diminished, for he has said so, but under Mr. McKinley mob violence has increased. . . . We again say that president McKinley is of no use to the Negro and no one but fools will say so."[43]

In an interview with the *New York Times*, Turner denied that he was a Democrat and promised that he did not intend to "stump the country for Mr. Bryan." However, Turner did concede his dislike of President McKinley's "attitude towards the Negro" and that he intended to "vote for Mr. Bryan in the belief that any change is better than none." This was no new change of heart, Turner reminded readers. He had been "cooling toward the Republican Party for sixteen years—ever since the decision of the Supreme Court held that "a negro had no civil rights." He also based his decision to vote for Bryan on his belief that "McKinley had done nothing for the Negro except appoint a few of them to office."[44]

In an interview published September 29, 1900, in the *Cleveland Gazette*,[45] Turner argued that the Republican Party "no longer allied to the human interests of the past." He reasoned that it was a "commercial party, pure and simple. They care very little about human suffering." He further maintained that the Republican Party "cared very little about the colored citizen and did not care whether his suffrage was restricted of not."

For Turner, it did not matter whether the Republicans in Congress had a majority or minority, because the "Democrats will go on curtailing the right of citizenship whenever and wherever they choose." "Democratic congressmen and senators," he argued, "will stand in the congressional halls" and "admit that they murder, cheat, and outrage colored citizens without fear of being bitterly assailed by a Republican." He surmised that there must be a "tacit understanding between "white Republicans and Democrats," because southern states that passed laws to "disfranchise the colored vote would not have dared to if they were sure Republican leaders would object."[46]

While acknowledging that some disagreed with his position, Turner argued that he had "more respect for an open enemy than a deceitful friend." "I believe," he continued, "that the Republicans want our vote very badly now, but after the election," he surmised, "they will give our people the same cold shoulder they have been giving them for years." He closed the interview by noting:

> So far as I am concerned, I am led to the positive conclusion that the present managers of the Republican Party regard my people as a dead load which they are tired of carrying. No colored man of any self-respect and intelligence will consent to further aid a party to hold the reins of national government. Republicanism doesn't mean now what it used to. If it did, I would be in it. I believe that in due course of time, thousands of men will see as I see today. Then I will not be regarded with so much special concern.[47]

In another interview, published October 27, 1900, in the *Cleveland Gazette*, Turner turned up his criticism of the Republicans. He suggested that the Republicans "lied" to African Americans about their freedom. "Our freedom was a war necessity," Turner argued, that "was dearly bought with colored arms 200,000 strong." Therefore, Turner continued, contrary to the "emotional idea that the Republican Party has an unlimited mortgage on the suffrages of the colored man," it is the Republicans that should be grateful to African Americans. Turner argued that for thirty-three years African Americans had delivered the vote to the Republican Party like a "poor man gives his pound of flesh to the shylock," while African Americans received nothing in return.[48]

However, the more Turner said that he would not stump for Bryan, and the more he reminded his audiences that he was not a member of the Democratic Party, the more the newspapers in the country continued to say otherwise. Turner's support for Bryan had now become an all-out endorsement for the Democratic Party and its policies—and many newspapers, especially African American ones, were not happy.

On September 28, 1900, the African American newspaper the *Seattle Republican* devoted a front-page editorial to Turner's support of Bryan. Titled "Change of Heart: The Bryan Salvation,"[49] the paper did not hold back its frustration with Turner's position. The rumor was that Turner would not campaign for Bryan in the South, where the majority of African Americans lived, but in the North and the West. The *Republican* suggested that Turner would do this because he knew that Democrats had already disenfranchised African Americans in the South and charged Turner's support of Bryan as aiding Democrats to disenfranchise Blacks all across the nation. The paper also charged that Democrats in the South were responsible for doing nothing about the lynching and terrorism Blacks faced and were the ones who created laws that would force a "paralyzed" Turner to ride some "300 miles" in a "Jim Crow" car after suffering a stroke.

The paper also questioned Turner's loyalty to African Americans. When Black citizens called for a strike against streetcar discrimination in the city of Atlanta, the newspaper noted Turner was against the measure. They wrote he called the action "the height of folly," and instead, while the "boycott" was in effect, not only did Turner ride the cars, but some African Americans believed rumors that Turner received a "free pass." The paper further intimated that if Turner could "succeed in his undertaking, he will no doubt be most tenderly cared for the balance of his life by the Democrats." In framing Turner as a Democrat operative and one not loyal to the race, they issued a warning for their readers: "Always watch the white folk's nigger."[50]

The *Republican* continued its attacks the following month. Under its "Political Pot Pie" column published on October 5, 1900, editors questioned Turner's motives and sanity in his support of Bryan.

> Bishop Turner has either lost his mind or a mercenary greed for gain has come over him, and my intimate acquaintance with him causes me to believe that he is not a fool. Turner lives in a state that has been under Democratic rule since 1876, and is competent to testify as to Bourbon Democracy, a thing so delightful and pleasant to the Negro that he wishes it extended all over the country

and Bryan placed in the White House to make sure that Democratic prosperity and happiness would reign throughout the length and breadth of the land. Well, it just so happens that every colored voter has an intimate knowledge of what white Democracy stands for. It stands for mob law, it stands for Jim-crow cars, it stands for Negro disfranchisement and it stands for everything tending toward the degradation of the Negro. No one should or ought to know these facts better than Bishop Turner, for he has lived all his life right in the midst of it and enjoyed those Democratic blessings.[51]

Others followed in repudiating Turner's support of Bryan. Republicans from Turner's home state of Georgia openly denounced him and his support of Bryan at their convention meeting, and celebrated orators and even bishops from both the AME and AME Zion churches criticized his support. They argued that the Republican Party freed Blacks and was the party that gave African Americans the right to vote. They also maintained that the Republican Party would be the better of the two parties to protect the rights of African Americans.[52]

Rev. Dr. H. C. C. Astwood, the pastor of Bridge Street AME Church in Brooklyn, New York, echoed these sentiments when he made a plea for congregants to attend an upcoming rally in support of McKinley. "If McKinley is not elected President," he thundered from the pulpit of his church, "there is going to be trouble in this country and a terrible lot of it." For Astwood, African Americans must elect McKinley to "help save the nation and give protection to your mothers and fathers in the Southland." He argued that if "Tillman and Bryan and their gang get in control of the government, they will not only disfranchise the Negro in the South but will attempt to do the same in the nation." At the close of the speech/sermon, Astwood passed out copies of an article published in the *Brooklyn Defender* he wrote criticizing Turner for his support of Bryan.[53]

At the McKinley rally on October 3, 1900, AME minister Rev. Dr. William D. Cook, in a speech, had some harsh words for Turner. "I don't know what's the matter with my Bishop. I have followed him in many things, but when he can take in his system such a nauseous dose of Bryan, I cut away from him." Suggesting that Turner's place of residence may have led him to this position, Cook said, "[B]ut he's out in Georgia, and it's been said of Georgia that it's half a mile from hell. Well," Cook further argued, "when a man's in hell, I suppose he has to make a compact with the devil so as to keep matters quiet." He closed his speech by reassuring his audience that there was "no danger of our people falling in line on such a proposition."[54]

Three days before the election, the *Iowa State Bystander* wondered, "[W]hat reasons can any Afro-American, Bishop Turner, or any other, have for throwing his influence in favor of Bryan? The wisest man," the paper continued, "cannot assign a single reason for supposing that Bryan's election would effect any good whatever for the Afro-American race, for it cannot be shown that in any one of his numerous speeches he has ever hinted at any of the remotest plans for doing anything of the kind."[55]

To respond against the attacks on his position and personhood, Turner took to the columns of the *Voice of Missions* to address and answer his critics. In a series of editorials, Turner offered his defense as to why he supported Bryan. In a column first published in the *Atlanta Journal* and republished in the *Voice of Missions*,[56] he reminded his readers that the charge that he was a Democrat was wrong. Emphatitically, Turner declared that he was "not a Democrat and never will be." He was for Bryan not because "he was a Democrat" or because "McKinley was a Republican," but because "we have tried McKinley for four years, and he is no benefit to the black man." While he did acknowledge that McKinley gave some African Americans patronage jobs, he maintained, "[A] great bulk of my race receives no more recognition at his hands than a man who has been dead for twenty years."

Moreover, Turner reminded his readers that even if he wanted to, he could not make speeches on behalf of Bryan because of the effects of the stroke he suffered the previous year. "While I am a great deal better and can walk about in a limping condition," he wrote, "I could not canvass any state or go out on a speaking tour if I were ever so anxious. To take the stump in my condition would be impossible."[57]

Turner then shifted to a critique of McKinley. He reminded his readers that while McKinley did declare in his inaugural address that "lynching must stop"—giving African Americans hope that "better times were ahead"— McKinley did little to support anti-lynching measures while in office. Turner noted that McKinley did not comment on one of the "bloodiest episodes that ever took place." Turner stated that when asked for a comment about the atrocity, McKinley "refused to open his mouth." Turner wrote that McKinley did not even say, "I am sorry; such conduct is disgraceful" or indeed anything. Turner argued that McKinley did not use the "moral influence" of the presidency and wasted an opportunity to speak up and stand with African Americans by refusing to say anything about the lynching. He continued this line of thought by arguing that while lynchings happened "before Mr. McKinley became president," they have "increased threefold if not fourfold since he has become president."[58]

Not content just to criticize McKinley, Turner then turned his attention to reasons why he "favored" Bryan. While some African Americans questioned Bryan's monetary policy, Turner could not have cared less. Turner was more concerned about "discrimination, proscriptions, disenfranchisement, lynchings" and the "wholesale blood and slaughter" that went unabated in African American communities. Instead of reelecting McKinley to do nothing once again about these atrocities, Turner suggested that Bryan would indeed "stop" them or greatly "diminish" them. Reflecting on McKinley's silence in the lynching of Sam Hose in Atlanta,[59] Turner reasoned that unlike McKinley, Bryan was "too bold and manly to say nothing about it."[60]

Turner saved some of his most vicious invective for African Americans from the state of Georgia who challenged his decision to support Bryan by writing him "abusive letters about what they have read in the papers." Turner first criticized the letters—some, in his words, "being half spelled" and "scratched not written"—and claiming, "[I could care] no more about their opinions than I do for a fly upon my coat sleeve." He wondered aloud whether they and their families went to church and/or Sabbath school, subscribed to a newspaper, or had a liquor problem. He reminded them, "[I have been] fighting for you for at least the last forty-four years and if you have done anything to help yourself, beyond eating, laughing, and abusing somebody, I have never heard of it."[61]

Turner also had a message for northern whites who criticized him by writing that "the Republican Party set him free." Turner reminded them that he was not enslaved and that he was "born free." However, while not being enslaved, he undoubtedly understood his "freedom" was nebulous at best. He continued, "I was freed again by Mr. Lincoln's proclamation, and I was freed again by the constitutional convention of 1866, and I again was freed by the Amendment to the United States Constitution and I suppose I should be free enough at this late day to vote for whom I please and not vote for whom I please."[62]

In an editorial published in the same October 1900 issue, titled "Turner Is a Democrat,"[63] Turner maintained again that he was not a Democrat; he just preferred Bryan to McKinley. In addressing his attackers, Turner called them "miserable shuttle-cocks" who were not worth a "pinch of snuff" because they "have done as much for their race as a toad frog." He reminded his readers that he had done "more for the race and the Republican Party than ten thousand of them would do in five hundred years." In foreshadowing what activists today call "showing receipts," Turner demanded:

> Where were they before the war between the states, when we were pleading for their freedom? Where were they during the war when as a United States

chaplain, we were leading regiments into battle and inspiring tens of thousands to die for the freedom of our race? Where were they since the war, when we were delivering speeches all over Georgia, Alabama, South Carolina, North Carolina, Tennessee, Florida, and in many other states advocating for the Republican Party? Where were they, when thousands and thousands of dollars were placed in our hands to pay public speakers and we were sending them to the four corners of the globe? Where were they, when we were commencing to speak at 11 o'clock and spoke in one continuous strain until we would drop dead at 5 o'clock in the afternoon, six hours in succession? Where were they, when we were sitting up all night hundreds of times writing campaign documents till daylight in the morning? Where were they, when we were battling in their behalf with the most learned white men and challenging the education of the age to read more languages than we could?[64]

Turner, in closing this part of the editorial, wrote,

We do not say that we have done more or as much as some other men, but all are dead, white and black who have done as much as we have. Now, because we say that we will vote for W. J. Bryan before we vote for William McKinley, the whole parcel of human buzzards and dogs are trying to vomit and slobber over me. But we defy them and spit upon their entire head.[65]

Second, he maintained that the Republican Party had not done anything to stop "lynching, disfranchisement or mob rule." He reminded his readers that states had already "disfranchised" African Americans and that "twenty-seven thousand black men and women have been put to death in the most fiendish manner." He asked, "Who has opened his mouth in congress? What Republican in any of the legislatures has even denounced it? Where is the man that has even written a newspaper article against it without apologizing for his presumption?" For Turner, the party had changed from a freedom-loving party to one that was indistinguishable from the Democrats. Comparing Republicans of his time with the ones before, Turner wrote, "We are not talking about Republicans fifteen to forty years ago who dared to speak and write and vote, but we are speaking about these milk and water Republicans, these Negro-hating Republicans." Turner continued:

We have been waiting for sixteen years for the Republican Party to do something to remedy the hellish decision of the Supreme Court. They have met in congress, in national conventions, in state legislatures, in state conventions and in every manner that men can meet, and they have not said a word nor offered a bill, nor proposed a measure, nor passed a resolution to remedy this abominable state of things. Yet they will call upon black men to fight, bleed and die for the rotten country. . . . [H]ad the Republicans half tried, the status of the black man would have been ten times higher.[66]

Since the *Voice of Missions* was a monthly, the November issue was the last one Turner had in which to convince readers to vote for Bryan. In that issue Turner wrote three editorials not only supporting Bryan but also criticizing many of his detractors. In one titled, "He Is a Democratic Bishop," Turner chastised fellow AME ministers who, upon learning of his support of Bryan, threatened to withhold money from the church. While insisting, as he always had, that he was not a Democrat and never would be a Democrat, the ministers' threats did little to bother him. "Those who do not want to give any money," he wrote, "because we will not stand by and see a Republican president do nothing or say nothing against these outrages can keep their money, so far as we are concerned." Turner called them "miserable fools and hypocrites" and wondered why they "proposed to go to hell to get revenge out of us."[67]

In his "Negro Office Holders" editorial, Turner states that McKinley supporters' only argument rested on the number of offices or positions in the government he had given to African Americans. "If some colored men get an office," Turner reasoned, "the balance must content themselves with being shot, hanged, burned, proscribed, discriminated against, Jim-crow carred and every other species of devilment." He reasoned, "[W]hat is an office to a few to be compared to the degradation and inhuman treatment which millions and millions of our race are victims of?" He therefore suggested that many of these officeholders were "miserable pap suckers" who were willing to "kiss the posterior of any white man to get an office." For Turner, receiving an office that way only "degrades and enslaves" the person and denies that person the freedom of being their own person.[68]

It was the third editorial where Turner just let all inhibition go. In "Fool Negroes Crazy about President McKinley," Turner declared that African Americans could no longer rely upon any political party and that he, for one, was willing to "try another white man." He started the editorial by telling his readers that he did not want to "say anything" about the upcoming election through the columns of the *Voice of Missions*, but since he thought that newspapers across the country misrepresented his onetime support of Bryan, he felt the need to say something. He reminded his audience that since he came out in support of Bryan, many thought that he had "perpetrated a great crime," and that led many to challenge him as a leader of the people and as a Black man.[69]

To address these concerns, Turner offered a twofold argument. First, Turner drew upon his Civil War experience to argue that he "knew what the liberation of our race cost." He argued, "Had some of our assailants gone through the battles we have, they would know the value of manhood and know such a rotten nation as ours should be blotted out of existence unless better management can be given." He recalled the battles he participated in during the war when he wrote, "We have seen again and again and again during the war black men, to say nothing of white men, piled upon each other like trees in a forest after a dreadful tornado. We have had men shot down on the right and on the left and have seen them writhing and quivering in death till breath left their body to give freedom to the bondman and liberty to the slave." By foregrounding the bravery of these men who died on the battlefield, Turner connected their sacrifice to the positions some African Americans enjoyed. "How come so many deacons, elders, doctors, Bishops, churches, lodges, captains, majors, colonels and other big dignitaries in the land today whose black backs would have been scars and whelps [sic] if these gallant and grand men had not died to knock the shackles from around their limbs?"[70] However, for Turner, they were only "miserable fools" and "contemptible asses," because they were the ones who were now assailing him for his support of Bryan.[71]

Second, Turner addressed those who would criticize his support of Bryan by writing that he wanted change. "We are willing to try another white man," he argued, "to see if he will do any better than the milk-and-water-white Republicans we have had in the White House for the last four years." He maintained that African Americans could no longer trust any party, for the "Republican Party is no better, so far as the Negro is concerned than the Democratic Party." In Turner's estimation, the Republican Party had not done anything for African Americans for the last "twenty years" except "take away the rights that the grand old Republicans gave us when the Republican Party was a symbol of liberty and manhood." He further charged that "contemptible scoundrels and a parcel of fool Negroes" that did not have as "much sense as a bat" made up the current Republican Party anyway. "But they may say what they please," he argued, "get mad or not, like it or dislike it, if we vote at all, we shall vote for W. J. Bryan."[72]

Third, Turner addressed what he argued was the main issue at hand. Political parties were not "against" African Americans—it was "white against black." For Turner, "white means to kill out black, or to enslave it, or to degrade it to a worse condition than slavery." To make his argument, he reasoned in closing,

> If Bryan does nothing, should he get to be president, he will be as good as McKinley, for McKinley has done nothing except to appoint a few colored men

to office and Bryan will do the same, so that Bryan can make it no worse; for under McKinley we have been disenfranchised, hanged, burned, and killed in every form and it cannot get any worse. The only thing Bryan could do would be to bring up hell from below, if possible, and the sooner he would do it the better; for this country is the vestibule of hell anyway at the present time.[73]

In addition to the editorials, Turner published others' articles in the *Voice of Missions* that questioned McKinley's support of African American interests. In one he published an article from W. H. Scott, who listed nine reasons why African Americans should not support McKinley. Turner also republished an article first published in the *Savannah Morning News* in which he again attacked the Supreme Court and its decision that for Turner had "de-citizentized" African Americans. Moreover, the article was full of quotes from Turner attacking the McKinley administration for doing "nothing" on behalf of African Americans. However, despite Turner's efforts and his last-minute editorial campaign against McKinley, on November 6, 1900, William McKinley won reelection in a landslide—with many of those votes coming from African Americans.

In accepting defeat, Turner wrote an editorial for the *Voice of Missions*, published the following month, titled, "McKinley, the God of Fool Negroes, Re-Elected." Turner started his column by acknowledging the election of McKinley and that "a number of colored men almost lost their heads over him, despite, in Turner's opinion, McKinley's silence when it came to issues relevant to African Americans. "He has done nothing," Turner argued, "nor said a word about the colored man." It was because of McKinley's silence on issues affecting African Americans that Turner "entered protest against him, for which we have been classed as a Democrat and advocating bloody-handed lynchers." Turner suggested that he would rather be a Democrat than a "consummate fool"—void of sufficient discernment to detect the "rascality, treachery, and the deceptive deviltry of the latter-day Republicans." He noted that there was a significant difference between the Republicans during the days of Reconstruction and the current ones. He called the former the "grand galaxy of a reformer," and he suggested, "No grander men ever lived." The latter he called "deceptive pimps who are trying to palm themselves off as Republican benefactors."[74]

Turner not only leveled his frustration at McKinley but also had harsh words for African Americans. While conceding that African Americans who supported McKinley may be "wise and learned, believing that out of two evils that McKinley and his party is the least," Turner argued that many African Americans were "too ignorant to see that the Republican Party is making a tool and a fool of the Negro." Further, he would intone that the "great mass of Negro devotees believe that the Republican Party is first and that God is next."[75]

Turner's rejection of McKinley and support of Bryan was not without reasons. Turner claimed that Bryan had privately assured him that he would "endeavor to put a stop to this lynching, burning and other violence." McKinley, on the other hand, "had not done it," nor, for Turner at least, did he intend to do anything to stop the violence whites perpetrated upon African Americans. Further, Turner wrote,

> Mr. McKinley has already shown his hand. If we are to believe the daily papers, he has already said that in those states that have disfranchised the colored man, he intends to advocate full representation in Congress. In other words, he intends to veto any bill that may pass Congress not allowing white Democrats to represent the black man, though the states disfranchise him. This of course will be an inducement for all the southern states to disfranchise the Negro and take away his ballot. And McKinley is the first man to openly advocate that policy. Yet the Negro is not able to see it.[76]

Turner, however, connected the disfranchisement of African Americans with another one of Turner long-advocated ideas—emigration. He argued that God in God's "wise providence" might have a hand in this. It may be that the "God of the nations," Turner wrote, "is endorsing this method for the purpose of driving the Negro out of this country and making him a nation of his own." Turner noted that while "he had been called a fool by fools" many times because of his African emigration position, he did not see much future for the Negro in America. "We wish to tell the young men and women of our race," Turner declared, "there is as much future for the Negro in this country as there is for a frog in a snake den."

Further, he opined, "And as we shall not bother much in politics in the future, we wish to make this statement that coming generations may remember it. We stake our intelligence, reputation, judgment, statesmanship, and all that we are on that declaration. We repeat, THERE IS AS MUCH FUTURE FOR THE NEGRO RACE IN THIS COUNTRY AS THERE IS FOR A FROG IN A SNAKE DEN."[77]

This would be one of the last editorials he would write for the *Voice of Missions*. In the same issue, under the heading "The *Voice of Missions* Will be Turned into Other Hands,"[78] Turner bade his audience farewell as editor of the paper. Whether the church asked him to step down or Turner did of his own volition is still debatable. Turner, however, did mention in his editorial that he knew he made some of the bishops "blush" because of some editorials that some regarded as "vulgar and disgraceful." Also, Turner wrote that many disapproved of him publishing letters "just as they were written" from readers, and because of his pro-emigration stance. Those tensions, along with the name-calling and terse language that Turner used on multiple occasions aimed at his opponents, probably had a lot to do with the church asking him to step aside as editor.

Patrick J. Kelly notes the role that the memory of the Civil War played in McKinley's presidential campaign in 1896. Along with other historians, he argues that Republicans "shifted away from the racial commitments of the previous generation of party leaders" and adopted a "strategy that emphasized a renewed nationalism based on sectional reconciliation." He reminded readers that the 1896 Republican platform, for the first time since the Civil War, "omitted any demand that the Federal government use its police power to guarantee black suffrage in the South." The Republican Party, "indifferent to the intensified attacks on the social and political rights of African Americans and eager to promote a patriotic nationalism based on the reconciliation of whites in the North and South," argued Kelly, "distanced the party from its historical role in revolutionizing U.S. race relations during the Civil War and Reconstruction."[79]

McKinley won the election against Bryan in 1896 and brought the same strategy to the 1900 campaign. By this time Republicans had aligned themselves with race-neutral policies and corporate interests. They had adopted a states' rights position that allowed "separate but equal" laws and discrimination in its myriad of forms to go unabated. While many African Americans still remembered the Republican Party as the emancipation party of Lincoln, the party had long shifted from the protection of civil rights and property of African Americans and left them to the whims of segregationists and racist state legislatures.

Turner attempted to sound the alarm at the creation of this "new" Republican Party. As I demonstrate in chapter 1, Turner began noticing the change as early as 1883, with the Supreme Court, and finally reaching its apex in 1896 with the *Plessy v. Ferguson* decision. By the time of the 1900 election—and seeing African Americans still beholden to a party that no longer cared about their civil rights, Turner, adopting a prophetic persona, stepped away from the socially accepted norm of Black leadership at the time and publicly supported the Democratic nominee.

Understanding that he faced a rhetorical challenge, his strategy was threefold. First, by letting his readers know that he was not nor ever would be a

Democrat, Turner attempted to position himself as a principled leader—not one who would just go along with the masses, but someone who would look fairly at the issues and then decide whom to vote for based on who would best serve. He was careful to reiterate that while he supported Bryan, he would not make any campaign stump speeches for him. Turner aimed to find a middle ground—especially for African Americans who chastised him for his Bryan support.

Second was his sharp critique of the Republican Party and the McKinley administration. Turner charged that the Republicans had not done anything on the behalf of or for African Americans' protection and civil rights. His aim here was to get African Americans to see what the party was doing instead of focusing on what the party had done. He argued that African Americans were holding on to the ideas and struggles of the past and not noticing that the party had long moved from those positions.

Third was the change in his prophetic rhetoric. While Turner continued to aim his critiques at the government, political parties, the Supreme Court, and society in general, he also ramped up the critique and condemnation of other African American leaders. While they had always been a subject of Turner's fire at times, during this election they stayed more on Turner's radar.

The sharp invective aimed at fellow Black leaders would eventually lead some of them to disfavor Bishop Turner. As Turner continued to call fellow bishops and other leaders "miserable fools and hypocrites," "miserable pap-suckers," "scullions," "boot lickers," "spittoonlickers," and "contemptible asses," many of those who faced Turner's wrath enjoyed occasions when the bishop seemed to get his comeuppance. When many of them continued to chastise Turner after the election, it was the *Colored American* in Washington, DC, that came to Turner's defense when they ran a column first published in the *Christian Recorder*. "No one knew better than Bishop Turner that no words spoken by him or anyone else could seriously defect the vote of the Negro," wrote the paper, "but he adhered to his stand being willing to submit to abuse in order that by his protest he might make the nation see its wrong in treating with indifference his people."[80]

As a pessimistic prophet, Turner, knowing he was fighting uphill, still felt compelled to do something that others thought was not in his best interest. In his farewell editorial, Turner pondered on whether he would ever start another paper. At that time he was not inclined to do so, because he believed that he had "done enough to rest quietly from now until," he "reached the grave." His rest did not last long. Two months later Turner launched the *Voice of the People* and immediately began to revisit an idea that he did not believe would or could ever happen—emigration to Africa.[81]

5

"THE SALVATION OF THE NEGRO"
Turner and the Rhetoric of Emigration

The death of Bishop Morris Marcellus Moore came as a surprise to many in the AME Church. Elected as the twenty-seventh bishop of the AME Church in May 1900, Moore died on November 23 of the same year, serving as bishop for only six months. Moore's death prompted several inquiries from members of the church, especially from some of the bishops as to who would serve Moore's Episcopal conference. The immediate decision rested in the hands of Bishop Turner, who, as senior bishop of the church, served as president of the Bishop's Council. Turner initially did not want to make any selection—preferring only to order all of the AME churches to mourning until the House of Bishops could meet. However, after discovering that the church expected him to "make some disposition of the matter," Turner decided to reassign Bishops Abram Grant and C. T. Shaffer temporarily.[1]

According to Turner, he based his decision on what he thought would be preferable to the two bishops and what would be cost-effective. First, Turner assigned Bishop Grant to the two Louisiana conferences that Bishop Moore served. Turner's reasoning behind this selection was that Bishop Grant had already been assisting Bishop Moore while Moore was sick. Second, Turner assigned Bishop Shaffer to Africa, because, according to Turner, Bishop Shaffer told him at least a "dozen times" that he would like to visit Africa and even wanted the church to elect him Bishop of Africa." Turner reasoned that Shaffer would be "delighted in being relieved of the Puget Sound Conference" to have more time for the African work." His decision was also directed at saving money for the church. Again, Turner reasoned that if the bishop in charge of the California conference (Arnett) could also make time to serve the Puget Sound Conference, the church would not have to pay the expenses of two bishops traveling to the West Coast. However, Bishops Grant and Shaffer were displeased with the assignments. Instead of informing Turner of their displeasure, both "rushed to the public press" to express their unhappiness. Turner's frustration with the bishops' dissatisfaction with the assignments led him to announce his resignation as president of the Bishop's Council. In his resignation letter, published in the *Christian Recorder*, he wrote, "I did what I thought was wise and for the best interest of the church. I did not anticipate such a reception as we have had."[2]

How some ministers responded to their appointments had always been an issue for Turner. He openly complained about ministers wanting the security that better assignments could offer and about how when bishops would move ministers from "a good appointment," which Turner called a "misnomer," they would charge that the bishop had "something personally against [them]."[3] He argued that there was a belief in the church that "nothing could be done for God without a goldmine"; it had gotten so bad, Turner lamented, that when offered an appointment to the church, the minister would want to know "What is there?" Some even wondered when they did not receive a good appointment what they had done to receive such a punishment.[4]

In one letter Turner wrote that he had come to "deprecate the annual conference," because after he had "prayed, advised, counseled, considered and discussed with the presiding elders the merits and fitness of the ministers for this and that place, and after "exhausting every phase of light that God and nature could ever impart," the "flood gates of grumbles, whines and complaints still come." Turner believed that ministers who berate bishops about their appointments have as much "trust God" in their souls as "arsenic in [their] stomachs."[5]

While Turner was critical of ministers who complained about their appointments, he was favorable not only to ones who accepted their appointments but also to ones who were successful in their work. In one letter to the editor aptly titled, "Success under Disadvantages," Turner wrote about Rev. Robert Davis and how he willingly took on an appointment that others saw as a bad one. Instead of complaining about the Somerset appointment in Kentucky, Turner wrote, the Reverend Davis, with his "half-blinded eyes," took to the task of building a new church. "Space will not permit me to give in detail the labors of Brother Davis," Turner wrote. "Let it suffice that last Sabbath, the 15th inst.; I dedicated to the glory of God a church edifice at

Somerset . . . worth at least fourteen hundred dollars. The church ranks as third of the city, including all white churches." Turner's reason for his public acknowledgment of the Reverend Davis was "to show some of our ministerial grumblers what can be accomplished when there is a will to work and a character behind the will that merits respect and confidence."[6]

Despite Turner's offer to resign, Bishop Gaines quickly reminded him that he could not officially resign his position as president of the House of Bishops, that by being the senior bishop, he automatically served as president of the House of Bishops.[7] Also, because the presidency was not an elected position, one could not resign. Writing the following week in the *Christian Recorder*, Bishop Gaines suggested that the best Turner could do was not to preside, thereby giving the bishop next in seniority the role of president. Turner could have resigned his role of bishop, but not the presidency of the House of Bishops.

With frustration mounting in his role as president of the House of Bishops, and his recent dismissal as editor of the *Voice of Missions* newspaper, Turner turned his attention to his next venture—starting another newspaper, the *Voice of the People*. While Turner founded the *Voice of Missions*, it became an official organ of the Missionary Department of the AME Church. The *Voice of the People*, however, would be different. As Turner noted in one of the first editorials, in February 1901, this would not be a "religious paper or a church paper, nor a paper for the contributions and correspondence of our ministers and people." Undoubtedly still stinging from his firing as editor of the *Voice of Missions*, the *Voice of the People* would be a paper operated and owned by Turner.[8]

Another thing would be different with this paper—Turner would not send free copies to anyone—especially not to ministers, general officers, and Bishops. If people wanted the paper, "they must pay for it." He did, however, expect people in his Sixth Episcopal District to support the efforts of the paper—but not as an "organ of the church," but simply as an "organ of the Bishop."[9]

In the following month's issue, Turner articulated the aim, function, and role of the paper thoroughly. Not only did he not want the paper to be a religious or church paper—thus making it a secular paper—he also wanted it to publish it in the interest of African emigration. "In other words," he wrote, "we shall advocate gradual African emigration, not wholesale, but a slow return to our fatherland." He closed his editorial by reiterating what he wrote earlier, "This paper will be chiefly devoted to African emigration and the manhood of the race."[10]

Turner's decision to start the *Voice of the People* coincided with ongoing renewed interest in emigration. With racism, Black subordination, and oppression continuing throughout the country, many believed that it was time to address the idea of relocation—again. In the South, small groups such as the Liberian Colonization Society, which took the place of the recently defunct International Migration Society and the International Migration and Steamship Company, headed by J. C. Bulis, began to promote African emigration. They both promised safe passage to Africa, and when the migrants arrived, they would have land to farm and work. However, both groups struggled, because while there was interest in going to Africa, or just escaping the place in which many African Americans found themselves, many did not have the money to emigrate. This renewed impetus for emigration led Turner to believe that the time was ripe for not only emigration but to found a shipping line between the United States and Liberia. He would have a chance at an upcoming emigration convention in Nashville to share his ideas and to again try to launch a mass exodus of African Americans to Africa.[11]

In this chapter I not only examine Turner's role at the convention but also discuss his rhetoric of emigration leading up to and after the convention. As I hope to demonstrate, Turner's rhetoric of emigrations shifts over time. From his belief in bringing Christianity to the continent of Africa as a reason for relocation to a place of refuge for African Americans, to eventually a place where African Americans can learn "true" civilization, Turner's rhetoric over the years shows just how malleable and fluid it was.

Moreover, depending on the context, Turner did not have any problem partnering with any group—including the despised American Colonization Society (ACS) to achieve goals. As a pragmatic prophet during much of the post-Reconstruction period, Turner aimed to eventually found a ship or an organization that would assist in his emigration efforts. Although emigration never happened on the scale he would have liked, his rhetoric did spur many, especially in the South, to reevaluate who they were and to discover their own agency. They may not have had the money and resources to emigrate to Africa, but many inspired by Turner did leave the South looking for a better way of life.

The Spirit of Emigration

For many African Americans, the thoughts and ideas on emigration were not new. Falechiondro Karcheik Sims-Alvarado has noted that due to the denial of civil liberties, "as early as the eighteenth century, African Americans had articulated their desire to resettle in West Africa." During what she has called the "proto-emigration" period, from 1773 to 1815, Blacks "capitalized on the revolutionary thinking of the time and advocated for emigration abroad and the end of slavery." Inspired by the Black Loyalists—American Blacks who joined the British Army during the Revolutionary War and who, after the war, emigrated to Sierra Leone, the desire for land and independence appealed to American Blacks faced with similar living conditions as Blacks in Canada and England. Free Blacks formed the first emigration associations and petitioned government officials for assistance in transporting them to West Africa. However, Sims-Alvarado has reminded us that the "necessary financial resources of blacks, compassionate whites, or the government did not coalesce to meet the growing demand by blacks to leave the U.S. during this period."[12]

Incidentally, it would not be "compassionate whites" or the government that would finance the first trip of Black Americans to Africa. That honor would go to Paul Cuffe, a wealthy Black shipowner who would launch what Sims-Alvarado has called the "first wave" period of emigration, from 1815 to 1865. Using $4,000 of his assets, Cuffe assisted thirty-eight free Blacks in resettling in Sierra Leone. Cuffe argued that establishing a community of formerly enslaved and freed Black people in West Africa was "vital to bringing Christianity to Africa, eradicating the illegal trading of African captives, and establishing commercial opportunities through land ownership and global trade for Africans on both sides of the Atlantic Ocean." As Cuffe prepared for his second voyage, he became ill and died of natural causes.[13]

Seeing that there was a desire among Blacks to emigrate to Africa, white organizations formed to assist freed Blacks who wanted to go. One such group was the American Colonization Society (ACS). Founded in 1816, this white-led organization founded by Robert Finley "introduced plans to resolve escalating racial tension in America by assisting free (as opposed to enslaved) blacks in traveling to and resettling in West Africa." According to Sims-Alvarado, the ACS presented itself as a "benevolent organization," and they hoped that "colonization, together with Christian conversion and civilization of Africans by African Americans would win the support of free blacks."

Sims-Alvarado continued:

> The ACS argued that resettlement outside the United States would allow blacks to vote, hold political office, and serve on a jury; obtain land granted by the colonization society; establish autonomous religious, educational, and economic institutions; and enjoy life away from hostile whites. But despite these enticements, the ACS found it difficult to recruit passengers. With the face of the leadership, leading advocates, and financial contributors of black emigration changing from black to white, blacks became less inclined to emigrate to West Africa.[14]

A closer look at the ACS may indicate why Blacks were less likely to support their efforts—Blacks simply did not trust the ACS. Many of the founders of the society were former owners of enslaved Africans, and while putting on a benevolent face, many of these elite white men were still unabashedly racist. Additionally, according to Sims-Alvarado, "potential settlers feared recapture and sale by Europeans and Africans involved in the ongoing illegal trans-Atlantic slave trade." However, despite the misgivings, the ACS did succeed in transporting 16,486 Africans and persons of African descent to Liberia, with 10,350 of that number coming from the United States.[15]

While not trusting the ACS and their emigration plans, many Blacks still found the idea of emigration appealing. According to historian Howard Bell, by 1847 at the National Negro Convention in Troy, New York, delegates were ready to listen "respectfully to a plan for a commercial venture involving blacks in Jamaica, The United States, and Africa." Influenced by Liberia gaining its independence and becoming a nation in 1847, many prominent Blacks during the antebellum period started to promote the idea of emigration anywhere outside of the United States. People such as Henry Highland Garnet, Martin Delany, Mary Ann Shadd Carey, Samuel Ward, Mary Bibb, Alexander Crummell, and others argued for the merits of emigration.[16]

The frenzy of activity surrounding emigration culminated in the 1854 National Emigration Convention held in Cleveland, Ohio, in 1854. Called and led by Delany, the convention focused exclusively on emigration, as a response to a previous convention led by Frederick Douglass a year earlier.[17] Delegates wrestled with issues centering around questions such as "should Blacks leave the United States and go abroad in order to establish a safer, more functional community of their own" or "should they remain in a nation that has endlessly oppressed them, while it also could hold the key to the success and solidification of their communities?"[18]

The highlight of the convention, however, came from Martin Delany. In delivering the keynote address of the convention, "The Political Destiny of the Colored Race,"[19] Delaney drew from work two years earlier, *The Condition, Elevation, Emigration, and Destiny of the Colored People of the United States.*[20] In his address to the convention, Kahn argued that Delany continued some of the same arguments found in the earlier work, for instance, his "denunciation of the Fugitive Slave Law, an appeal to natural law, and a chronicle of black contributions to American society." In this speech to the convention, however, Delany "embellishes his basic argument and produces a fascinating restatement of ideological preference."[21]

With the ending of the Civil War and the ratification of the Thirteenth Amendment that abolished chattel slavery, African Americans hoped for a brighter future. Discussions of emigration began to dissipate as formerly enslaved people navigated their newfound freedom. As the joys of freedom gave way to the sad realities of Reconstruction, African Americans found this other side of freedom, in many ways, just as treacherous as their enslaved existence. As frustration mounted, many newly freed people started thinking about the possibilities of emigrating out of the South. For instance, 194 Blacks in Macon, Georgia, in July of 1866, eight months after the ratification of the Thirteenth Amendment, partnered with the ACS to resettle in Liberia. Grassroots efforts such as this one and another in Sparta, Georgia, renewed interest in African emigration throughout Reconstruction.[22]

Interestingly, at the time Turner claimed that he opposed emigration. In a letter to the *Christian Recorder* published November 24, 1866, Turner wrote, "I have been a stern opposer of that scheme for many years," and "prior to the emancipation of our people I looked upon the colonization scheme as one of the tricks of slavery, to rid the country of free negroes." However, seeing these African Americans leave for Liberia led Turner to rethink his position. In the same letter, while disagreeing with the move, Turner also celebrated those that decided to go. He wrote that it was their God-given right to leave and go wherever they pleased. Though even at this time he thought that fortunes for African Americans would improve in the United States, he also admired those who would bid "goodbye" and take "to the road." He would soon ask others to do the same.[23]

Turner's Early Emigration Rhetoric

Turner's interest in and support of emigration is hard to pinpoint. According to Turner in a letter to the editor of the *Washington Post* in 1895, he became a "convert" to African emigration after hearing Alexander Crummell speak upon the subject in May 1862.[24] However, in a letter to Rev. G. W. Ottley, Turner claims he been writing and speaking on emigration ever since he preached on "The Redemption of Africa and the Means to be Employed" before the Philadelphia Conference in the spring of 1860.[25] While the origins of Turner's interest in emigration may be suspect, we do know that he at least is sympathetic to arguments supporting emigration as early as 1861.

In a letter to the *Christian Recorder* published December 14, 1861, Turner rebuffed arguments against emigration made by Rev. T. Strother—who claimed that the primary reason why he was against emigration was that the "whites wish to get rid of us" and the "desire us to leave." For Turner, it did not matter whether or not white people wanted to get rid of African

Americans; Turner maintained that Black people should decide their fates. Turner wrote that he did not "care what [white people's] intentions [were], for Turner reasoned that "God had often made the devil and his instrumentalities to work out for his people ineffable blessings." Turner argued that African Americans should discuss emigration and "let those go who wish, and let those stay who desire; let us have a free expression about it, for all this helps to develop intellect; it sets men to studying the physical and geographical condition of the globe. But to talk about moving the colored people from this country is foolishness."[26]

He vigorously refuted a report that he was a prime mover of President Lincoln's meeting with Black leaders in Washington, DC, to discuss a Central American emigration plan. Turner wrote that he "hated the scheme of compulsory colonization" as much as his opponents. However, despite the overwhelming opposition to emigration from leading Black abolitionists such as Robert Purvis and Frederick Douglass, Turner continued to insist that emigration proposals should have a "hearing in Washington."[27]

Despite his protestations to the contrary, Turner was in contact with officials from the American Colonization Society (ACS) as early as 1866. In a personal letter written to William Coppinger, secretary of the ACS, on July 18, 1866, Turner not only advocated for emigration but also asked for support in becoming a lecturer on the subject. Anticipating arguments that he would use later in his career in supporting emigration, Turner wrote, "I am taking the ground that we will never get justice here," Turner wrote. He argued that "God is and will [continue to] withhold political rights from us, to turn out attention to our fatherland." He saw this as an opportunity to become "missionaries to the millions in Africa.[28]

Disputing what he wrote later in 1895 as to the time he became an emigrationist, Turner, in his letter to Coppinger, wrote that he became a convert to emigration only "five weeks ago while riding in the cars," and since becoming a convert, he wanted to "advocate" for it as much as possible. "What will your Society give me to become a lecturer on the subject," Turner asked, because "thousands of people [in the] South would hear of this thing who can't read and know nothing of it." Turner argued that the Society needed people in the South who were skilled to meet the "argument of the whites" because they were "terribly opposed to it." Turner closed the letter by writing, "[I]f you will offer me some inducement, I will speak and write on the subject and I know I have as much influence as any man South of color."[29]

Many in the African American community criticized Turner's close association with members of the ACS. On March 27, 1873, Frederick Douglass, editor of the *New Era* newspaper, criticized one of Turner's speeches as one "made in the interest of the Colonization Society" and one that "aided the Colonization Society." Turner took offense at the charge and wrote, "I never have had, nor do I ever expect to have, anything to do with the Colonization Society. And more, I want nothing to do with it. I am neither its advocate nor opponent. If it is doing any good may the Lord be with it, and if it is doing harm may it be cut short. I know nothing of its operations." Turner argued that what he said in his lecture about Africa were his own "personal views," and while he "never expected to go to Africa himself, he hoped for the day that his sons could and dispelled the gloom of ignorance from the mental and moral sky of those two hundred millions of human beings, who are as much in need of civilization as any people upon whom the sun ever shone."[30]

Twelve days later, in his speech "The Negro in All Ages," delivered on April 8, 1873, in Savannah, Georgia, Turner used the occasion to address Douglass again. He reminded his audience that Douglass earlier accused him of "clandestinely aiding the Colonization Society." In doing so, Turner said, Douglass "hurled his philippics at [him] in a most frightful manner." However, since that time, Turner said he had "read some works" on colonization that "opened his eyes, enlarged his "store of information," and had allowed Turner to "form an opinion." Turner later explained:

> I believe the Colonization Society has done good, is doing good, and will ultimately be adored by unborn millions. Through this very Colonization Society some of the posterity of Mr. Douglass may yet sway the scepter in that now darkened and despised country, but then enlightened and civilized nation, that will rank their names beside such men as Alexander and Charlemagne who are now sleeping in the womb of the future. But for the Colonization Society there would be no communication between here and our Fatherland and there would be no medium through which to convey the waters of life to that famishing people.[31]

Though he offered a full-throated defense of his support of the ACS, Turner also suggested at this time that he did not endorse "African emigration." He believed, however, that it was "our duty to civilize the fatherland and the only way to civilize a people is to move into their midst and live among them. As for people who argued that the ACS was not "noted friends of the Negro," Turner did not see this as a problem at all. He saw the hand of God at work—overruling evil for good.[32]

Despite what Turner had said in the past about the ACS, nearly three years later the society made Turner one of its honorary vice presidents. Turner seemed to be happy about the position. In a letter to the society, Turner expressed thanks for his "election," and he "promise[d] to render full service to the best of [his] ability." While Turner was appreciative of the position, he reminded the society that he had never been a "colonizationist," as popularly understood by African Americans. For Turner, the "founders, supporters and directors" of ACS were "actuated by pure impulses and Christian desires, having constantly in view the gradual abolition of slavery in the United States, and the civilization and evangelization of the millions of Africa." Addressing those who argued that the ACS should disband because of the elimination of slavery in the United States, Turner wrote,

> In my judgment, there is more occasion for it than ever before. Every right-thinking man, who will ponder the Negro question twenty-four hours, must come to the conclusion that my race cannot long remain in the land of its centuries of thralldom unless it be a state of serfdom or ward-espionage. This I know would be revolting to its every member and to its friends. But just so long as we are a people within a people vastly our superiors in numbers, wealth, &c., having no government of our own, we shall be nothing, and be so treated by the civilized world. The Negro may wax as eloquent as Demosthenes, Pitt, or any of the renowned orators of the past ages; still he will be considered a cipher until he wins distinction in manipulating and running the machinery of government. Nothing less than nationality will bring large prosperity and acknowledged manhood to us as a people.[33]

He suggested that African Americans could accomplish this not by "constantly complaining of bad treatment; by holding conventions and passing resolutions; by voting for white men for office; by serving as caterers and barbers, and by having our wives and daughters continue as washerwomen and servants to the whites." Turner argued that "a government and nationality of our own can alone cure the evils under which we now labor, and are likely yet the more to suffer in this country." Turner believed that the time was near for "American people of color" to start thinking about building the "United States of Africa."[34]

Turner's "election" as one of the vice presidents of the dreaded ACS did not sit well with many African Americans. The editors of the *Savannah Colored Tribune* issued a warning to Turner and wrote that he should "reflect well before he attempt[ed] to work in the interest of the Society." Turner, in his letter published February 19, 1876, reminded the editor that he had been "reflecting upon the status of the negro in this country for many years," and that the more he reflected, the more he believed that "our salvation as a race depends upon a negro nationality, either in Africa or in South America."[35]

Further, Turner shifted the argument back at his detractors and challenged them to come up with better solutions.

> I am startled at times at the ignorance displayed by many of our prominent colored men, upon the real condition of our race in this country. Don't you see it's a white's man Government? And don't you see they mean at all hazards to keep the negro down? And don't you see the negro does not intend to stay down, without a fuss and an interminable broil? Then why waste our time in trying to stay here? Why not do as the white settlers of this country did, leave and build up a country and Government of our own; and have our own negro Presidents, Governors, Judges, Congresses, Legislatures, etc; yes, kings and queens if we choose. Then, and not till then, will the nations of earth respect us, and admire our manhood and genius.[36]

In another letter to the editor, published March 18, 1876, in the *Savannah Colored Tribune*, Turner defended yet again his emigration position. While noting "[S]everal exceptions have been taken to my position in regard to going to Africa and establishing a negro nationality," Turner argued that he was only trying to protect African Americans from a "set of ravenous white wolves, who are preying like the vampires of hell upon our people." For this he opined that he had been "called a fanatic, a fool, an aspirant for royal honors, the would be king, etc.," and wondered just "how long can the negro race last in this country at such a ratio of murdering as is now in process of operation in this state?"[37]

With the election of many conservatives to state offices, and along with the patronage given by national Republicans to southern white Democrats as part of the 1877 Compromise that effectively ended Reconstruction, many other Blacks at the grassroots level began to look at emigration possibilities. One group, however, did not favor emigration—the AME Church. Despite Turner's view on emigration, the overwhelming majority of the leadership of the church vehemently opposed emigration. According to Bailey, the "growing vehemence with which many AME ministers denounced African emigration exemplifies the increasing divide between leaders and laity, urban and rural, middle class and poor in African American communities. For many 'ordinary' black Americans, America was far from a paradise, and some sought a new life abroad. Prominent white and African Americans heralded black progress in America, particularly in the realm of education."[38]

For instance, in 1878 at a preachers meeting in Philadelphia, the church issued a statement that called emigration "absurd." It also argued that despite emigration efforts happening at the grassroots level—especially in the

South—that did not mean that there was support among the church leadership for emigration. In a resolution members wrote of their "unfaltering opposition" to emigration and reasoned, "[I]f we could endure the hardships in the years of slavery, when we were only chattels, we can contend with the remaining prejudices, now [that] we have our liberty, and enjoy our rights as citizens." They argued that emigration movements "not only serve to unsettle and distress our people, but to encourage the hope in our enemies, that they may succeed in converting their former kidnapping into emigration, and thus beguile us away from your own country poor and penniless while they invite others to come." They further called on those who "perpetuate" such movements to "show their faith by their works in going to that land, and staying there until they accomplish something and tell us from experience that it is a good land which the Lord our God giveth us." They close the resolution by writing that "until some such proof is given, we recognize all such efforts as coming from selfish motives, for causes unknown to us."[39]

The resolution adopted at the preachers meeting did not stop Turner from proclaiming his position on emigration. In the same year, Turner watched the launch of the *Azor* that carried 206 African Americans to Liberia. Even though he argued that it did not go far enough, Turner supported Pap Singleton's effort that led fifty thousand African Americans from the South out west—to states such as Missouri and Kansas. Therefore, Turner, led by both the grassroots emigration movements and a desire to refute church-leader arguments on emigration, develop his own theory of emigration, which he published under the title *Emigration of the Colored People of the United States*.

In this pamphlet, after a lengthy introduction of the history of emigration, Turner first argued that emigration had the "sanction from heaven and has been the theory, as well as a cardinal practice of all nations of antiquity." Second, he said that emigration is a "pre-requisite to the material, social and intellectual growth of a people," and as such, it is not "disgraceful, humiliating, or destructive to society." Finally, Turner stated that emigration is an honorable solution for a people who are "subjected to ill treatment, persecution, proscription, outrage and other forms of injustice."[40]

Moving to his African American critics—who argued that Blacks should not be concerned with emigration to Africa or anywhere else, because "colored people are to the manner born and, as such, are citizens of the United States," Turner called their arguments "illogical." He believed the problem many Blacks had with emigration came from their dislike of the American Colonization Society (ACS) and offered four primary reasons for African Americans to consider emigration. First, African Americans should take pride in their homeland. Second, Africa's land and climate offer some of the best advantages of planting and farming. The third reason had to do with Blacks' treatment in America, and finally, he predicted "bad times" were ahead for America, which meant even worse times for African Americans.[41]

After the church elected Turner bishop in 1880, the defense of his emigration policies and beliefs became even more argumentative as his status, as a bishop had a larger platform to share his views. Turner found himself at the center of the "African Question" debate in the pages of the *Christian Recorder*. For instance, when Benjamin Tanner began to criticize Africa and argued that African Americans couldn't care less about Africa, Turner forcefully disagreed. In one letter, published on January 4, 1883, Turner wrote, "[T]here are a host of us who see our condition from another standpoint, and our future equally as differently, and that host believes that Africa somehow is to give the relief for which our people sigh."[42]

In what would become a constant and consistent refrain throughout the rest of his life, Turner argued that many of these "recognized leaders" were simply out of touch with the majority of African Americans—many of whom resided in the South. When challenged that the majority of African Americans did not care about Africa, Turner wrote that in "some portions of the country it is the topic of conservation, and if a line of steamers were started from New Orleans, Mobile, Savannah or Charleston, they would be crowded to density every trip they made to Africa." He argued that there was "general unrest and a wholesale dissatisfaction among our people in a number of sections of the country to my certain knowledge, and they sigh for conveniences to and from the continent of Africa. Something has to be done."[43]

In another letter, published in the *Recorder* on January 25, 1883, Turner suggested that Black ministers and the Black elite were out of touch with the overwhelming poverty and struggle that faced the majority of African Americans. He noted that it was a "very easy thing for a few ministers in Philadelphia" to meet and have a "jolly time dealing in technicalities and theories, but it is another thing to have your sweat and blood devoured yearly by the vampires of a nation which is deaf to your cries and blind to your agonies. Justice in this country for the black man, from the Supreme Court of the United States down to the City Recorder, is a farce."[44]

Turner later asked rhetorically:

> Do you know of any instance in the world's history where a people shut out from all honorable positions, from being kings and queens, lords, dukes, presidents, governors, mayors, generals, and all positions of honor and trust, by reason of their race, ever amounted to anything? No sir, I will answer for you. There is no instance on record, except where preceded by revolution. People

must have one like them on high to inspire them to go high. Jesus Christ had to take upon himself our very nature before his plan of redemption was a success. It required a God-man on the throne of the universe to awaken the inspiration of a world. And till we have black men in the seat of power, respected, honored, beloved, feared, hated and reverenced, our young men will never look up.[45]

The debate between Tanner and Turner led Turner to offer a response in an article published by the *Recorder* on February 22, 1883. First, Turner grounded his emigration position in the argument that no race "will ever be respected, or ought to be respected, who do not show themselves capable of founding and manning a government of their own creation." He suggested that the "civilized negro" had yet to do this and that the "Colonization Society propose[d] to aid him in accomplishing that grand result. They are our best friends and greatest benefactors, as the stern and inexorable logic of facts will soon show."[46]

Second, while Turner argued that slavery was not a "divine institution," he did argue that it was a "providential institution" that God intended to make as the "primal factor in the civilization and Christianization of that dark continent." Turner went so far as to argue that "any person whomsoever who opposes the return of a sufficient number of her descendants to begin the grand work, which in the near future will be consummated, is fighting the God of the universe face to face."[47]

Third, Turner argued that if people around the world are "turning their attention to Africa," America should too and that the United States "should awake to her share of duty in this great movement." He also wrote that the United States owed African Americans "40 billion dollars" for the services rendered during slavery—estimating, according to Turner, "one hundred dollars a year for two million of us for two hundred years."[48]

Fourth, Turner reiterated his argument he was not for wholesale emigration, because he did not believe that all African Americans or Africa were prepared to receive that level of emigration. Here he called only for "five or ten thousand" per year and argued that he could "establish a government, build a country and raise a national symbol" with the people who were sent to jail, hung, or lynched. Turner proclaimed, "empty me your jails and penitentiary, and in ten years, I will give you a country before which your theories will pale and disappear."[49]

Fifth, Turner refuted arguments about the climate in Africa. He argued that "such language not only charges God with folly but contradicts the teachings of both science and philosophy. They have not even learned that man is cosmopolitan, that his home is everywhere upon the face of this globe. They have not read the history of this country that they pretend to love so well. God have mercy upon their little heads, and smaller hearts is my prayer."[50]

Lastly, Turner argued for emigration because he could "see through the dim future a grand hereafter for the Negro." He predicted that African Americans would grow in numbers, especially in the South, more rapidly than whites. However, he also predicted something else—a continued white backlash to this growth. For Turner, there was no "peaceful future" in America for Black people.[51]

While many argued that Turner wanted all Black people to go to Africa, he consistently denied that he would want everyone to go to Africa. In a letter to Rev. G. W. Ottley, published in the June 21, 1883, edition of the *Recorder*, Turner wrote:

> If all the riffraff white-men worshipers, aimless, objectless, selfish, little souled and would be white Negroes of this country were to go to Africa, I fear it would take a chiliad of years to get them to understand that a black man or woman could be somebody without the dictation of a white man. For the truth is, two-thirds of our race has no faith in themselves, and because they have none in themselves individually, they do not have any in each other. To them the white man is all and in all, therefore, it is useless to attempt to be anybody, especially where the white man does not hold sway; and where he does sway the scepter of power, he uses it to the degradation and dehumanization of the black race.[52]

In his open letter to B. K. Sampson, published in the *Memphis Daily Appeal* on November 8, 1883, Turner proudly proclaimed to be an "African emigrationist." Here, his reason for his position centered on his belief that the United States was not the "ultimate home" for African Americans. "I believed that the prejudice of the white race would either drive us out of the country or reduce us to a state of vassal degradation that could be more intolerable than slavery itself," wrote Turner. He wrote that he had no "faith in the race love of the South and less in the North," and as soon as African Americans were not a "political power in the South," Turner argued, the papers in the North started berating African Americans. He consistently lamented that because he "dared to tell my race they would have to leave the country at an early day or go from bad to worse, I have been denounced in public conventions and ostracized by the colored papers all over the country."[53]

Later in a letter addressed to B. K. Bruce of Mississippi, published March 27, 1890, in the *Recorder*, Turner would make his case in a sharper tone when charged with wanting all African Americans to immigrate to Africa. In an elongated invective, Turner wrote:

Thousands of us would be a curse to the continent, especially that portion of us who have no faith in the Negro, or his possibilities or even his future possibilities, who worship white gods, who would rather be a white dog on earth than a black cherub in heaven, who are fools enough to believe the devil is black, and therefore that all who are black are consanguineously related to him; ignorant black preachers who will stand up in the pulpit and represent this and that species of crime and vice as being as black as sin; and still another portion of us, who will study for years in college and even graduate, to follow the high calling of a waiter or a bootblack, as though classic lore was a prerequisite to such an exalted occupation; who had rather be a white man's scullion than a black man's prince, who regard Africa as being next door to hades, while it is the richest continent under heaven. And still another class of us, who will work as hard to dissuade young ministers from going with the gospel to the land of our progenitors as if they were going to leap over a fatal precipice; who pretend to be serving God, and have no aim higher than to get to heaven to be white; who profess faith in a bodily resurrection from the dead, and yet expect that resurrected and glorified body to be white; that class of us who would rather go forty miles to hear a white ass bray than a hundred yards to hear a black seraph sing . . . [54]

"Every colored man in this country who is not proud of himself," wrote Turner, "his color, his hair, and his general make-up is a monstrosity. He is a curse to himself and will be to his children. He is lower than a brute and does not deserve the breath he breathes, much less the bread he eats. Any man, though he be as black as midnight, who regards himself inferior to any other man that God ever made, is simply a walking ghoul and ought to join his invisible companions at the first opportunity, unless he does it to the extent of his natural or acquired ability."[55]

African Trip

In 1891 Turner took the first trip to Africa. Several pastors had emigrated to Africa already, and while there, they started churches under the AME banner. However, the churches struggled financially as they ministered to natives, newly arriving immigrants, and even a few dissatisfied members of white churches and missions. Understanding that the churches and ministers needed some help and encouragement, the AME Council of Bishops agreed to support Turner and authorized a trip for him to visit Africa. As Redkey noted, "although officially Turner was sent to organize the AME Churches for better supervision and financial support, the bishop viewed his trip as a pilgrimage and a chance to compare the real Africa with his dream Africa."[56]

Turner arrived in Sierra Leone on November 8, 1891. According to Angell, for the next ten days, Turner preached on several occasions to "overflowing crowds." While there he also convened the first Sierra Leone Annual Conference and ordained three deacons. From there he went to Liberia, where he received an "ecstatic" welcome. Of his welcome Turner wrote, "I never saw such rejoicing over the presence of a bishop as there is in Liberia. The preachers seem to have forgotten God and gone to bishop-worshiping. I have reproved them repeatedly, but it does no good." Turner's activities were not limited only to the church. He visited the grave of his aunt, Hannah Greer, who died in 1888 and spent time relaxing and fellowshipping with his Liberian host Samuel Campbell on his hundred-acre coffee farm. As he did in Sierra Leone, Turner convened the first Liberia Annual Conference and ordained six deacons.[57]

Turner chronicled his trip to Africa in letters to the *Christian Recorder*. Two years later the AME Publishing Board collected the letters and published them as a book titled *African Letters*. In the letters Turner offered glowing reports of both the land and the people of Africa. Turner was impressed with the native Africans he met on the ship. In writing about one African, Matthew Thomas of Lagos, Nigeria, Turner wrote that he was one of the "most learned men" he had ever met. Thomas read and spoke five different languages and understood Greek, Latin, Hebrew, Syriac, and Arabic. "Talk about the African being ignorant," declared Turner. "Here is one who has no superior for book learning in our country, yet he is only 37 years of age."[58]

After arriving in Sierra Leone, Turner wrote that he thought it was a "low, swampy lagoony town, with narrow, muddy streets, as filthy as a cesspool." However, he was surprised with its "cleanliness, pavements sidewalks, rock-sewers and decency everywhere." Impressed by the "fine buildings" he saw, Turner was surprised that "they all belong to black men." Turner wrote, "When I inquired about the great cathedral, with tower and clock, and other large churches, with spires, domes, and steeples, and was told they were black people's churches, I had to say, thank God for this sight!"[59]

Also impressive were the people Turner met. Wrote Turner, "[W]hat fools we are to suppose these Africans are fools!" In one worship service, Turner wrote that "twenty different languages were used but a large number would understand everybody and tears would be shed." In his retelling of this worship experience, Turner wrote, "Great heavens, how white people on one hand, scullion negroes upon the other, have misrepresented Africa! Some who got up in that love-feast to talk were what they called heathens, right from the bush, with a mere cloth over them, and while I could not understand a word, you could see they were full of the Holy Ghost." His general experience with African people was that the native African has no fear, no cowardice, no dread, but feels himself the equal of any man on earth. The land as far as I went, is rich, water streams in abundance, fruits of every kind, flowers of every beauty, and while I saw many doing nothing at all, I saw many hundreds at work, and hard at work, too."[60]

If Sierra Leone was a pleasant experience for Turner, Liberia was much more. In writing about Liberia, Turner wrote that it was one of the most "paradisical portions of earth my eyes ever beheld." He argued that "any person who cannot live here with reasonable health cannot exist anywhere." Turner wrote that this was the only country that "everybody could have a stream of water running through his yard. It is the most perfectly watered region I have ever witnessed. The water, too, is clear as a crystal, and rapidly flows wherever seen." Turner enthusiastically wrote:

> If some of our rich colored men in the States would come here and open up the coal mines at Carrysburg, they would be worth millions in a few years. The steamships would buy the coal by millions of tons. The coaling stations at Grand Canary and Sierra Leone, now supplied with coal shipped from England, would be transferred to Liberia, and wealth untold would be the result. They have coal, marble, silver, gold, tin and diamonds, all in Liberia. I never had over-much admiration for Liberia until since my arrival here. I thought it was a second-class portion of Africa, but it is the richest region of the globe I ever saw. There is no place in the United States that will begin to compare with it. Any man who will run down Liberia, so far as its natural resources are concerned, is a fool and an ass. I am not talking about what I have heard, either. I am speaking of what I have seen with my own eyes, and handled with my own hands.[61]

After his trip to Africa, Turner believed the time was right to start seriously promoting his vision of emigration. With the rising tide of white supremacy, Turner argued that things were not going to get better for Blacks and that emigration was the only viable option. In a letter to the editor of the *Indianapolis Freedman*, Turner wrote, "I have said, and say yet, that there is no more hope for the black man in this country to become a civil and political factor than there is for a frog in a snake den. And any man who is too idiotic to see it ought to go and hang himself."[62]

National Negro Convention

Two years later Turner issued a call for African Americans to convene in a national convention, because, for Turner, the time had come for Blacks to consider emigrating out of America. Turner wrote in the call:

> I do not believe that there is any manhood future in this country for the Negro, and that his future existence, to say nothing of his future happiness, will depend upon his nationalization. . . . But knowing that thousands and tens of thousands see our present conditions and our future about as I do, and after waiting for four years or more for some of our colored statesmen or leaders to call a national convention or to propose some plan of speaking to the nation or to the world, or to project some measure that will remedy our condition, or will even suggest a remedy, and finding no one among the anti-emigrational party or anti-Negro nationalization party disposed to do so, and believing that further silence is not only a disgrace but a crime, I have resolved to issue a call in the near future for a national convention to be held in the city of Cincinnati, where a spacious edifice is at our disposal, to meet some time in November, for the friends of African repatriation or Negro nationalization elsewhere, to assemble and adopt such measures for our actions as may commend themselves to our better judgment.[63]

Despite the persistent and adverse reactions to emigration, the attendance was better than Turner expected. About eight hundred delegates registered, along with many local Blacks from host city Cincinnati, who all came to hear the emigration-minded bishop speak. In delivering his keynote address, I have argued, Turner "adopted a prophetic persona of a pragmatic prophet and issued a (re)constitutive rhetoric[:] mission-oriented prophecy—one that calls an audience active within a divine mission.[64]

Throughout the speech, Turner offered many of the same reasons why African Americans should consider emigration as a viable option to rid themselves of the abuses they had to suffer in America. How one that was new within his emigration argument was his call for reparations. Turner argued that America owed Blacks "billions of dollars" for slavery, making Turner one of the first to call for slavery reparations.

> This nation justly, rightly, and divinely owes us work for services rendered, billions of dollars, and if we cannot be treated as American people, we should ask for five hundred million dollars, at least, to begin an emigration somewhere, for it will cost, sooner or later, far more than that amount to keep the Negro down unless they re-establish slavery itself. Freedom and perpetual degradation are

not in the economy of human events. It is against reason, against nature, against precedent, and against God.⁶⁵

Turner grounded his call for reparations in what is *"just, right and divine,"* thereby elevating the discussion of reparations and placing it in a moral sphere. Turner not only invited his audience to see this position and take it seriously but also invited the audience to reflect on the fairness of the country. "Turner's aim of course," was to get the audience to "*see* what he sees—that America has not been fair to African Americans, therefore, they should consider emigration as a viable option and that African Americans should receive compensation to support this emigration enterprise."⁶⁶

According to reports, throughout the speech the audience "shouted and cheered," and after Turner finished, he received sustained applause. By the end of the convention, it was clear that the overwhelming majority of delegates were not in favor of emigration anywhere. Instead of an emigration plan, the only recommendations that came out of the convention were to establish the National Equal Rights Council, with Turner acting as chancellor, and to continue to appeal to Congress, governors, and the American people for fair and equal justice.⁶⁷

If naming Turner chancellor was an attempt to get Turner to support the efforts of the Council, it did not work. In an article published in the *Voice of Missions* in January of 1894, Turner sarcastically asked, "What under heaven would [I] want with a national convention of over seven hundred delegates to endorse African emigration, when at least two million of colored people here in the South are ready to start to Africa at any moment, if we had a line of steamers running to and fro."⁶⁸

Frustrated by the outcome of the convention, Turner was correct about one thing; there were many African Americans ready to board ships and leave, heading to Africa or anywhere that they could escape the oppression they found in America. The fact of the matter was that Africa was an expensive trip, always a stumbling block for those who wanted to go. So Turner turned his attention to not only advocating emigration but also to securing the means for people to get to Africa. For Turner, that meant providing a steamship that would sail to Africa. He would have his chance with the formation of the Colored National Emigration Association.

Turner and the Colored National Emigration Association

In 1901 G. T. Adams led efforts to hold an emigration convention October 7–9 in Nashville, Tennessee. Despite previous attempts at an emigration plan, Turner quickly supported the proposed convention by promoting it in his *Voice of the People* newspaper. While the records of the meeting have been lost to history, we do know several things that came out of this gathering. First, delegates formed the Colored National Emigration Association to raise $100,000 to purchase a used steamship for emigration and commercial purposes. By doing this they were able to merge several of the struggling emigration groups into one organization. Second, women were allowed to not only serve as delegates but also to speak at the convention. Third, the delegates elected AME minister Dr. W. H. Heard as president of the association and Abrams as vice-president. The delegates selected Heard because he had spent four years in Africa and could "tell so much about foreign travel, foreign countries and knew so many people abroad." The group also estimated that they started with about four thousand members and expected more organizations to join.[69]

The association also agreed on two more important matters. First, the association would not limit emigration to Africa. They resolved to emigrate anywhere—"South America, Central America, Cuba, Santiago, Mexico, Hawaii," any place outside America. They denounced the "worthless vagabonds and Negro villains" who criticized emigration but yet posed no remedy "for the ills" that plagued African Americans. Delegates at the convention likened "such Negroes" with the "murderers" trying to "exterminate African Americans from the "face of the earth."[70]

Second, the association not only made Turner their chief financial officer in the roles of chancellor and treasurer but they also named Turner's *Voice of the People* as their official organ. In his role as chief financial officer, Turner promised that if African Americans would meet him halfway, "he would have a ship or die." In an address to the convention, Turner sought to relieve fears that some may have had regarding financial oversight that had sunk previous emigration efforts. Turner promised that "every penny paid for investment in a ship would be held in a sacred trust to be refunded if the ship was not purchased."[71]

However, in his address to the convention, Turner aimed the majority of his critiques against the nation for not protecting African Americans' civil rights and liberties, as well as at some African Americans who remained passive about their conditions. Turner reminded his audiences that African Americans had only to be charged with a crime and they are then "hung, shot, burned, or mutilated." For Turner, "American justice does not any more regard him as entitled to consideration than if he was a venomous snake." He further said he sometimes feared that the charge that the "Negro is of an inferior race" could be more "truth" and "poetry," because, as he reasoned, "for any race that will submit to the abuses heaped upon it such as the Negro is subjected to today, and virtually say nothing is evidently very weak." However, he closed the speech on an up note. He claimed that he was "happy that there are enough with courage and manhood to start this national movement who are not satisfied with the conditions that are pressing the life out of us in the United States." They concluded their three-day convention by agreeing to meet the following May in Chattanooga.[72]

During the months between the conventions, Turner did not waste any time promoting the association's efforts and the merits of emigration. Through the *Voice of the People* and other newspapers, Turner wrote a series of columns that focused on the reasons why African Americans should turn their attention toward emigration. First, Turner grounded his arguments in the way society treated African Americans. For example, in one column, published in the *Colored American* in Washington, DC, Turner argued that African Americans had "no protection at all from the United States government." Further, he wrote,

> We have no rights in the public highway, none in the jury box, none in the ballot, none anywhere. We are hanged, we are shot; we are burned; we are disfranchised; we are outlawed whenever and wherever a mob chooses to do it. Jails are merely a place of safe keeping till drunken bands have time to form and take our lives in the most inhumane manner and then telegraph over the country that we assaulted or tried to outrage some white woman that was never born. At least, this is the case ninety times out of every hundred and the whole nation accepts the verdict of the drunken and inhuman mobs.[73]

Turner also refuted arguments made by those who opposed emigration. For instance, some in the African American community did not believe that it was necessarily the color of Black people that whites objected to; it was the lack of resources. They argued that as soon as African Americans got money and wealth, then white people would be able to look past color and treat African Americans as equals. Turner quickly picked up on this fallacious line of thinking. In a letter to the editor first published in the *Voice of Missions* and then excerpted in the *Washington Times*, Turner used the backlash behind President Roosevelt's invitation to Booker T. Washington to dine at the White House[74] as an example of how white people felt even about an African American who, by all accounts, had acquitted himself appropriately. Turner wrote,

> Most of the stay-here crowd, in speaking of the ridiculosity of our emigration position have said: "Oh, it is not your color the white people object to; it is your poverty. Get the dollar and everything will be alright." But I reckon everybody sees now. Billions of dollars would not remove the curse of being a Negro.

President Roosevelt simply dined with Booker T. Washington, who was a representative of twelve million of his supporters, tax-payers, flag defenders by land and by sea and yet two-thirds of the country are cursing, bellowing, vomiting, and disgracing themselves because a colored man ate dinner with a white man. We will say no more about the fool stuff uttered by fool negroes. We wish they had some resolve.[75]

Another argument that opponents used against emigration was to declare that African Americans were superior to Africans. In an open letter in response to fellow AME minister Rev. R. Seymour, Turner refuted the charge. While conceding that African Americans had some advantages, Turner argued that the African had more "common sense" and "business qualities," and "knew how to make a living upon his own merits, without being "hirelings" or "scullions." He further wrote that "one African has more manhood in him than fifteen American black men. He has more business sense than twelve American Negroes." While Turner did admit that African Americans knew more about Christianity, he also wrote that they were "helpless, cowardly, dependent; has less faith in himself and is more worthless generally than the native African." He closed the letter by writing that Rev. R. Seymour says, "Bring the African to this country, educate him and let him go back. God forbid, God forbid. I fear we would educate him to be a coward."[76]

Still another way opponents of emigration attacked Turner was to misappropriate and misrepresent his arguments and positions. For example, an Associated Press dispatch published in the *Atlanta Constitution* said that Turner was encouraging African Americans to immigrate to Tunis and that the French government supported the effort. Turner, in response, denied "knowledge of the affair." While he wrote that he would not have any problem with people who wanted to go there, he was in favor of the "black man emigrating to a portion of the world where he will be at the head of his own government." Turner never questioned whether or not African Americans could run a government because, as he argued, he had "seen too much and [knew] too much of his ability in that direction to doubt it." Further, he wrote

> I know he will never be a man, he will never have the instincts and promptings of manhood as long as he is regarded a mere creature for others to control, nor will he ever play his part in the civilized world while he is thus shackled and hampered. We had as well remain here as a race as to emigrate where the French have absolute control. The thing I am clamoring for is for negro merchants, negro statesmen, negro courts, negro legislatures and governments, and to be masters of themselves.[77]

Turner continued to spread the news about the association and its upcoming convention. They promoted the convention as a "grand mass meeting" for those in favor of leaving the United States for Africa, Cuba, Hawaii, or "any other part of the world where the Negro can have manhood, civil, and political rights, regardless of color." In the call they advertised that the purpose of this meeting was to "devise some scheme upon which all can unite." Further, they claimed that the convention would be the "most important convention ever held by the race."[78]

In an editorial written by Turner and published in the *Voice of the People*, he bragged how the stock price had gone up since the initial offer at the October meeting. Many Blacks, frustrated by the oppression they faced throughout the South, formed chapters of the association. One man, C. W. Brown, formed a chapter in Vancouver, Canada. On seeing the support for the effort, Turner started to promote the upcoming Chattanooga convention even more. He expected the association to grow with new members and increased financial support.

Outside of Turner's *Voice of the People* and a few other sympathetic newspapers, the media did not comment much on the event. They did, however, take the time to criticize emigration efforts. For example, the *Hattiesburg Daily Progress* declared that no good and sensible African American would want to leave the South for "Massachusetts or Liberia," arguing that the African American "who works for a living is satisfied here, and you couldn't pull him away with a half dozen yoke of oxen." It suggested that America was the best place for African Americans and that the southern people were friends to African Americans. However, it did encourage the "sorry class of African Americans to "go to Liberia."[79]

The *Seattle Republican* added that "Congress will not appropriate that amount of money nor any amount of money for colored folk to leave this country, and if Congress did do it there is not a baker's dozen of colored folk who would avail themselves of the opportunity." It argued that America was the home of the "colored man just the same as the white man, and here he proposes to stay and battle it out whether the contest be long or short, and here he proposes to succeed as do other nationalities."[80]

Even before the convention, one newspaper called it a "waste of time" after Turner called African Americans to discuss the issue of emigration at a church before Sunday service. The *Hartford Courant* wrote that "nothing good" or "nothing practical" would come from the meeting. "Turner's idea of a great race exodus from this country to Central Africa is fantastic and preposterous." The editors argued that "intelligent, industrious Negroes would not want to go to Africa any more than they want to go to Labrador or Patagonia." The editors suggested that only a few could go if they wanted to and that if they did go, the editors surmised, African Americans "would be lamenting their folly and wishing themselves home again in the United States before the first year was out."[81]

AME minister A. Benjamin Cooper, writing in the *Southern Christian Recorder* offered a scathing critique of the meeting. He started his critique by noting that both the president of the association, William H. Heard, and Bishop Turner elected not to stay after visiting Africa. He suggested that they both go to Africa and "remain there for a few years" to "get things in shape" for those who will be prepared by the time the company prepares its first Great Ship." He however, not only doubted that Heard and Turner would lead the way but also questioned the association's methods. He wrote, "I am afraid, by the time all these promoters get their expenses for holding the conventions and going to them and paying speakers and a thousand and one other expenses; the "ship money" will be but a few pennies." Further, he wrote, "[D] own with the African movement. Up with something that will help us, one and all, to see the right, do the right, and be the right."[82]

The convention was a disappointment for Turner. Only a hundred delegates attended, and while the delegation represented members throughout the nation, they did not raise as much money as they hoped. Many Black leaders simply ignored the convention. However, the convention did produce a petition that, as one newspaper reported, cited "a long train of abuses which it asserts the negroes are subject to among which is denial of all social and political recognition, and violation of his constitutional rights and asked Congress for 500 million dollars towards emigration." At the end of the convention, the delegates decided to hold another convention in Charlotte, North Carolina, in October. However, due to timing and interest, the association rescheduled the meeting for May 1903 in Montgomery, Alabama. In the interim, Turner continued to promote emigration and address his critics.[83]

Though disappointed with the convention, Turner continued to promote emigration as the solution to the problems African American faced in the United States. In a letter published in the *Hartford Courant* in response to the paper labeling Turner a "foolish old mischief-maker" for his support of emigration, Turner wrote, "Yes, I favor emigration for my race. Let them leave a cruel and ungrateful nation like this." Repeating the paper's accusation, Turner continued, "I am a fool and mischief-maker because I am not willing for my race to sit down and quietly be murdered in every conceivable form and for the nation to say, well done by its silence. A fool because a savage country can outrage and murder my race in every manner, and I am not willing to hold my tongue while it is being done."[84]

In an article published first in the *New York Tribune* and republished in Turner's *Voice of the People*,[85] Turner offered his full-throated support for emigration. He started by commenting on how both whites and African Americans have "roundly abused" him for his emigration position. He wrote that he had always been open about his views, and he aimed to give his emigration mission the "widest publicity possible." Turner argued that the future of the African American race was in Africa, and the sooner that African Americans immigrated to Africa, the better it would be for the entire race. Turner's reasoning for the move was that African Americans were "dying out." He argued that the "Negro race is not growing healthier, wealthier, wiser or anything else which goes to make life worth living."[86]

Turner also addressed a question that his critics lobbed at him at every turn—if he thought that Africa was so great, how come he did not go to Africa and stay? Turner suggested that he was needed in America but that when he could get "fifty or one hundred thousand Negroes to go with me" he he would be "off like a quester horse," adding that he believed it would be his "best day's work ever." For Turner, African Americans could never hope to be more than "hewers of wood and drawers of water." He argued that legislatures, especially in the South enacted laws meant to "keep the negro down," and since this was the case, he rhetorically asked, "[H]ow can the negro ever hope in this county to attain the full stature of a citizen or a man?"[87]

To heighten his effect, Turner turned to fear-based appeals. He warned that if African Americans remained in the United States, white people would soon "exterminate" or reenslave them. Realizing that many African Americans did not share his bleak outlook, Turner argued:

> Some people are unkind enough to say that this kind of talk comes from a disordered brain. That kind of prating does not annoy me in the least. I am too much in earnest in this work to give any worry to such stuff. I have been called uncivilized and a heathen, but I believe I am doing my Master's work in these efforts to better the condition of my people. The Negro can never hope to attain respectable recognition here, and I think he should go where he can. Here he is only a slave and a menial for the giant race. That is all he can ever hope to be in this land.[88]

In the March issue of the *Voice of the People* in 1903, Turner published (and probably wrote) the call for the second annual convention of the Colored National Emigration and Commercial Association to commence on June 24, 1903, in Montgomery, Alabama. The signatories invited both men and women, including those who took issue with emigration but had other plans to present. However, they warned that the "scullionized portion" of the race, those that had "nothing but negative babble to present," were not invited and would be "regarded as intruders." After listing reasons and grievances for emigration, Turner reminded his readers that the convention was an attempt to do something. "Silence," he wrote, "upon our part any longer bears the stamp of acquiescence and is a declaration of our willingness for the condition to continue." He closed the call stating, "God will crown our efforts with consequences that will be long remembered."[89]

Despite the efforts of Turner and the association, many saw the convention in Montgomery as a failure. According to historian Edwin Redkey, while several local Blacks attended, on the opening day of the meeting, there were only forty-five delegates registered for the convention. During the meeting Turner was able to secure $150 worth of stock, and the delegates voted to charter a ship in 1904, rather than wait until they could buy one outright. They drafted a petition to give to Congress, and after some "rousing speeches," the conference ended.[90]

The convention turnout disappointed Turner. Despite attempting to stay positive about the fundraising efforts, he had to admit the reality. In an article published in the *Voice of the People* newspaper that September,[91] Turner lamented that they were "making poor headway" in raising funds. He wrote that the association had secured only $26,000 toward their goal of $100,000. A frustrated Turner blamed the failure on the bulk of African Americans' "sitting down waiting for others who have some heart and soul to invest their money in the scheme to do it." Turner argued that African Americans did not want to help themselves, but if there was "dirt-eating, foot-kissing and humiliation, any condescension any dog-fawning needing to be done," African Americans were "ready to do it."[92]

"Help yourself," Turner continued, was not "characteristic of the American Negro." Turner argued that the African American was more interested in spending his money on "excursions or some other nonsensical way than to invest it to do himself some good." Speaking of Black leaders, he wrote, "[T]here are a set of ignorant and fool advisors in the country telling our people to be quiet and not help ourselves, and it appears like they are the ones our people are listening to." For Turner, these leaders were white men's "scullions," who grew up to manhood in this position and could not help but be "miserable mendicants." As the year ended, Turner began to see reality. In an appeal to members of the association, he wrote, "The members of this association appear to have gotten tired of sending in their dues and enlisting new members. The way we are going on, we will not be able to purchase our contemplated ship in twenty-five years." He wrote that he was "becoming discouraged" and wished that "members would pay their quarterly fees and work for the organization" or meet in convention to "disband the organization," so that he could return everyone their money. "There's a perfect lag in our association," he wrote. "Is it possible the American Negro can start and finish nothing?"[93]

Bishop Turner would eventually lose interest in the association, and the group would later disband. In a letter to Secretary Wilson of the American Colonization Society, Turner wrote, "[F]or some time you may have noticed I have not said or done very much in the interest of Liberian colonization." He continued

> I attempted to organize an association that would raise a hundred thousand dollars . . . but after raising a few thousand . . . a lethargy or seeming indifference appeared to come over our organization. . . . As treasurer of the organization I just returned the money . . . to those who had given it and invested and disbanded the institution. I did this at the protest of our president, Dr. W. H. Heard, and some of the most influential members of the organization, for the reason that I did not intend to have anyone say they put money in my hands and that I had spent it or robbed them of it.[94]

While Turner would continue to advocate emigration as the solution to the ills and issues facing African Americans, this would be his last organized attempt at emigration to Africa.

Melbourne Cummings, in her dissertation on Turner, noted that Turner's emigration campaign was extremely productive in other ways. First, drawing from the work of Charles W. Lomas, she called Turner's emigration campaign a "revolutionary agitation campaign." According to Cummings, Turner's rhetoric was "directed against entrenched conditions that had existed for years in the social, political and economic order of the United States as it related to black people." Second, Cummings noted that Turner's rhetoric was "always the search of dignity, pride, and 'manhood' future for black people." Third, again, while emigration did not happen on the scale that Turner would have liked, Cummings reminds us of one crucial fact—Turner was successful at persuading many to emigrate. "Considering the numbers," Cummings noted, Turner was far more successful in his emigration efforts than Martin R. Delany or Marcus Garvey." Cummings wrote, "But even Marcus Garvey's phenomenal movement has been termed the largest Black Nationalist movement in the

United States, few, if any, blacks actually emigrated. Turner, on the other hand, was responsible for the actual emigration of at least one thousand Southern blacks to Liberia."[95]

His rhetorical eagerness to justify and persuade his audiences of the merits of emigration was moving and motivating to many, but Turner's rhetoric was also problematic. For instance, well into his rhetoric of emigration, Tunde Adeleke has argued, to justify his emigration plans Turner "purified and rendered positively" the "negative and painful historical experience of slavery. Therefore, "slavery became a divine strategy meant to bring heathen and backward Africa in contact with civilization." Adeleke argued that Turner therefore was guilty of practicing "slaveocentrism—one that identifies slavery and the American experience, rather than Africa, as the foundation for constructing a black American identity."[96]

For Adeleke, even Turner's time spent in Africa did not erase his Eurocentrism. For instance, while Adeleke argued that Turner, while visiting Africa, significantly reduced the "civilization gap between African and America," his letters still confirmed "certain shortcomings in the condition of Liberians." Adeleke wrote that after his African visits, "indigenous Africans were not completely backward, they nevertheless retained certain anachronistic habits and customs and remained in need of spiritual salvation."[97]

While Turner did not start as a promoter of emigration, textual evidence demonstrates that he was at least sympathetic to the idea as early as 1862. He argued that African Americans should at least debate the merits of emigration, and if anyone wanted to emigrate, they should. As he would fully develop later in his career, Turner believed that Black people should determine their own fates—Black agency was sacrosanct. Early in his career, though he called talk of emigration "foolishness," Turner believed not only that everyone should make up her or his own mind about emigration but that the African American community should support people's decision to leave.

As time went on, however, and as the promise of Reconstruction did not deliver the freedom that African Americans expected, Turner began to revisit the subject of emigration. He first started courting the American Colonization Society in hopes that he could land a lucrative contract to become a speaker and writer on the topic of emigration. At this time Turner saw emigration and his role in it as one that would help send missionaries to Africa. While many in the African American community criticized Turner's overtures to the ACS, Turner remained steadfast in his belief that the ACS was doing good work. He saw ACS only as an opportunity to get missionaries to Africa and to "civilize the fatherland" and, at least publicly, did not endorse emigration.

In 1876, however, Turner dropped all pretense and came out as an endorser and supporter of emigration. After accepting the honorary title as one of the vice presidents of the ACS, he began to argue that African Americans should start thinking about building the "United States of Africa." No longer just sympathetic to emigration or only helping missionaries arrive, Turner began to argue that African Americans needed a "government and nationality" of their own and that would be the only thing that would "cure the evils" under which African Americans found themselves living daily.

After the publication of his *Emigration of the Colored People of the United States* in 1879 and his election to bishop in 1880, Turner became more argumentative as he continued to promote his emigration positions. First, Turner refuted the charge that no one really cared about emigration, claiming that millions of people were ready to leave America if there were a line of steamers prepared to sail. Second, he claimed that many of the Black elite and northern leaders were simply out of touch with what Black Americans in the South were thinking. Third, while many claimed that Turner was proposing that all African Americans emigrate, he argued vehemently that this was false. For Turner, only the ones who had faith in themselves and did not see whiteness as the be-all and end-all were ready to emigrate to Africa or anyplace else.

It was his trip to Africa that would not only give him more of a desire to promote emigration but also expand his vision of what it would mean. Seeing Africans, talking with them and engaging them as equals, Turner no longer saw them as "ignorant" and in need of civilization. He lamented how white people and African Americans had misrepresented Africa and its culture. As for differences in religious expression, Turner noted that one could still see that they were "full of the Holy Ghost." It was seeing Africa in all of its majestic beauty that led Turner to continue to promote his vision of emigration.

After the failure of the Negro Convention in 1893 to move the majority of the delegates to support emigration, Turner began to seek a way to secure a steamship to promote his emigration vision. He also shifted his arguments in support for emigration. First, he began to focus on how society treated African Americans. He reminded his audiences that Black people had no protection from the United States government. Second, he offered refutations of the line of thinking that color was not the issue in the discrimination against African Americans. Third, he refuted arguments that would declare African Americans "superior" to native Africans. He reminded his audiences of his trips to Africa, and the pride carried by Africans ."

However, for all of his hard work and rhetoric supporting emigration, African Americans did not emigrate at the levels desired by Turner. While Turner did succeed in motivating some African Americans to emigrate to

Africa, the numbers were not enough for the emigration movement to be successful in the ways Turner envisioned. Therefore, on the surface it would seem that Turner's rhetoric ultimately was a failure. However, I suggest that we need to examine Turner's emigration rhetoric anew.

While promoting emigration as a panacea for Blacks dealing with the American apartheid system, Turner's rhetoric also produced some of the earliest notions of Black self-esteem, identity, and personhood.[98] Cummings noted this when she wrote of Turner's emigration campaign that he was able to instill in African Americans "a kind of black pride and hope for their salvation and future that had not been felt since emancipation."[99] While many scholars start with the work of W. E. B. Du Bois in race and Black identity studies,[100] I suggest that Turner's work and rhetoric in this area predates that of Du Bois. For Turner, some African Americans did not want to emigrate because they did not believe they could. Turner argued that spoke to a much larger issue—that they suffered from an inferiority complex that hindered them from trying to do something on their own.

Turner explicated this line of thinking throughout his rhetoric on and in support of emigration. As already mentioned, early in Turner's career he was sympathetic to emigration. He thought that African Americans should at least be open to debating the matter. Turner saw African Americans as part of the body politic, and they should be free to discuss openly any matter about them. While at this time he did not publicly support emigration plans, Turner did argue for a "flowing conversation about African Americans' options" for what "was possible in their lives."[101]

For instance, in 1862, when there were talks of a possible plan of emigration to Central America, Turner opined, "[L]et it be discussed and let those go who wish, and those stay who desire; let us have free expression about it, for all this helps to develop intellect."[102] According to historian Kate Masur, "Turner emphasized individual self-determination" by "stressing the multiplicity of African Americans' aspirations and destinies." For Turner during the Civil War, an understanding of freedom meant an "opportunity to pursue one's dreams, whatever they may be," and if this included the possibility of emigration, that would have been fine. It would be African Americans making decisions about their own destinies, because Turner never voiced doubt that Black people were "capable of sorting through the arguments [about emigration] and making informed decisions."[103]

For much of his career, Turner attempted to get African Americans to see their value and worth and not dwell in feelings of inferiority. It was the same inferiority that made African Americans believe that everything white was godly, and everything Black was evil. As discussed in chapter 2, Turner thundered, "God is a Negro," not because he literally believed that God was Black, but because he thought that Blacks must believe in a God that looked like them to feel affirmed in a world that told them that they were not worthy. This was essentially the same argument that James Cone would make some seventy years later in his work on Black Theology.[104]

Turner also preached that "degradation would only beget degradation"—that Blacks who felt bad about themselves would only pass this feeling down to their posterity "ad infinitum." He wrote and spoke about how Blacks wanted to be white but could not, and how in essence, since they could not be white and did not want to be Black, they in turn became monstrosities. He vehemently criticized Blacks for hating themselves and in turn hating Africa. Thus, Turner eventually saw emigration as necessary for the emotional and spiritual, as well as the physical well-being, of African Americans. America was not the land of the free for African Americans, in Turner's estimation; it had become Babylon, and only escape from its tentacles could bring the much-needed relief that African Americans desired.

After four trips to Africa, after the establishment of the AME Church on the continent, after much dialogue with African governmental and tribal leaders, after seeing much of the spirit by and from Africans, Turner concluded that African Americans must emigrate to Africa for another reason. While for much of his life Turner argued that Blacks needed the crucible of slavery to learn civilization, it was indeed the other way around—Blacks needed to emigrate to Africa now because it was the place in which African Americans could finally learn civilization.

Turner concluded that America was not a civilized country, and it did not practice the tenets of Christianity—at least not when it came to Black people. Turner argued that Blacks should emigrate because in Africa "human life is sacred and no man is deprived of it or any other thing that involves his manhood without due process of the law."[105] While this may be a romanticized version of Africa, Turner began to lay the foundation for a Pan-African movement that did not look at Africa disparagingly but respected Africa as an equal partner with much to offer.

In promoting emigration as an option for African American well-being, Turner offered a *third way* in African American rhetorical discourse in the late nineteenth and early twentieth centuries. Many historians and rhetoric scholars see this period of African American history as the "Washington and Du Bois" era. Many maintained that African Americans wanted either accommodation or integration. However, Turner rejected both positions and offered emigration as a possible solution to the problems African Americans faced. While the majority of Blacks did not accept emigration as a solution, many did. And African Americans would need this encouragement because, as they soon would discover, white supremacy and white nationalism were becoming pervasive throughout the land—for African Americans, things were about to get much worse.

6

"HELL IS AN IMPROVEMENT SO FAR AS THE NEGRO IS CONCERNED"

Turner and the Damning of America

On May 18, 1905, the AME Church convened to celebrate the twenty-fifth episcopal anniversary of Turner. Despite the disagreements and differences Turner had with other bishops and members of the church, a large audience crammed into St. Paul Chapel AME Church in St. Louis, Missouri, to celebrate the senior bishop of the church. Bishop W. J. Gaines, who served as the presiding officer for the event, opened the occasion with a brief address acknowledging that only a few of those present in 1880, when the church elected Turner bishop, were present at this event. He celebrated the "remarkable providence of God" in preserving Turner and "prospering the church." Bishop B. W. Arnett read the roll and minutes of the 1880 General Conference, and other officials read the many letters from other ecclesiastical leaders from different church denominations that came in support and celebration of Turner.[1]

The three-day event was made up of over twenty presentations that spoke to Turner's role in the church and society. Church leaders delivered papers celebrating Turner that carried titles such as "Bishop Turner, His Birth, Rearing and Education," "H. M. Turner as a Statesman," "Bishop H. M. Turner as Missionary and Promoter of Missions," "Bishop H. M. Turner as a Race Leader," and "Bishop H. M. Turner as a Publisher." The papers provide an overview of the life and legacy of Turner, and it also allowed those who did not know of Turner's earlier career to begin to reassess what they may have thought of Turner.

By all accounts, with sessions starting early in the morning and lasting well into the night, the event was a rousing success. One writer proclaimed that the event would go down in history as a "red-letter event in African Methodism." After commenting on the "beauty and magnificence" of the event, the writer added, "Nature smiled upon the occasion, and ministers and laymen of his own and other churches vied with each other in doing honor to the most noted Negro churchman living."[2]

One day later, after the celebration, Turner delivered the Sunday sermon at St. Paul AME Church. Turner's text for the day was Psalms 20:14: "Offer unto God thanksgiving and pay thy vows unto the Most High." One reporter that witnessed the sermon wrote that Turner seemed "inspired" and that he was "unequaled" in "depth of thought and Biblical research." After demonstrating how nature, animals, and even plants give thanks to God, Turner then shifted his attention to himself.

> For forty years, I have been trying to preach the Gospel and to give thanks to the Most High; but I have, in a measure failed. My feeble voice is not adequate to so stupendous a task; for when I consider the heavens, the work of His fingers, the sun, moon, and stars which he has ordained, what am I but an atom, whose feeble voice cannot swell the strains of the volume of music which sings the praises of the ubiquitous God? The Most High God, that is, he is highest of the high, a stupendous height to which human conception cannot attain. Therefore, if we would contribute to the glory of God in giving thanks to the Most High, we must seek in all of our actions to be right, with conscience void toward God and man; each making his contribution with the passing days.[3]

The celebration rejuvenated Turner. With the failure of his last emigration effort and his relinquishing of the editorship of the *Voice of the People*, Turner began to reassess his role in the church as well as within society. As the celebration reminded him, he had been on the forefront of many of the issues facing African Americans since the Civil War—and while not everyone agreed with his positions on all the issues and problems faced by African Americans, many still respected him for the work he had done. However, it seemed that the tide was turning against Turner. A new generation of voices, removed from the brutality of slavery, had come on the scene—new and younger voices vying for the attention of African Americans. These voices wanted to celebrate the dawning of the twentieth century as a new day in the life of African Americans. Many celebrated the schools and churches African Americans built. They also celebrated the property gains that African Americans achieved. While celebrating this optimistic vision for Black America, they did not want to talk about the ills of slavery; those days were long gone. They also did not want to talk about the failures of Reconstruction; those days, too, were long gone. They wanted to only look toward the future, and while not everything was as perfect as it could have been, some African Americans learned to find their own way to gain some measure of success.

Turner did not share this optimism. He consistently said publicly that there was no future for African Americans in the United States. He argued that there was nothing that African Americans could attain by staying in the United States. The reason was that, for Turner, at its core America was a racist country incapable of appreciating the gifts and efforts from African Americans. He concluded that there was no amount of education, no amount of money, and no amount of business acumen that Black people could achieve that would make white people respect them as human beings. In this chapter I examine Turner's understanding of race and racism and how it developed through Reconstruction into the early twentieth century.

Turner and the Understanding of Race and Racism

Early in Turner's career, his writings suggest that he supported the idea that if Black people had an opportunity to show their worth, then white people would respect them. In 1863 Turner called on African Americans to love their enemies. During the Civil War, in his sermon "Colored Men and the Draft," Turner suggested that there was "too much hatred" and posited that God would not deliver Black people while they cherished such "hellish feelings." Turner further said:

> Look at this nation. We are hating each other. The dominant, or white race, are hating us, and abusing us, every opportunity, heaping upon our heads indignities of every kind, and even murdering in cold blood, as they did in New York. And we, in turn, have the same revengeful feeling toward the white race. Think you, my brethren, we can ever obtain the favor of God, with the blessings of peace as a nation, while he witnesses such murder in our hearts, as many of us now cherish? We have got to put away these abominations. It is the cause of our troubles. We have been cherishing the feeling of hatred, until we have gone to butchering each other by the thousands. We must love our enemies and pray for them which despitefully use and persecute us.[4]

While serving as a chaplain, Turner wrote that he felt "proud of the term negro." When I am walking the streets of a city," wrote Turner, "and hear someone say, there goes a negro preacher, or a negro chaplain, I feel a peculiar exaltedness. I say, thank God, that a negro can be a preacher or chaplain."[5]

In a January 10, 1863, editorial in the *Christian Recorder* after President Lincoln issued the Emancipation Proclamation, Turner argued that African Americans could now "assert [their] rights and feel [their] manhood." While admonishing African Americans, he argued that no longer can the "men of our race be legally made to quaff up the scorn and derisions of a misanthrope rabble, many of whom are so inexplicably depauperated from licentious lives and devilish habit, that if they were sent as delegates to form an integral part of a dog's assembly or sent as ambassadors to the wild cats of the forest, they would be denounced as trying to insinuate themselves into ranks superior."[6]

Early on, however, Turner did see how the "curse of slavery" affected the "greatness" of his race. "It has not only depressed and horror-streaked the should-be glowing countenances of thousands," Turner wrote in a letter to the *Christian Recorder* published February 25, 1863, "but it has almost transformed many into inhuman appearance." In writing about his experience of two men escaping slavery, Turner wrote, "There were two men came in the night before last, and had I met either by myself, I should have run for my life—supposing him to be the devil. But what capped all was, when I commenced to converse with them, one seemed to be intelligent, and I could not imagine where he kept his intelligence, for I could see no place in his head to keep it; but it was there, and could not be counteracted."[7]

After slavery, Turner wondered aloud what would freedom mean without having any resources to become productive and enjoy the fruits of freedom. Turner argued that this "guarantee of liberty," this "superficial freedom," does not cancel the debt of obligation" that the country owed the formerly enslaved. Writing a letter for the *Christian Recorder* published on August 5, 1865, while appreciating the work of the "societies" and "benevolent institutions," Turner maintained that the country needed to do more. "They have established several schools," suggested Turner, "but have not met the wants of our people by a hundred degrees. They have educated and are still educating thousands, but millions have not seen their teachers yet. They have given them raiment by thousands, but millions are still clad in the coarse, tattered garments of slavery." Turner argued that the formerly enslaved people were without "money, land, homes, and houses; and many, to all noble purposes of life, are insensible," and that they were in need of instruction in the "economy, industry, and thriftiness of every species. They need to be taught the value of wealth," he continued, "and to desire the acquisition of money; for I hold it to be a part of our nature to strive after this. They want to know what to do with freedom, its resources, responsibilities, liabilities, dangers, and securities. It is not natural that a people who have been held as chattels for two hundred years, should thoroughly comprehend the limits of freedom's empire: the scope is too large for minds so untutored to enter upon at once."[8]

As the Union victory gave way to Reconstruction, Turner, like many African Americans during this time, believed that the Reconstruction measurers were going to lay a foundation of equality. However, violence and threats of violence against Black bodies increased. On one trip to Alabama, Turner, in a letter published June 23, 1866, in the *Christian Recorder*, shared the story of the beating of Rev. Robert Alexander—a minister who wanted to preach and start a school in the area. "Four white citizens broke into his room at midnight," Turner wrote, "and beat and stabbed him until he appeared like a lump of curdled blood." When the women ran screaming to the agent of the Freedmen's Bureau for help saying, "[C]ome and save our minister from being murdered," the agent only replied, "I can't do anything for you," and he "never got out of his bed." Turner closed the letter with a lament: "O God! where is our civilization? Is this Christendom, or is it hell? Pray for us."[9]

Turner, while a member of the Georgia House of Representatives, had an opportunity to participate in a joint committee to investigate the Georgia penitentiary system. During Turner's investigation, he discovered that Black women not only were on chain gangs but also were "whipped on the butt in the presence of men" and made to relieve themselves in front of men. Then there was a story of a man only known as Aaron whom prison guards whipped with a "double strap."

> They stripped him stark naked and tied him with the shackles around the crosstie and then stretched him out, with his belly down on the crossties. He fell off and was then whipped on the privates. As we were going home at night he stopped and said, "Good-bye boys, I am going to die." DeVancy then said, "If you want to die, I'll help you." He then whipped him about ten minutes, when he fell dead. He was buried just about day the next morning.[10]

Even when prisoners became sick, they were subject to beatings. Turner learned of a sick man that instead of getting treatment was bludgeoned to death by the doctor. There was no inquest held over the body, and a fellow prisoner had to make a box for the dead prisoner.[11]

Turner testified before Congress on November 3, 1871. When asked about the "lawless violence and outrages" perpetrated by the Ku Klux Klan, Turner talked about how "night prowlers" threatened his own life. "I am satisfied that on two or three occasions," Turner answered, "I may say in a dozen instances, if I had not secreted myself in houses at times, in the woods at other times, in a hollow log at another time, I would have been assassinated by a band of night-prowlers, or rovers, I will call them."[12]

Turner then shared about the time he was in Columbus, Georgia, and how a Mr. Ashburn was with him on the stage as Turner delivered a speech. "About a half an hour after I came out," Turner told the committee, "a band of organized Ku Klux, or assassins, went to Mr. Ashburn's house and murdered him." Turner told them that he also learned from someone that if the killers had known where he was, they would have murdered him as well.[13]

When asked by a member of the committee if he knew of any people "injured" by "night marauders," Turner answered that he had seen "scores of them.": "I have seen men who had their backs lacerated. I have seen other men who had bullets in them; I have seen others who had their arms shot off, shot so badly that they had to be amputated; I have seen others with legs shot off. I have heard of any quantity of horrible deeds."[14]

When asked how many murders had been committed in the state since the spring of 1868, Turner responded: "We held a Southern States convention week before last in Columbia, South Carolina, at which place there were delegates from all the Southern States. We meet together at the request of the committee on murders and outrages, and according to the best of our knowledge and belief it was estimated that since reconstruction between fifteen hundred and sixteen hundred had been perpetrated."[15]

When his interlocutor asked "in the South," Turner answered, "No, in the State of Georgia." When pressed on how many murders had happened in all the southern states since 1868, Turner responded that it had not been "less than twenty thousand." That number, Turner noted, was what delegates had agreed upon based from the reporting that each delegate made to the "murder and outrages" committee.[16]

In his many letters to editors, Turner chronicled the extrajudicial and state-sponsored violence perpetrated against African Americans. In one to the *Colored Tribune* published March 18, 1876, Turner wondered just how long African Americans could last in America. "I have just figured up the reported number of colored persons who have been brutally killed within the last twenty-five days in this State alone," Turner wrote, "and find the sum to be twenty-seven." Moreover, the twenty-seven Turner wrote could have been "augmented to thirty-seven if all the facts were known through the State," and that "no white man has been or will be arrested if he kills forty Negroes." In a letter to the editor of the *Christian Recorder* newspaper, dated January 4, 1883, Turner wrote that it had been estimated that the murders and outrages perpetrated upon Black people since 1867 were somewhere in the neighborhood of 200,000.[17] Quoting an article in the *New Orleans Christian Advocate*, Turner, in a letter to the editor dated February 22, 1883, wrote that "there is not a night that some colored person is not lynched in the State of Louisiana. . . . There is not a night, or a day either, the year-round that our people are not most brutally murdered."[18]

After Reconstruction, the *Christian Recorder* asked Turner for his thoughts on the 1880 presidential election that would eventually pit the Republican nominee, James Garfield, against the Democratic nominee, Winfield S. Hancock; Turner lamented that he did not care. In writing about how the nation treated African Americans, Turner wrote,

> I think my race has been treated by it with the kindness that a hungry snake treats a helpless frog. I am as near a rebel to this Government as any Negro ever got to be. My race has been treated with so much treachery, vile contempt and diabolical meanness, that I have but little in the country anyway, except to eke out my existence and get out of this world with a prospect of finding a better. I am not talking at random. I have been in nearly all parts of the entire nation within the last four years, and know whereof I speak, and have studied the Negro phase as thoroughly as my ability would enable me, for I have "the negro on the brain." And I wish had never been born, so that I might not have been a witness to the deviltry perpetrated upon my people by a so-called civilized country.[19]

However, as the racism and racist attitudes of America continued, Turner's rhetoric on race became even more pessimistic. In an open letter to the Rev. G. W. Ottley, Turner, while discussing and supporting his call for emigration, wrote:

> The whole tendency of our ignoble status in this country is to develop in the Negro mean, sordid, selfish, treacherous, deceitful and crank sided characteristics. There is not much real manhood in the Negro in this country to-day. There is far more learning and general intelligence, I grant, but far less race patriotism, and wherever race patriotism does not exist among people treachery in its worst form does. The American Negro does not possess half the respect for himself to-day he did fifteen years ago and it only requires a little sober sense to see it.[20]

Turner also worried about arguments that would effectively "bleach out the Negro race." According to Turner, some Blacks had argued that if African Americans and white people were allowed to intermarry, Blacks would be effectively "bleached out," and racism would disappear. Turner called the idea an "impossibility." For Turner, it was an impossibility for two reasons—first, there would be "such shooting, hanging, lynching, burning and flow of blood [as] has [not been] seen since the world began," and second, "such a fuss and bustle as would arise from colored women has never been predicted." Therefore, for Turner, "every man who advocates the bleaching out of the Negro race, is an absolute fool, or he is a monster in human flesh."[21]

While admitting that some who thought this were good people, he nevertheless argued that they were "so dwarfed in intellect, so twisted in the idea that white is God, they have thought so narrowly, read so little philosophy, so destitute of a knowledge of the scientific operations of nature, have studied so little about the fitness of things in the economy of race relations, and man's complex unity, that they have no proper conception of the infernalness of their hateful theories." For Turner, they do not "seem to realize themselves as advocators of the meanest form of lasciviousness, and that they are infusing in our young the basest sentiments that were ever distilled in the devil's laboratory. They are worse than cannibals, more to be dreaded than wild tigers; their tongues are a thousandfold more poisonous than the fangs of a rattlesnake."[22]

This inferiority thinking led many African Americans to complain about their physical features, something that frustrated Turner greatly. In one letter published in the *Recorder* on November 22, 1888, Turner wrote of two Black women discussing another woman's "beautiful hair" that hung "way down her back." Turner lamented that the "inference was that if it did not hang down her back, it would not be beautiful." Turner wrote, "This country is full of just such black and yellow fools. Instead of thanking God for what he has given us, and taking care of it, we are always whining because God did not make us something else." He argued that he did not see any "hope for the Negro race while he complains about his hair, color, and other specialties peculiar to himself. A stately black man and a refined black woman has no superior, in looks, upon earth."[23]

A *Baltimore American* reporter, in an interview reprinted by the *New York Times* on May 5, 1884, asked Turner if African Americans have sufficient advantages in America. Turner responded, "No, for no people can advance who are treated as we are." In anticipating his later theological outlook, Turner continued, "In some places in America black is supposed to symbolize the devil and white to represent God. But this is partially wrong for the devil is white, and never was black. There are as many blacks as whites in the universe. There are black worlds, and I believe millions of black angels in Heaven—in fact, there are angels of all colors there."[24]

In a political forum for the *AME Church Review* in its January 1885 issue, Turner responded to the election of Grover Cleveland by writing that he "cared very little about it," wished it nothing but "ill and misfortune," and hoped that it would be "blotted from the pages of history." His bitterness stemmed from the 1883 Supreme Court decision that overturned the 1875 Civil Rights Act (see chapter 1). He argued that the decision "sold out at publication seven million of my race, and wickedly, cruelly and infernally turned us over to the merciless vengeance of the white rabble of the country" and "a man who loves a country that hates him, is a human dog and not a man."[25]

For Turner, America associated all notions of whiteness with God, and thoughts of Blackness with the devil. Anticipating arguments from Malcolm X and the Nation of Islam in the twentieth century, Turner wrote that "white is perfection, greatness, wisdom, industry, and all that is high and holy. Black is ignorance, degradation, indolence, and all that is low and vile, and three-fourths of the colored people of the land do nothing day and night but cry: Glory, honor, dominion, and greatness to White." Turner argued that many African Americans were "contaminated with this accursed disease, or folly as well as the thoughtless masses." He reasoned that as "long as such a sentiment pervades the colored race, the powers of heaven cannot elevate him. No race of people can rise and manufacture better conditions while they hate and ignore themselves. A man must believe he is somebody before he is acknowledged to be somebody."[26]

In another interview published in the *Recorder* on April 17, 1890, when asked by a reporter if he had any hope for the future for African Americans in this country, Turner responded, "I have no faith in our permanent future here, for the reason that, while the Negro shed the first blood for American Independence and also freely spilled it in every war since for the maintenance of her institutions, yet he is looked upon as an alien race."[27]

In an interview published in the *Atlanta Constitution* on July 14, 1890, Turner told a reporter that Blacks and whites could live peaceably together, but he believed that they would not. He reasoned that white people could not live with any race of people unless they were the masters of the situation. For Turner, whites were already treating African Americans as an "alien race." Turner argued that African Americans would not be "satisfied with such a condition," because Blacks felt that they too had shed blood in every war for the establishment and maintenance of this country from its inception, and by that, they were "entitled to a full citizenship." Turner maintained that as long as African Americans did not receive full citizenship status, they were going to be irritated and "keep the country stirred up." Turner reasoned that

African Americans were too much like white people to be "treated as an alien" and be at "peace themselves or let white people be at peace."[28]

In an interview with the *Chicago Daily Tribune*, published July 11, 1891, Turner declared that there was a "deep, racial prejudice between the whites and blacks in this country." He suggested that this prejudice was increasing, "thus widening the chasm which separates the two races." The reason for this in Turner's estimation was that the "bar of social contact" was so "severely maintained" that white and Black people could not get to know each other. "I maintain," Turner said, "that all history will justify my position that two alienated nations cannot occupy the same territory and be at peace, for one will dominate the other."[29]

In a letter published February 2, 1895, by the *Washington Post*, Turner visited a familiar theme. "It is well known to the nation that I see no manhood future in this country for my race," Turner wrote. "I mean unconditional, unrestricted manhood, civil, political, social and every privilege, immunity and opportunity to achieve distinction and honor, without which no people or race can progress and develop the mighty powers, that lie dormant within them." After suggesting that the "social chasm" between white and Black was widening, Turner reflected on his past thinking about race and how wrong he was.

> Many years ago, I said in my speeches and articles for public press, that as soon as the negro acquired education and wealth, we would be brought in touch with each other, but I have lived to see the day, when the negro graduated from the first colleges of the land, abound upon the right and the left, and thousands can count their wealth by hundreds of thousands of dollars, and instead of being looked upon and appreciated by the dominant race of the land, as more entitled to a favorable consideration, they are regarded in most instances as more pestiferous and dangerous, and are the victims of more ridicule and contempt. Therefore, the theory is a phantom, and every man with common sense fully realizes it.[30]

Turner reasoned that African Americans would never reach the place of "social recognition as menials and scullions." Virtues such as "bravery, self-reliance, conscious endeavor, and success despite opposition were the ones, for Turner, that commanded respect as opposed to a "don't-care, do-nothing, servile submission." Therefore, for Turner,

> Degradation begets degradation, while respect and honor beget respect and honor. For not more than one man out of every hundred thousand rises above his environments, and our degradation in breeding contempt for each other every hour of the day; and it has gone on to such an extent that nearly every colored person who can is trying to pass for white and another portion is

buying this deadly hair-straightening drug and are trying to pass for Indians. Cubans, Mexicans, and anything rather than negro. I have had applications from churches as a bishop praying that I would not send them a black pastor. A third of our race today had rather be monstrosities than black gentlemen."[31]

Later in the letter, responding to one of his contemporaries who argued that African Americans did not want social equality with white people, Turner stood firm. "The Negro who does not want social equality anywhere and under any circumstances, must necessarily want degradation," argued Turner. "For when he is out of social touch he is out of civil touch, political touch, judicial touch, financial touch, business touch, religious touch, literary touch, and every other touch that involves manhood and respectability. For social touch is the pivoted point of every form of respectability. All the doctor [J. T. Jenifer] asks, he says, is to be let alone, yet remain here—an absolute impossibility."[32]

In a letter to the editor of the *Independent*, Turner argued that African Americans confronted either "emigration of extermination." The African race in this country can no more hope to stand up under the present pressure than a man could hope to shoulder and walk off with the Rocky Mountains," wrote Turner. "And any white man who thinks so has only to blacken his face and travel a few days through the country." Believing that the white race will always reign supreme in America," Turner claimed that African Americans were "dying out" and certainly not growing "healthier, wealthier, wiser, or anything else which goes to make life worth living."[33]

As time went on, Turner became more frustrated about the prospects of African American achieving any sense of dignity and self-worth in America. Realizing that African Americans were not going to Africa in the numbers he advocated for a change to happen, Turner resigned himself to staying in America and speaking out against the injustices that Black people faced daily. In a speech to an AME conference in Atlanta, Georgia on May 7, 1904, Turner boldly declared he was "unwilling to sing *America*" until the country became "what it claims to be, "sweet land of liberty." In another speech, delivered later that month in Chicago, Turner told his audience, "Don't learn songs like, "wash me, and I will be whiter than snow." He said that he would not tolerate anyone singing that song in his presence.[34]

The year 1906 did not start well for Turner. His third wife, Harriett Wayman Turner, formerly the widow of Bishop Wayman, died in Philadelphia in January of 1906. She had been sick for two years, and family members shipped her body to Baltimore, where she was finally laid to rest on January 14, 1906.[35] Surprisingly, Turner remained quiet about his wife's death. Unlike for his first two wives, Turner did not offer a glowing eulogy of Wayman Turner. Maybe his grief was unspeakable, as he never spoke of the deaths of his children with his first wife either. Maybe Turner would have gotten around to reflecting on his wife's death, but the reactions to his speech in Macon, Georgia, on February 13, 1906, would divert his attention away from anything else.

The Flag: A Contemptible Rag

In 1905 W. E. B. Du Bois planned to organize a conference to "oppose firmly present methods of strangling honest criticism; to organize intelligent and honest negroes and to support organs of news and public opinion." Du Bois's salvo was meant as a direct affront to the accommodationist strategies and politics of Booker T. Washington. The conference would become known later as the Niagara Movement, and though its members hailed from thirty-four states, according to Godshalk, it had "deep Atlanta roots." Looking to develop those roots even more, Du Bois and local members of the Niagara Movement partnered with Turner and local Baptist minister and publisher William J. White to convene the Georgia Equal Rights Convention (GERC) in Macon, Georgia.[36]

Over two hundred delegates attended the two-day GERC convention that started on February 13, 1906. According to the organizers, the meeting was "harmonious and enthusiastic." During the convention, delegates adopted resolutions that asked for the abolition of Jim Crow cars and lynching, the rights to join the militia, representation on juries and trials by one's peers. At the close of the meeting, the delegates decided to form a more permanent organization, and by the end of the convention, eight hundred people were in attendance.[37]

The highlight of the convention was Turner's opening speech that Godshalk called "courageous" and the "high point of the convention." However, there is not an existing copy of the address available. What we have are newspapers reports of the speech. For instance, on February 16, 1906, the *New York Times* reported that "in an address before 500 delegates at a convention of Negroes, Bishop H. M. Turner declared the American flag to be a dirty and contemptible rag and that hell was an improvement on the United States when the Negro was involved." They also added that Turner said in closing, "[If]f a little ignorant and stupid white man who was never heard of and never would be heard of until ten thousand years after the resurrection trumpet wishes a little notoriety, he begins to belie and slander the Negro and bounds into popularity."[38]

Other newspapers quickly picked up this news story and added their own headlines. The *Salt Lake Herald*'s headline read: "Negro Bishop Turner Slanders 'Old Glory.'"[39] The *Wenatchee Daily World* ran with the headline: "Bishop Turner Denounces Flag."[40] The *Cairo Bulletin* led with the headline "Is a Dirty Rag."[41] Turner would insist that the paper misquoted him, but that did not stop the onslaught of criticism hurled Turner's way.

The *Lancaster News* of South Carolina published a letter to the editor from someone who lived in Macon, Georgia. The person, calling herself or himself "Former Lancastrian," wrote that Turner failed to receive the sanction of the other Negroes in the convention and was "doubtless surprised." The person continued by writing that "such leaders as Turner will never contribute much to the uplifting of his race."[42] The *Tallahassee Weekly True Democrat* suggested that newspapers were making a mistake in publishing what he said in the speech. "What the decrepit, old idiot has to say about the nation, the flag and our people hurts no one, and the best of his own race pays no attention to his periodical squeaks." They advised to stop giving Turner publicity and if they do, "he will quiet down." They held up the work of Bishop Benjamin Tanner Tucker as an example of how Black leaders should lead. "He is doing a good work among his people and is bending all efforts to uplift, improve, and thus make them better citizens," they wrote, and "no small part of his efforts is directed towards creating kindly feelings between white and colored citizens."[43]

The *Bamberg Herald* reported that letters flooded the mayor's office in Macon, Georgia "protesting the utterances" of Turner. It wrote that the "most spirited disapproval" came in a letter from Indianapolis that read: "If there are any white men in Macon they ought to thrash that dirty black brute within an inch of his life." Another letter read: "We think he deserves the full extent of Macon's wrath and the prosecution of the government. Really such a mild punishment is far too dignified a method in which to handle a fiend."[44]

Nine days after the speech, Turner responded in an editorial published in the *Atlanta Constitution*. In a letter titled "Turner Denies He Cursed the Flag,"[45] Turner started by denying that he ever called the "flag of the nation a dirty and contemptible rag." After sharing with his readers how he has seen the flag honored all across the country and even in "foreign nations," Turner wrote that for him to make such a statement would be to proclaim himself a "fool of fools." Turner wrote that he did say that "there was not a star on the flag that the Negro could claim, or that recognized his civil liberty and unconditional manhood, more than if it was a dirty rag." He reminded his readers that he was talking to African Americans and not white people. He lamented that the newspapers "did not publish everything that he said," because if they would have, Turner argued, "the papers would have seen the people at the meeting that night as the country's revolutionary sires complaining about their "grievances."[46]

Turner wrote that he did say that African Americans were "not citizens of the United States since the delivery of that monstrous decision by the United States Supreme Court on October 15, 1883, and May 18, 1893. Further, Turner wrote that he did say that "there [was] more color babble in the United States than in hell itself; that color was unknown there," and "that men went there on account of crimes and vicious lives, but [in] the United States everybody's "value or non-value depended upon color."[47]

Moving away from what he did say in the speech, Turner turned his attention to how African Americans are a "motor force." Turner reasoned this because of the many newspapers, political speeches, and sermons that focus on the life of African Americans. However, Turner argued that the people who spend so much time talking about African Americans do not know of what they speak or write. According to Turner,

> Those who assume to know the most about the Negro never visit his churches to hear him preach, nor his lyceums to hear him debate and discuss questions, nor his homes to inspect his furniture, to hear his wives and daughters play the piano and organ, to examine his libraries and see his books, or inspect his schools and colleges to see what the youths of the race are doing toward preparing themselves for future usefulness.[48]

It is more popular, according to Turner, to "prate about the inferiority of the Negro and compare him to a monkey, orangutan, or a common animal." Turner noted the hypocrisy in this, because while society saw African Americans as animals, "hundreds of laws must be passed" and "judicial decisions delivered" to keep African Americans oppressed.[49]

Turner then reassured his readers that while African Americans were calling more state conventions than ever, white people need not worry about their effectiveness. "Nothing more than petitions through communications and delegations will be the result," Turner wrote. "The government will be asked for better conditions, or help to help ourselves." After reminding his readers that he had been before the people of Georgia for forty-eight years and had not "hurt anybody yet," and was "too old to hurt anything," Turner did promise to do all he could, not to "pull down the white man," but to "lift up the black man."[50]

If Turner hoped that his letter would calm down the critics, he was sadly mistaken. Instead of focusing on his response, many newspapers still focused on the speech and his denunciation of the flag. The *St. Paul Appeal* wrote that while Turner was a "well-meaning" and "imprudent man," they wrote that the speech only "excited prejudice against the people with whom he is identified." They argued that "racial prejudice" was already "strong enough without any increase and that for the sake of his people, Bishop Turner should talk more wisely or hold his peace."[51]

The *Richmond Planet* wrote that Turner should "damn the hypocrites," but not "denounce the flag."[52] The *Montana Plaindealer* wrote that while always an admirer of Turner, it could not support his "recent utterances about "America and the flag."[53]

The Black-owned newspaper the *Atlanta Independent* criticized Turner as well. Publishing in the *Richmond Times-Dispatch*, the editors of the *Independent* wrote, "Nobody takes [Turner] seriously." They called Turner a "freak" and wrote that his words were "incendiary" "treasonable," and sacrilegious." They suggested that Turner's "utterances no more represent the conservatism and representative character of the race in the state than did the convention." While they did admit that the flag has different meanings for both Blacks and whites, they argued that Blacks do not have anything to gain and could not hope for any "additional protection from its significance by denouncing it and its sentiment." They closed with a stinging rebuke of Turner and his speech.

> If the good bishop believes what he said, then he is a fraud and ought to have the moral courage to stand up in an open meeting and tell his people that the Christian religion is a humbug. The Bishop's sacrelegion against the flag of his country cannot but prove menacingly hurtful to the race and people he was seeking to help. His language was not only unfortunate and hurtful to the Negro masses, but it argues our innate inferiority.[54]

News of Turner's speech even reached the White House. According to historian Stephen Ward Angell, "white people bombarded President Theodore Roosevelt with demands that Turner be indicted for treason." Roosevelt asked Booker T. Washington to investigate, and despite Washington's defense of Turner, Roosevelt still sent a letter to Turner asking him why he should not be arrested on the charge of treason. In a private correspondence to Washington, Turner thanked him for his support and explanation to Roosevelt. However, he did add that if the president brought charges against him, he would at least have an opportunity to defend himself. "And I think I shall be able to prove forty times more treason perpetrated against my race under the shadow of the United States flag than they can establish against me." Turner closed the letter reassuring Washington that "should it come, I will try and be ready." Thankfully for Turner, the issue died down, and no charges were ever brought.[55]

If both Roosevelt and Washington thought that Turner would calm down, they were sadly mistaken. When white business owners complained that African Americans were leaving the state and, as a result, there was no one to work the farms, Turner responded that the reason was not that Blacks were lazy or did not want to work. They left because they were looking for better and more favorable conditions. It did not help that the Democratic gubernatorial primary had been unmercifully anti-Black. "The fact is," declared Turner, "that a hundred thousand have left the state in pursuit of better conditions and to get rid of the eternal Negro howl that is heard from year to year. He is the burden of every speech and almost every newspaper article." He wrote that he believed at least "fifteen thousand stump and platform speeches have been delivered since the present gubernatorial campaign has been going on, and not one of those speeches has been void of the Negro."[56]

Turner's argument about the rhetoric of the gubernatorial campaign was not hyperbole. Hoke Smith campaigned on the outright disenfranchisement of Black voters. Despite the veneer of a city being the beacon of interracial progress, the racist Democratic campaign for governor exposed what brewed underneath the surface. In September of 1906, when Smith defeated Clark Howell for the nomination, a few days later, behind the rhetoric of the campaign and a consistent theme of anti-Blackness in the media and popular press, white people in Atlanta exploded into a bloody rampage against Blacks. Aptly misnamed the Atlanta Race Riot, at the end of the three-day orgy of violence, dozens of Black people were dead, and property and businesses in the Black community were destroyed. If it had not been for Black people finally taking up arms in self-defense, it could have been worse.[57]

After the massacre city officials seemed to be more concerned about the city's image than anything else. Both Black and white ministers in the city began to campaign and refocused their efforts on establishing law and order. Interracial dialogues started that led to the creation of the Atlanta Civic League and the Colored Co-Operative Civic League. While white ministers united in their belief in white superiority and the need for racial segregation, Black ministers joined efforts to close many of the "dives" where working-class black patrons were described as "vicious rounders, loafers, and grossly ignorant criminals" and whose passions were "stirred by mean liquor."[58] In providing leadership to their respected communities, both Black and white ministers took public roles in closing down the bars in the Black community. Many African American ministers felt that if they took a strong position against the perceived idleness and shiftless attitudes of the working-class and lower-class Blacks, they would find a measure of favor from white people.

That white people massacred Black people did not surprise Turner. He had been warning African Americans about this for years. Moreover, he argued that the ministers were focusing on the wrong issues in addressing the massacre. In a speech on November 7, 1906, in Bainbridge, Georgia, Turner told his audience that the "Atlanta episode a few weeks ago was the greatest misfortune that had ever happened to the two races in this section. It was all the worse," continued Turner, "for the reason that the better classes in both races looked to Atlanta for intelligence, forbearance, Christianity, and race respect, the one for the other." In Turner's estimation the massacre caused "more suffering, wounded feelings, and families wrecked for all time." He reminded his audience of his continued calls to emigration to Africa and said that the "Atlanta trouble is the greatest proof of the wisdom and judgment of my project than anything." He closed by asking, "In the name of all that is good and righteous what do you see in this country for the black man but constant trouble?"[59]

The following year in April of 1907, at a meeting held at the People's Tabernacle in Atlanta for the purpose of "bringing better understanding between the races" and toning down some of the more incendiary rhetoric between the races, Turner delivered a speech that again shifted the focus from blaming African Americans for the massacre to getting his audience to see the much larger picture. Turner declared that "enough innocent blood had been shed to drown Congress, the Supreme Court, and President Roosevelt." He argued that the courts were keeping African Americans in "subjection" and that all the laws favored white people, and he "bitterly assailed" Georgia senator Ben Tillman for his anti-Black rhetoric. Turner also challenged Tillman to select any jury "of his own picking" as to the "relative refinement and education" of both men and openly declared that if he failed to win, he was "willing to be hanged." Most of the newspapers reporting on the meeting called Turner's speech a "surprise" and said that he made a "bitter attack" at a meeting that organizers had hoped to be uncontroversial. However, despite the criticisms leveled at the country and Senator Tillman, African Americans in the audience "wildly cheered" Turner's speech.[60]

Later, Turner revisited an issue that had gotten him into trouble the previous year—the flag. If the thought of being brought up on treason charges and having both Blacks and whites upset with him entered his mind, it was not enough to stop Turner's prophetic denunciations of how Black people were treated in America. In a speech delivered at the AME conference in New York at Bridge Street [Brooklyn] Church, Turner started by commending the heroics of the man who introduced him, Dr. D. French Hurley. Then Turner shifted. "I used to love the American flag once myself. But I now despise it because America is the most horrible color-prejudice nation on earth. Here Negroes can be lynched, burned alive and skinned and nothing is done about it."[61]

Turner told the crowd that his loyalty to the country was like the loyalty of Jefferson Davis. "I know I have been criticized and called a fool because I believe in negro nationality," Turner said, "but I don't care anymore for my critics than I do for the bark of a dog." He argued that whites "proscribe" African Americans because of the "whimsical prejudices of misanthropes" and that African Americans were "just sitting there and whining." In closing he did not apologize for advising African Americans to leave the country that was "saturated with prejudice." He continued to argue that it was the best option for African Americans.[62]

Unlike the last time that his flag comments caused a stir, this latest dust-up did not register too much on the national scene. For many, Turner's rhetoric became old and tired. However, there was one notable exception. Anna Mixon wrote a letter to the editor responding to Turner's speech. She started with, "If the daily papers correctly reported the utterances of Bishop H. M. Turner, the race should hang its head in humiliation for the hopeless perverted state of a very narrow mind." Mixon argued that "stirring up feelings of hatred, pandering to the tastes of the hot-headed and ignorant is not going to better matters—in fact, it really hurts the cause." She suggested that "hurling insults at the flag will not add to his list of friends" and that "every colored man and woman should rise up and condemn him."[63]

For some, however, Turner's rhetoric, although fiery and bombastic, hit all the right notes. Back home in Georgia, on November 14, 1907, Turner spoke to an audience of four hundred ministers of the Southwest Georgia Conference and delivered a "remarkable and stirring address" that was "enthusiastically received." In addressing plans from the state legislature to follow through on disenfranchising African Americans, Turner declared, "We are passing through a fearful exercise now. It is apparent that the hand and circle of dominant power is against us." He argued that the "effort to disenfranchise and rule us out of the pale of humanity is an effort to disgrace us, a scheme put in operation by malicious and misanthropic men to tie us to the wheel of degradation."[64]

Turner, in a strongly worded critique aimed toward African Americans, lamented:

God and nature help those who help themselves. If we had stood up as we should have done, we would not be puppets of degradation or if we had manhood and dared to defend our rights, there would be no Jim Crow cars.... I will say one more word, and you may infer my meaning, without the consent of the Negro, no cars could run in Georgia. I am sorry to say they are running by our cowardice and disunited action.[65]

There is no harmony among us; Turner conceded, "no concern about our rights and the rights of our children and our children's children." He suggested that everyone who sits quietly was "tying their children's children" to the "wheels of degradation for a hundred years to come." Turner reasoned that such people should not become parents and that African Americans must start to reclaim their own agency.[66]

In our study of the rhetoric of Martin Luther King Jr., Anthony J. Stone and I noted the shift in King's rhetoric. Early in King's career, they argued, King produced what Sunnemark called a "common discourse." King aimed this type of discourse to be as inviting as possible for as many as possible." King meant for this type of discourse to be "non-offensive," as this rhetoric was to focus on "recognition and affirmation." Drawing from the work of Sunnemark, we argued that this type of rhetoric had a "vague generality," meaning that this type of rhetoric can mean many different things to many different people.[67]

However, King's rhetoric in the last year of his life cannot be used in this way. Drawing from Anthony Cook, we suggested that King began "to understand the hegemony of repressive ideologies, and to deconstruct the limits they appear to set on the possibilities of change" and became "deeply committed to the reconstruction of a social reality based on a radically different assessment of human potential." They argued that the reason for the change was King's "growing understanding of race and racism" and part of the reason for his growing understanding of race and racism was that King adopted a persona as a pessimistic prophet. Nearing the end of his life, King held that what kept America from becoming truly great was its racism.[68]

Turner took the same rhetorical trajectory. He too started out optimistic and not understanding how race and racism worked. As I note in chapter 2 and this chapter, Turner did not see just how race functioned during the Civil War. He argued that slavery was the cause of the war and that God was angry at both Blacks and whites for the roles they played in perpetuating slavery—whites, of course, for enslaving Blacks, and Blacks for hating whites and having "revengeful feelings towards them." Echoing Jesus, Turner called on African Americans to "love their enemies and pray for them who despitefully use and persecute us."[69]

After Lincoln issued the Emancipation Proclamation, Turner felt that the time had come for African Americans to reflect on their actions and begin to operate in their freedom. For Turner, that meant that African Americans had to rid themselves of their "licentious lives" and "devilish habits." He even would blame slavery itself and not necessarily how whites treated African Americans as the cause of the formerly enslaved's rough and rugged appearances. Turner radically believed that after the war, and with the evil of slavery gone, America was going to live up to the ideals that many espoused for the nation. Finally, for Turner, African Americans could eventually take part in the covenant agreement of what it meant to be an American.

As the end of the Civil War gave way to Reconstruction, Turner began to notice that not everyone shared his optimism. As he readied himself for the work of Reconstruction, Turner saw the increase of violence against Black bodies. Although Turner used his influence to report as much of this as possible, not much was done in the way of protecting African Americans from lynch mobs and wholesale massacres. However, up to this point, Turner still had a faint belief that if done correctly, the Reconstruction measures could work and produce the lasting change that he had hoped for.

Sadly, that would not be the case. Instead, violence and outright lawlessness continued to go unabated against African Americans. Turner would come to see that this was more than prejudice against specific individuals. After the failure of Reconstruction, Turner began to offer an analysis that implicated the nation in its racism toward African Americans. Moreover, he began to argue that this racist behavior by society started to affect African Americans' self-esteem and self-worth. Grounded in much of his emigrationist rhetoric as discussed in chapter 5, Turner argued that racism, or what he called having the "Negro on the brain," also limited Black people's agency to do things for themselves in positive and productive ways.

Additionally, Turner argued that the racism experienced in the country also led many African Americans to hate themselves. This self-hatred led Black people to criticize each other for their skin, hair, and facial features. Moreover, this self-hatred led to degradation that many African Americans would pass down to their children. Turner argued that degradation begets degradation and that trying to pass for anything but Black was not good for the long-term future of African Americans in this country.

Many wanted to erase "Black" altogether—even claiming that God was white. As discussed in chapter 2, Turner argued that people who do not believe that they look like the God they claim to serve are a helpless people. For Turner, as long as "Black" symbolized the devil and "white" symbolized God, there would be no hope for African Americans, because they would continue to cry "glory, honor, dominion, and greatness to White."[70]

Turner's analysis of the condition of African Americans would shift to an examination of whiteness. He argued that white people could not live with any other race of people unless whites were "masters of the situation." Moreover, according to Turner, white people did not want to know Black people anyway. To have social contact with members of the Black race would have meant, in the eyes of white Americans, social equality. Turner keenly discerned that the term "social equality" was the idea that kept white people "legally" separated from African Americans in public spaces. However, argued Turner, white people could not simply leave Black people alone—the only interaction and relationships whites wanted were based on the master/servant relationship. Anything else constituted social equality—making Blacks equal to whites.

Turner's pessimism was now complete. Frustrated at the failures to emigrate to Africa in the numbers that he had hoped for, along with the continued violence aimed at African Americans and the rising tide of white nationalism that discredited and denied African Americans at every turn, Turner sought to speak truth to power at the risk of alienating relationships with both Blacks and whites. As the responses to his critiques of the flag and nation demonstrate, Turner's words provoke harsh feelings from his critics. Many did not understand, however, that Turner had lost hope and faith in the country a long time ago. While others critiqued Turner, he was busy being the prophet that African Americans needed. His pessimistic hope was to uplift the race by telling the truth about their situation.

CONCLUSION

Reclaiming the Pessimistic Prophecy of Bishop Henry McNeal Turner

On October 13, 1913, the seventy-nine-year-old bishop spoke to a packed house at the Institutional Church in Chicago, Illinois. As reported by the *Chicago Daily Tribune*, Turner, while "white haired" and slow walking, still had a "powerful voice" that reached the distant corners of the church. When he stood to speak, in a showcase of oratorical prowess, he told his audience, "I am no good tonight." Then, as if on cue, he turned and looked at the chairman of the event and asked, "What shall I speak about?" The chair responded, "Speak about the moon, Bishop." Turner responded in kind and began an extemporaneous speech about the moon.

After speaking about the moon, Turner shifted his focus and began to speak more poignantly on a subject many in the audience came to hear him talk on—race. While commending the white race, he also condemned the race. He admonished his audience to "help the white man up but help yourselves while you do it." Further, he charged the audience to "let your sons and daughters go to colleges and schools. Give them opportunities, for the black race needs them." After calling slavery a "providential" and not a "divine" institution, Turner foresaw the time when Jim Crow legislation would happen not only in the South but in the North as well. Then Turner gave a chilling warning—he prophesied that there were a "lot of hard times coming—times we have not passed through yet." In an eerie prediction, Turner closed his speech by saying that these tough times "will come before you have gone from this earth, but while I am sleeping in my grave, my words will still be ringing in your ears."[1]

Those tough times would come for African Americans, but Turner would not be around much longer to experience them. In 1912 the AME Church assigned Michigan and Canada under his supervision, and in May 1915 Turner planned to attend a church conference held in Ontario. Despite his frail health, Turner would not be dissuaded from attending the conference. Arriving in Detroit, Turner boarded a ferry heading for Windsor, Ontario. When he arrived, Turner suffered a massive stroke and collapsed on the wharf. Bishop Flipper afterward suggested that Turner went to the conference because he had a "premonition of his death" on this trip and proceeded anyway. Turner shared that he didn't want to die in America, because of its denial of citizenship rights to Blacks, and on May 8, 1915, he died several hours later, not on American soil, but in Ontario, Canada, at a Windsor hospital.[2]

Turner's body arrived back in Atlanta on May 10 and lay in state for a week at Howard and Son Funeral Home. An estimated twenty-five thousand people viewed the body of Turner and paid their respects, and on May 18, 1915, another fifteen thousand were able to attend the funeral service held at Bethel AME Church in Atlanta. The two-hour service celebrated the life and legacy of Turner. Ponton wrote of the service, "The church was profusely decorated to suit the occasion and in deference of the great personage in whose memory the obsequies were being held." The floral arrangements that decorated the casket of "America's greatest Negro" came from all parts of the country. The love and appreciation shown to Turner at his funeral according to Ponton, "demonstrated that he who was loved during his life time was not forgotten in his death."[3]

Many notable African Americans took time out to eulogize Turner. *AME Review* editor Reverdy Ransom remarked that Turner was a "remarkable man, whose like does not appear more than once in a century, the like of whom we shall not see again." Further Ransom wrote:

> Bishop Turner was a staunch defender of his race. His scathing denunciations of lynching and mob violence, his severe arraignments of the courts for unjust decisions and his oppositions to all forms of Jim Crow legislation made him one of the foremost defenders of his race. He stood for the manhood and equality of his race and sought to arouse and stimulate this sentiment among his people. His flaming wrath against traitors, trimmers, sycophants, and cowards among his people revealed the intensity of the fire of his earnestness.[4]

Other contemporaries praised Turner as well. Bishop Evans Tyree remarked, "Bishop Turner was a powerful man. He loved his race, his church, and his God from the depths of his soul," while R. R. Wright Jr., then editor of the *Christian Recorder*, simply wrote, "Henry McNeal Turner was the most remarkable Negro of this generation." Henry Lincoln Johnson, columnist of the newspaper the *Atlanta Independent*, wrote: "The travail of his people always appealed to Bishop Turner and the lamentations of the negro always found in him an abundant sympathizer and a most distinguished advocate. On the lecture platform, in the public forum, in magazines, in newspapers, indeed everywhere Bishop Turner has brought to bear all of his great learning, research, heart, and soul for the advancement and edification of the Negro the world over."[5]

W. E. B. Du Bois, who would go through a prophetic trajectory similar to Turner's, wrote,

> [Turner] was a man of tremendous force and indomitable courage. As army chaplain, pastor and bishop, he has always been a man of strength. . . . In a sense, Turner was the last of his clan: mighty men, physically and mentally, men who started at the bottom and hammered their way to the top by sheer brute strength; they were the spiritual progeny of ancient African chieftains and they built the African church in America.[6]

Although celebrated royally at his death, soon thereafter Turner quickly became a footnote in history. Religious ethicist Gary Dorrien, who reclaimed Turner as one of the earliest proponents of the Black social gospel, remarked that Turner was forgotten even by "scholars of black American history and religion." Dorrien noted that John Hope Franklin "mentioned Turner only in passing," and Rayford Logan and Vincent Harding "barely mentioned him, once each." Benjamin Qualls and James M. McPherson "referred to him zero times in one book and once in another." E. Franklin Frazier "reduced Turner to a page on Reconstructionist political religion," and Carter G. Woodson "did the same." Outside of Ponton's uncritical biography of Turner two years after his death, there would not be another scholarly writing on Turner until 1938 with the publication of J. Minton Batten's *Henry M. Turner, Negro Bishop Extraordinary*.[7]

Batten called Turner "one of the most influential of the Negro prophets who sought to solve the problems of his race and to guide his people along the paths that lead to God." In writing about Turner's sixty-plus years of public activity, Batten wrote that Turner "helped the Negro to adjust himself to a social environment which prescribed changes in his status with a most confusing persistency and frequency." He closed his biographical essay by noting that "few men of the Negro race have had careers more varied or more influential."[8]

I am often asked, "What would Turner's positions be on issues of today?" While of course we will never know, I would like to think that Turner would be the same pessimistic prophet today that he was during his day. For instance, while he would undoubtedly celebrate some of the country's successes, I see Turner still raining down anathemas on the Supreme Court for many of their decisions that, just as in his day, affect African Americans and all people of color. Take the example of voting rights, the decision to allow unregulated money in elections; the decision to strip Section Five, better known as a preclearance section of the Voting Rights Act; decisions that uphold voter ID laws; and the decision to allow partisan gerrymandering—all would have come under Turner's criticism. Moreover, Turner would not only criticize African Americans for not being more outraged over these decisions but would lament how many people do not use the vote they have. If he were here today, I argue, Turner would make the connection between not only federal, state, and local elections but also the appointment power associated with those various offices. He would give us lessons in civics that we would not soon forget.

If Turner were here today, he would love the many different theological expressions. He would have loved James Cone's work on Black Theology because it would have given him language to describe what he was doing in his day. He would definitely be a liberationist, and he would explore other faith traditions. He would have appreciated many of the efforts of feminist and womanist theologians and would have used much of their work to support his own views on women's roles in the church. He would be open to much in the way of New Age spirituality and the group of people who declare themselves to be spiritual but not religious.

However, he would have some issues with the church. Turner would be critical of white churches and their steadfast refusal to understand race and racism in America. He would frown on the politics of many white churches. For instance, he would have not understood how 81 percent of voters who self-identify as white evangelicals voted for Donald Trump and still support him in high numbers. He would not understand why many white churches are silent on the border crisis and why we as a country are standing by, allowing the government to detain these refugees and to separate them from their families. He would also wonder why Black churches have remained silent as well and why some even adopt a white supremacy theology on issues of race and social justice.

I believe Turner would still be antiwar. He would take issue with the fact that the country has military bases all over the world. It probably would shock him to see that Guam and the Philippines are still territories of the United States. He would today have huge problems with the country's foreign policy and how the commander in chief acts on the world stage. However, he would be downright apoplectic about the ongoing "war on terror." He would lament the fact that the United States has been in a sustained "war on terror" for almost two decades with no end in sight. He would question our elected leaders and government officials about this and demand that troops be sent home.

On the political front, Turner would be an active participant. However, neither party would like what he would have to say. Turner would critique both the Democrats and Republicans, as he did in his day, as not being responsive to the needs of African Americans. He would still try to shake up conventional political thinking and probably would ultimately push for a third party. He would find home with Cornel West and others who critique both parties as being loyal to only the rich while the poor people continue to suffer. I also believe that he would openly support any candidate that he felt would have the people's best interest at heart.

I do not think Turner would push for emigration to Africa in today's political climate. Part of his argument for emigration was that African Americans needed a place that would afford them safety from the tentacles of white supremacy. He would see today that it is global. There is no place on earth one could go to get away from white supremacy. However, he would still champion many of the things that came out of his emigrationist rhetoric. The role of Black agency, self-esteem, personhood, and identity would center much of his rhetoric. He would champion immigrant and refugee rights and wonder aloud what America is doing at the border. He would applaud the efforts of activists with Black Lives Matter, and he would especially appreciate the women who lead much of the effort. He would challenge Black people to live up to the ideals espoused and critique anyone who thought Black people could not do anything they put their minds to.

Lastly, Turner would have a lot to say around race in America. Turner would have harsh critiques against the country that just not too long ago, was making pronouncements that it had become postracial. He would remind us that racism is still alive and well in America. From the policing that goes on in Black and brown communities, to voter suppression efforts, to our immigrant and refugee crisis and even the racist language from elected officials, Turner would have a lot to say.

In short, Turner would have been as relevant today as he was in his time. But the question remains, how did such a towering figure, one during his lifetime named as one of the Four Horsemen of the AME Church, become relegated to a footnote? I suggest two main reasons. First, when Turner died in 1915, African Americans embarked on an integrationist program in dealing with the issues germane to African Americans, and it has remained a part of the tradition. In short, led by figures such as W. E. B. Du Bois and members of the NAACP, Blacks started to focus on fighting for civil rights and integrating society. Proponents of this optimistic rhetoric argued that if African Americans could show loyalty to the nation, show their piety by being good American citizens, that the country would respond in kind. It is no accident that Evelyn Brooks Higginbotham constructed her notion of a "politics of respectability" from the women's movement in the Black Baptist church that started at the end of the nineteenth and the beginning of the twentieth century. African Americans were simply too busy proving themselves to focus on or highlight any type of pessimism.[9]

The second reason connects to the first. Maybe history forgot Turner because up until now Turner's writings had not been available for study. Unlike some of his contemporaries, Turner does not have a traditional archive housed in an institutional repository. Because of the integrationist focus and the period of progressivism that many promoted at the time of Turner's death, African American scholars did not collect Turner's works or, again, promote Turner as someone worthy of study.

An analysis of Turner's rhetoric from 1896 to 1915 would demonstrate that Turner anticipated future movements within the African American rhetorical tradition. For instance, Marcus Garvey's Back-to-Africa movement is largely indebted to the rhetoric of Turner as is the rhetoric of Malcolm X and Black Power advocates. Turner's prophetic pessimism even found its way into the rhetoric of Martin Luther King Jr. as he neared the end of his life.[10]

I argue that to reject Turner's prophetic pessimism is also to reject the hope that prophetic pessimism provides. Unlike Afro-pessimism, which suggests there is no such thing as human agency, prophetic pessimism's hope is for people to (re)claim that agency and operate with self-determination. While Turner would agree with Afro-pessimists that Black people cannot overcome their suffering in society through the "grammar of rights, respect and compassion," Turner's hope had been getting African Americans to see this. Drawing from Afro-pessimistic language, Turner wanted Blacks to see themselves as "sentient beings" and not necessarily as humans or, Turner's word, "citizens" of the United States. Turner's hope was to get Black people to use their agency to become woke to the real situation and leave America to make a better situation. While emigration may have been problematic on multiple levels, Turner's call for emigration is what Black people's agency and decision making looks like in a real world. It was Turner's prophetic pessimism and bearing witness to the ills faced by many African Americans during this time that gave many African Americans a sense of pride and the courage necessary to face whatever came their way.

NOTES

Introduction: The Prophetic Pessimism of Bishop Henry McNeal Turner

1. D. W. Culp (ed.), *Twentieth Century Negro Literature: Or a Cyclopedia of Thought on the Vital Topics Relating to the American Negro* (Naperville, IL: J. L. Nichols, 1902), 5–6.
2. R. S. Lovinggood, "Will It Be Possible for the Negro to Attain," in Culp (ed.), *Twentieth Century Negro Literature*, 49.
3. J. W. Hood, "Will It Be Possible for the Negro to Attain," in Culp (ed.), *Twentieth Century Negro Literature*, 56.
4. L. S. Holsey, "Will It Be Possible for the the Negro to Attain," in Culp (ed.), *Twentieth Century Negro Literature*, 46.
5. Henry McNeal Turner, "Will It Be Possible for the Negro to Attain," in Culp (ed.), *Twentieth Century Negro Literature*, 42–43.
6. Turner, "Will It Be Possible for the Negro to Attain," 43.
7. Turner, "Will It Be Possible for the Negro to Attain," 43–44.
8. Turner, "Will It Be Possible for the Negro to Attain," 44.
9. Turner, "Will It Be Possible for the Negro to Attain," 44.
10. Turner, "Will It Be Possible for the Negro to Attain," 44.
11. Turner, "Will It Be Possible for the Negro to Attain," 45.
12. Turner, "Will It Be Possible for the Negro to Attain," 45.
13. According to the United States Chaplain Corps, Turner applied in July of 1863 and received his commission on September 10, 1863. https://www.facebook.com/Army ChaplainCorps/photos/a.408322599243107/598311413577557/?type=1&theater.
14. For research on prophetic rhetoric, see George Shulman, *American Prophecy: Race and Redemption in American Political Culture* (Minneapolis: University of Minnesota Press, 2008; Robert E. Terrill, *Malcolm X: Inventing Racial Judgment* (East Lansing: Michigan State University Press, 2007).
15. Andre E. Johnson and Anthony J. Stone, "The Most Dangerous Negro in America": Rhetoric, Race and the Prophetic Pessimism of Martin Luther King Jr., *Journal of Religion and Communication*, vol. 41, no. 1 (2018): 11.
16. Kristen Lynn Majocha, "Prophetic Rhetoric: A Gap between the Field of Study and the Real World," *Journal of Religion and Communication*, vol. 39, no. 4 (2017): 14.

17. Andre E. Johnson, *The Forgotten Prophet: Bishop Henry McNeal Turner and the African American Prophetic Tradition* (Lanham, MD: Lexington Books, 2012), 7.

18. Alan D. DeSantis argues for the inclusion of a third type: Amostic prophecy. Derived from the biblical prophet Amos, this is when the speaker (prophet) speaks as one outside the covenant as she or he exhorts the audience to live up to their own covenant. See "An Amostic Prophecy: Frederick Douglass' 'The Meaning of July Fourth for the Negro,'" *Journal of Communication and Religion*, vol. 22, no. 1 (1999): 65–92.

19. Barry Brummett, *Contemporary Apocalyptic Rhetoric* (New York: Praeger, 1991).

20. Brummett, *Contemporary Apocalyptic Rhetoric*, 10.

21. David Howard-Pitney, *The Afro-American Jeremiad: Appeal for Justice in America* (Philadelphia: Temple University Press, 1990), 5.

22. Howard-Pitney, *Afro-American Jeremiad*, 5.

23. Sacvan Bercovitch, *The American Jeremiad* (Madison: University of Wisconsin Press, 1978), 7.

24. Howard-Pitney, *Afro-American Jeremiad*, 7.

25. Bercovitch, *American Jeremiad*, 7

26. Andre E. Johnson, "To Make the World So Damn Uncomfortable: W. E. B. Du Bois and the African American Prophetic Tradition," *Carolina Communication Annual*, vol. 32 (2016): 22.

27. There have been books that attend to the African American jeremiad tradition. See David Howard-Pitney's *The African American Jeremiad: Appeals for Social Justice* (Philadelphia: Temple University Press, 2009); and Willie J. Harrell, *Origins of the African American Jeremiad: The Rhetorical Strategies of Social Protest and Activism, 1760–1861* (Jefferson, NC: McFarland, 2011).

28. Christopher Hobson, *The Mount of Vision: The African American Prophetic Tradition, 1800–1950.* (New York: Oxford University Press, 2012), 38.

29. Hobson, *Mount of Vision*, 39.

30. Hobson, *Mount of Vision*, 40–41.

31. Johnson, *Forgotten Prophet*, 115.

32. David Zarefsky, *Rhetorical Perspectives on Argumentation: Selected Essays* (New York: Springer, 2014), 11.

33. Zarefsky, *Rhetorical Perspectives on Argumentation*, 11.

34. Zarefsky, *Rhetorical Perspectives on Argumentation*, 11

35. Kathleen J. Turner (ed.), *Doing Rhetorical History: Concepts and Cases* (Tuscaloosa: University of Alabama Press, 1998), 4–5.

36. Johnson, *Forgotten Prophet*, 10.

37. Johnson, *Forgotten Prophet*, 10.

38. Johnson, *Forgotten Prophet*, 10.

39. Johnson, *Forgotten Prophet*, 14.

40. Johnson, *Forgotten Prophet*, 10, 14–15.

41. Peter L. McLaren and Michael Dantley, "Leadership and a Critical Pedagogy of Race: Cornel West, Stuart Hall, and the Prophetic Tradition," *Journal of Negro Education*, vol. 59, no. 1 (1990): 39–40.

42. Michael Dantley, "Purpose Driven Leadership: The Spiritual Imperative to Guiding Schools beyond High-Stakes Testing and Minimum Proficiency," *Education and Urban Society*, vol. 35, no. 3 (2003): 274–75.

43. Johnson, *Forgotten Prophet*, 15.

44. Patrice Douglass, Selamawit D. Terrefe, and Frank B. Wilderson, "Afro-Pessimism," Oxford Bibliographies, August 2018, http://www.oxfordbibliographies.com/view/document/obo-9780190280024/obo-9780190280024-0056.xml.

45. Douglass, Terefe, and Wilderson, "Afro-Pessimism."

46. Ta-Nehisi Coates, *Between the World and Me*, 1st ed. (New York: Spiegel & Grau 2015); Frank B. Wilderson, *Afro-Pessimism: An Introduction* (Minneapolis: Racked and Dispatched, 2017).

47. Johnson, *Forgotten Prophet*, 105.

48. Kofi Agyekum, "Invective Language in Contemporary Ghanaian Politics," *Journal of Language and Politics*, vol. 3, no. 2 (2004): 347–48.

49. Mary McEdwards, "Agitative Rhetoric: Its Nature and Effects," *Western Speech*, vol. 62, no. 1 (1968).

50. McEdwards, "Agitative Rhetoric," 36–37.

51. McEdwards writes,

> Invective is the result of a direct one-to-one relationship of the speaker to his single enemy rather than a multiple relationship of a speaker to the enemies of a particular group in a society. The agitator has not been hurt personally by an individual or situation as is the case with the user of invective. Invective has personal bitterness for its primary quality and is addressed to an individual who has directly harmed the speaker—or so the speaker assumes. Agitative rhetoric generally lacks this bitter and spiteful tone. Its final purpose is extreme change in the status quo to benefit others besides the speaker rather than a narrow personal attack to benefit only the revengeful attacker. The agitator in society deliberately tries to select the diction, the imagery, the syntax that will move his audience emotionally and intellectually to call for change; the bitter speaker uses invective for catharsis of self alone. The language of invective is churlish, malicious, and surly; agitative language is jolting, combative, and passionate—in the fullest sense of the term. (37)

52. McEdwards, "Agitative Rhetoric," 43.

53. Ibram X. Kendi, *Stamped from the Beginning: The Definitive History of Racist Ideas in America* (New York: Nation Books, 2016), ch. 10.

54. Henry McNeal Turner, "The American Negro and the Fatherland," in *Africa and the American Negro: Addresses and Proceedings of the Congress on Africa*, edited by J. W. E. Bowen (Atlanta: Franklin, 1896), 194.

55. Anthony Moran, "Identity, Race, and Ethnicity," in *Routledge Handbook of Identity Studies*, edited by Anthony Elliott, 170–85 (New York: Routledge, 2011).

Chapter 1: "An Abominable Conclave of Negro Hating Demons": Turner and the *Plessy* Decision

1. Thomas Ross, "The Rhetorical Tapestry of Race: White Innocence and Black Abstraction," *William and Mary Law Review*, vol. 32, no. 1 (1990): 5–6, https://scholarship.law.wm.edu/wmlr/vol32/iss1/2/.

2. Ross, "Rhetorical Tapestry of Race," 6–7.

3. *Abbeville Meridional*, May 23, 1896, p. 2.

4. "Jim Crow Car Unconstitutional," *Louisiana Democrat*, May 27, 1896, p. 2.

5. "Equality, but Not Socialism," *New Orleans Daily Picayune*, May 19, 1896.

6. *Cleveland Gazette*, May 30, 1896.

7. See "Supreme Court Decision," *Omaha Enterprise*, May 30, 1896; "That Decision," *Cleveland Gazette*, May 30, 1896.

8. "The Jim Crow Case," *Indianapolis Freedman*, May 23, 1896.

9. Kirt H. Wilson, *The Reconstruction Desegregation Debate: The Politics of Equality and the Rhetoric of Place, 1870–1875* (East Lansing: Michigan State University Press, 2002), 17–18.

10. F. Michael Higginbotham, *Ghosts of Jim Crow: Ending Racism in Post-racial America* (New York: New York University Press, 2013), 63–64.

11. An Act to Protect All Persons in the United States in Their Civil Rights and Furnish the Means of Their Vindication. Thirty-Ninth Congress, 1st Session, chapter 31 (1866), https://www.loc.gov/law/help/statutes-at-large/39th-congress/session-1/c39s1ch31.pdf. For a look at the debate of the 1866 Civil Rights Act, see Mark Shawhan, "By Virtue of Being Born Here: Birthright Citizenship and the Civil Rights Act of 1866," *Harvard Latino Law Review*, vol. 15 (2012).

12. G. Edward White, "The Origins of Civil Rights in America," *Case Western Reserve Law Review*, vol. 64, no. 3 (2014): 772.

13. White, "Origins of Civil Rights in America," 773.

14. *Memphis Riots and Massacres* (Washington, DC: Government Printing Office, 1866), 22.

15. Bernice Bouie Donald, "When the Rule of Law Breaks Down: Implications of the 1866 Memphis Massacre for the Passage of the Fourteenth Amendment," *Boston University Law Review*, vol. 98, no. 6 (2019): 1607–76, 1654–55.

16. Orville Vernon Burton, "The Creation and Destruction of the Fourteenth Amendment during the Long Civil War," *Louisiana Law Review*, vol. 79, no. 1 (2018): 189–240, 212–13.

17. Burton, "Creation and Destruction of the Fourteenth Amendment," 214

18. Burton, "Creation and Destruction of the Fourteenth Amendment," 215.

19. Andre E. Johnson, "I Have Had to Pass through Blood and Fire: Henry McNeal Turner and the Rhetorical Legacy of Reconstruction," in *Remembering the Memphis Massacre: An American Story*, edited by Beverly Bond and Susan O'Donovan (Athens: University of Georgia Press, 2020).

20. "A Minister's Life in Danger," *Christian Recorder*, February 23, 1867.

21. Andre E. Johnson (ed.), *An African American Pastor before and during the American Civil War*, Vol. 3: *The Literary Archive of Henry McNeal Turner: American Reconstruction, 1866–1880* (New York: Edwin Mellen Press), 206, 209.

22. Henry McNeal Turner, *A Speech on the Benefits Accruing from the Ratification of the Fifteenth Amendment and Its Incorporation into the United States of America* (Atlanta: New Era Printing, 1870).

23. For more on the 1875 Civil Rights Act, see Richard Gerber, *Civil Rights Act of 1875: A Reexamination* (New Haven: Yale University Press, 2008).

24. For a detailed examination of the debates and rhetoric centered around the passage of the Civil Rights Bill, see Wilson, *Reconstruction Desegregation Debate*.

25. Johnson (ed.), *African American Pastor*, Vol. 3, 245.

26. Johnson (ed.), *African American Pastor*, Vol. 3, 245.

27. Johnson (ed.), *African American Pastor*, Vol. 3, 247.

28. Johnson (ed.), *African American Pastor*, Vol. 3, 248.

29. Johnson (ed.), *African American Pastor*, Vol. 3, 91.

30. Johnson (ed.), *African American Pastor*, Vol. 3, 92–93.

31. Legal rhetorical historian Sally F. Paulson has argued that the decision in the Slaughter House cases helped lay the foundation for the court's decision to find the 1875 Civil Rights Act unconstitutional and eventually set the stage for the separate but equal doctrine. See her *Desegregation and the Rhetorical Fight for African American Citizenship Rights* (Lanham, MD: Lexington Books, 2018), especially chapter 2.

32. US Supreme Court, Civil Rights Cases, 109 U.S. 3 (1883), https://supreme.justia.com/cases/federal/us/109/3/case.html.
33. US Supreme Court, Civil Rights Cases, 109 U.S. 3 (1883).
34. US Supreme Court, Civil Rights Cases, 109 U.S. 3 (1883).
35. Andre E. Johnson (ed.), *An African American Pastor before and during the American Civil War*, Vol. 4: *The Literary Archive of Henry McNeal Turner, 1880–1892* (New York: Edwin Mellen Press), 40.
36. Johnson (ed.), *African American Pastor*, Vol. 4, 40–41.
37. Johnson (ed.), *African American Pastor*, Vol. 4, 40–41.
38. Johnson (ed.), *African American Pastor*, Vol. 4, 40–41, 42.
39. Henry McNeal Turner, *Civil Rights: The Outrage of the Supreme Court of the United States upon the Black Man* (Philadelphia: AME Church, 1889), 14.
40. Turner, *Civil Rights*, 15.
41. Turner, *Civil Rights*, 15, 7.
42. Turner, *Civil Rights*, 15, 9.
43. Turner, *Civil Rights*, 15, 9–10.
44. Henry McNeal Turner, *The Barbarous Decision of the United States Supreme Court Declaring the Civil Rights Act Unconstitutional and Disrobing the Colored Race of All Civil Protection* (Atlanta: Bishop H. M. Turner, Publisher, 1893), 3.
45. Turner, *Barbarous Decision of the United States Supreme Court*, 3.
46. Turner, *Barbarous Decision of the United States Supreme Court*, 3.
47. See the Supreme Court case *Charley (Charles) Smith v. The State of Mississippi*, 162 U.S. 592 (1896).
48. Henry McNeal Turner, "Farewell Negro," *Voice of Missions*, June 1896.
49. Turner, "Farewell Negro."
50. Henry McNeal Turner, "The United States Supreme Court," *Voice of Missions* (June 1896).
51. Turner, "United States Supreme Court."
52. Turner, "United States Supreme Court."
53. Turner, "United States Supreme Court."
54. Turner, "United States Supreme Court."
55. Turner, "Sackcloth and Ashes for the Negro," *Voice of Missions* (July 1896).
56. Turner, "Bishop Turner's Wail," *Cleveland Gazette* (July 18, 1896).
57. Turner, "Bishop Turner's Wail."
58. Turner, "Bishop Turner's Wail."
59. Turner, "Bishop Turner's Wail."
60. "Bishop Turner Rousing His Race," *Washington Post*, Nov. 18, 1899, p. 4; "The Negro De-Citizentized," *Voice of Missions*, November 1900.
61. "Races Must Separate," *Voice of Missions*, November 1903.
62. "Negro Bishop Protests," *New York Times*, May 7, 1904.
63. Robert Terrill, "Protest, Prophecy and Prudence in the Rhetoric of Malcolm X," *Rhetoric & Public Affairs*, vol.4, no. 1 (2001): 34–35.
64. See Andre E. Johnson, *The Forgotten Prophet: Bishop Henry McNeal Turner and the African American Prophetic Tradition* (Lanham, MD: Lexington Books, 2012).
65. See Benjamin E. Mays, *The Negro's God: As Reflected in His Literature* (Eugene, OR: Wipf & Stock; 2010); and Gayraud Wilmore, *Black Religion and Black Radicalism*, rev. 3rd ed. (Maryknoll, NY: Orbis Books, 1998).

Chapter 2: "Negroes Should Worship a God Who Is a Negro": The Making of a Black Rhetorical Theologian

1. "Bishop Turner Went Hungry," *New York Times*, Feb. 21, 1897.
2. "Called the Bishop a Negro," *Christian Recorder*, March 11, 1897.
3. Andre E. Johnson (ed.), *An African American Pastor before and after the American Civil War*: Vol. 5: *The Literary Archive of Henry McNeal Turner. 1883–1892* (New York: Mellen Press, 2016), 85–86.
4. Andre E. Johnson (ed.), *An African American Pastor before and after the American Civil War*, Vol. 6: *The Literary Archive of Henry McNeal Turner, 1893–1900* (New York: Edwin Mellen Press, 2018), 49.
5. Johnson, *African American Pastor*, Vol. 6, 49.
6. Despite the copious amount of material we have on Turner, there has been no thorough examination of Turner's theology. However, see Anthony Pinn, "Double Consciousness," in "Nineteenth-Century Black Nationalism: Reflections of the Teaching of Bishop Henry McNeal Turner," *Journal of Religious Thought*, vol. 52, no. 1 (1995): 15; and James Arthur Holmes, "Black Nationalism and Theodicy: A Comparison of the Thought of Henry Highland Garnet Alexander Crummell, and Henry McNeal Turner" (dissertation, Boston University, 1997), especially chapter 5 for an examination of Turner's theodicy.
7. Stephen Ward Angell, *Bishop Henry McNeal Turner and African American Religion in the South* (Knoxville: University of Tennessee Press, 1992), 253.
8. I am currently collecting and editing the writings of Turner under the title *The Literary Archive of Henry McNeal Turner* (Edwin Mellen Press). The first six published volumes cover Turner's career from 1859 to 1900 and contain over 250 writings. Also see Jean Lee Cole's *Freedom's Witness: The Civil War Correspondence of Henry McNeal Turner* (Morgantown: West Virginia University Press, 2013), and the Henry McNeal Turner Project, http://www.thehenrymcnealturnerproject.org/.
9. Angell, *Bishop Henry McNeal Turner*, 253.
10. Josephus Coan, "Henry McNeal Turner: A Fearless Prophet of Black Liberation, *Journal of the Interdenominational Theological Center*, vol. 1, no. 1 (1974): 12, 15.
11. Angell, *Bishop Henry McNeal Turner*, 253.
12. Johnson, *African American Pastor*, Vol. 5, 18.
13. Johnson, *African American Pastor*, Vol. 5, 18–19.
14. Samuel Wakefield, *A Complete System of Christian Theology* (New York: Carlton and Porter, 1862), 10.
15. Andre E. Johnson (ed.), *An African American Pastor before and after the American Civil War*, Vol. 1: *The Literary Archive of Henry McNeal Turner, 1859–1865* (New York: Edwin Mellen Press, 2010), 47–48.
16. Johnson, *African American Pastor*, Vol. 1, 186.
17. Johnson, *African American Pastor*, Vol, 2, 43.
18. For more on Turner's interpretation of slavery, see Johnson, *Forgotten Prophet*, 36–40.
19. Johnson, *African American Pastor*, Vol. 1, 90, 119, 157.
20. Henry McNeal Turner, "*A Speech on the Benefits Accruing from the Ratification of the Fifteenth Amendment* (Atlanta: New Era Printing, 1870); Memorial Services Tribute to the Hon. Charles Sumner, 1874.
21. Henry McNeal Turner, *Celebration of the First Anniversary of Freedom* (Augusta: G.U.L. of Georgia, 1866), 8.

22. Andre E. Johnson (ed.), *An African American Pastor before and after the American Civil War*, Vol. 4: *The Literary Archive of Henry McNeal Turner, 1880–1892* (New York: Edwin Mellen Press, 2015), 20.

23. Henry McNeal Turner, "The Colored Vote," *Atlanta Constitution*, Oct. 23, 1883.

24. "Bishop Turner Talks," *Atlanta Constitution*, July 14, 1890.

25. Henry McNeal Turner, "A Remarkable Letter," *Christian Recorder*, Feb. 14, 1889.

26. Johnson (ed.), *African American Pastor*, Vol. 3, 234.

27. Johnson (ed.), *African American Pastor*, Vol. 3, 236–37.

28. Dedicatory services of Bethel, Philadelphia, *Christian Recorder*, October 30, 1890.

29. Exhortations are typically extemporaneous sermons giving theoretically under the inspiration of the Holy Spirit.

30. Johnson (ed.), *African American Pastor*, Vol. 4, 72–73.

31. Johnson (ed.), *African American Pastor*, Vol. 4, 73.

32. Johnson, *African American Pastor*, Vol. 4, 111.

33. Andre E. Johnson (ed.), *An African American Pastor before and after the American Civil War*, Vol. 5: *The Literary Archive of Henry McNeal Turner, 1883–1892* (New York: Edwin Mellen Press, 2016), 33.

34. "A Female Preacher Ordained," *New York Times*, Dec. 2, 1885.

35. "Connectional AME Women in Ministry: Herstory," Connectional AME Women, http://www.amewim.org/our-herstory.html.

36. Johnson (ed.), *African American Pastor*, Vol. 4, 196–97.

37. Johnson, *African American Pastor*, Vol. 4, 203.

38. Henry Theodore Johnson, *Divine Logos, or the Wonderful World of John* (Boston: McDonald, 1890), 19, https://babel.hathitrust.org/cgi/pt?id=emu.010002588862; Johnson (ed.), *African American Pastor*, Vol. 5, 102.

39. Henry McNeal Turner, "The African as a Tradesman and Mechanic," February 15, 1893, 1–2, https://babel.hathitrust.org/cgi/pt?id=emu.010002585911;view=1up;seq=2.

40. On his first trip to Africa, Turner's cabinmate was an African by the name of Matthew Thomas. As related herein, in chapter 5, Turner wrote how impressed he was by this man and how much he learned from him. One thing Thomas shared with him is his belief that at the beginning of the creation of humankind, all races were Black. It was here that Turner was first introduced to the Blackness of humankind. Wrote Turner about Thomas's teaching on the subject, "Mr. Thomas reasons so masterly upon this . . . that I am almost a convert." See Henry McNeal Turner, *African Letters* (Nashville: AME Publishing House, 1893), 18–19.

41. Turner, "African as a Tradesman, 2.

42. Turner, "African as a Tradesman," 8.

43. "Black Adam in Eden," *Galveston Daily News* (Tex.), http://coloredconventions.org/items/show/1241.

44. *Savannah Courier* (Tenn.), Aug. 24, 1893, *Chronicling America: Historic American Newspapers*. Lib. of Congress. https://chroniclingamerica.loc.gov/lccn/sn89058248/1893-08-24/ed-1/seq-2/; *Sea Coast Echo* (Bay Saint Louis, Miss.), Sept. 30, 1893. *Chronicling America: Historic American Newspapers*, Lib. of Congress. https://chroniclingamerica.loc.gov/lccn/sn86074033/1893-09-30/ed-1/seq-2/.

45. *Grenada Sentinel* (Miss.), Aug. 26, 1893. *Chronicling America: Historic American Newspapers*. Lib. of Congress. https://chroniclingamerica.loc.gov/lccn/sn85034375/1893-08-26/ed-1/seq-4/.

46. *Omaha Daily Bee* (Neb.), Nov. 21, 1893. *Chronicling America: Historic American Newspapers*, Lib. of Congress. https://chroniclingamerica.loc.gov/lccn/sn99021999/1893-11-21/ed-1/seq-8/.

47. Henry McNeal Turner, "God Is a Negro," *Voice of Missions*, November 1895.

48. Henry Lyman Morehouse, "The Spirit and Policy of the American Baptist Home Mission Society in Its Work for the Colored People of the South," *Baptist Home Mission Monthly*, vol. 17, no.11 (Nov. 1895): 412–22, 414.

49. Morehouse, "Spirit and Policy," 414.

50. Turner, "God Is a Negro," *Voice of Missions*, February 1898. For a fuller analysis of Turner's editorial, see Andre E. Johnson, "God Is a Negro: The Rhetorical Black Theology of Bishop Henry McNeal Turner," *Black Theology Journal*, vol. 13, no. 1 (2015): 29–40.

51. Johnson, "God Is a Negro," 36.

52. Johnson, "God Is a Negro," 36.

53. Johnson, "God Is a Negro," 36–37.

54. Johnson, "God Is a Negro," 37

55. Genesis 1:1–2 (NRSV).

56. Johnson, "God Is a Negro," 37.

57. Johnson, "God Is a Negro," 37.

58. Johnson, "God Is a Negro," 37–38.

59. Johnson, "God Is a Negro," 38.

60. Johnson, "God Is a Negro," 38.

61. "Bishop Turner Speaks Boldly," *Richmond Planet* (Va.), July 9, 1898. *Chronicling America: Historic American Newspapers*, Lib. of Congress. http://chroniclingamerica.loc.gov/lccn/sn84025841/1898-07-09/ed-1/seq-4/.

62. *Daily Capital Journal* (Salem, Oreg.), Feb. 21, 1898. *Chronicling America: Historic American Newspapers*, Lib. of Congress. http://chroniclingamerica.loc.gov/lccn/sn99063955/1898-02-21/ed-1/seq-2/.

63. "Rev. Graham's Powerful Plea," *Richmond Planet* (Va.), Feb. 12, 1898. *Chronicling America: Historic American Newspapers*, Lib. of Congress. http://chroniclingamerica.loc.gov/lccn/sn84025841/1898-02-12/ed-1/seq-4/.

64. David Cunningham, *Faithful Persuasion: In Aid of a Rhetoric of Christian Theology* (Notre Dame, IN: Notre Dame Press, 1991), 5.

65. Cunningham, *Faithful Persuasion*, 5.

66. Cunningham, *Faithful Persuasion*, 5.

67. Stephen Ray, *Do No Harm: Social Sin and Christian Responsibility* (Minneapolis: Fortress Press, 2003), xvii.

68. Ray, *Do No Harm*, xxiii.

69. Dan Compier, *What Is Rhetorical Theology? Textual Practice and Public Discourse* (New York: Bloomsbury T&T Clark, 1999).

70. David Cunningham, *These Three Are One: The Practice of Trinitarian Theology* (Malden, MA: Blackwell, 1998), 19.

71. Cunningham, *These Three Are One*, 19.

72. Johnson, "God Is a Negro," 35.

73. Johnson, "God Is a Negro," 35.

74. Johnson, "God Is a Negro," 38.

75. Johnson, "God Is a Negro," 38.

76. Johnson, "God Is a Negro," 38.

77. Henry McNeal Turner, "Madam Turner Translated," *Voice of Missions*, February 1898.

Chapter 3: "An Unholy War of Conquest": Turner and the Creation of an Antiwar Protester

1. Named for Henry M. Teller, a Republican senator from Colorado, the amendment was a joint resolution from Congress on April 20, 1898, in response to President McKinley's declaration of war request. Congress granted the president's request but stipulated that America could not annex Cuba.
2. Howard Zinn, *A People's History of the United States of America* (New York: Harper Collins, 2004), 312–13.
3. Zinn, *People's History*, 313.
4. Zinn, *People's History*, 313.
5. Andre E. Johnson (ed.), *An African American Pastor before and during the American Civil War*, Vol. 1: *The Literary Archive of Henry McNeal Turner, 1859–1865* (New York: Edwin Mellen Press, 2010), 21.
6. Johnson (ed.), *African American Pastor*, Vol. 1, 39–40.
7. Johnson (ed.), *African American Pastor*, Vol. 1, 85.
8. Johnson (ed.), *African American Pastor*, Vol. 1, 44.
9. Johnson (ed.), *African American Pastor*, Vol. 1, 46.
10. Johnson (ed.), *African American Pastor*, Vol. 1, 29–32.
11. Johnson (ed.), *African American Pastor*, Vol. 1, 29.
12. Johnson (ed.), *African American Pastor*, Vol. 1, 29–30.
13. Johnson (ed.), *African American Pastor*, Vol. 1, 30.
14. Johnson, (ed.), *African American Pastor*, Vol. 1, 30.
15. Johnson, (ed.), *African American Pastor*, Vol. 1, 31.
16. Johnson (ed.), *African American Pastor*, Vol. 1, 32.
17. Jean Lee Cole, *Freedom's Witness: The Civil War Correspondence of Henry McNeal Turner* (Morgantown: University of West Virginia Press, 2013), 18.
18. Johnson (ed.), *African American Pastor*, Vol. 4, 209–10.
19. Johnson (ed.), *African American Pastor*, Vol. 3, 246.
20. For a fuller treatment of African American soldiers during the Spanish-American War, see Le'Trice D. Donaldson's *Duty beyond the Battlefield: African American Soldiers Fight for Racial Uplift, Citizenship, and Manhood, 1870–1920* (Carbondale: Southern Illinois University Press, 2020), especially chapter 2.
21. George T. Robinson, "Eight Months in Camp," *National Baptist Magazine*, vol. 7, November–December 1890, 120–25.
22. George P. Marks III (ed.), *The Black Press Views American Imperialism (1898–1900)* (New York: Arno Press, 1971), 18, 24, 29.
23. Marks, *Black Press Views American Imperialism*.
24. Marks, *Black Press Views American Imperialism*, 89–90.
25. Marks, *Black Press Views American Imperialism*, 59.
26. Marks, *Black Press Views American Imperialism*, 59–60, 101.
27. "Lawyer Thomas L. Jones Speaks," *Washington Bee*, May 7, 1898, p. 4.
28. Henry Hugh Proctor, *A Sermon on the War: The Duty of Colored Citizens to Their Country*. (Atlanta: Mutual Printing), 1898.
29. Proctor, *Sermon on the War*.
30. Proctor, *Sermon on the War*.
31. Proctor, *Sermon on the War*.

32. Proctor, *Sermon on the War*.
33. Edwin Redkey (comp. and ed.), *Respect Black: The Speeches and Writings of Henry McNeal Turner* (New York: Arno Press, 1971), 172.
34. Edwin Redkey (comp. and ed.), *Respect Black*, 173.
35. Henry McNeal Turner, "Cuba and the Negro," *Voice of Missions*, February 1898.
36. Henry McNeal Turner, "War with Spain," *Voice of Missions*, July 1898.
37. Turner, "War with Spain."
38. Turner, "War with Spain."
39. Turner, "War with Spain."
40. Turner, "Cuba and the Negro."
41. Turner, "Cuba and the Negro."
42. Turner, "War with Spain"; "The Color Line in Cuba," *Voice of Missions*, October 1898.
43. Untitled editorial, *Voice of Missions*, October 1898.
44. Henry McNeal Turner, "The Negro Should Not Enter the Army," *Voice of Missions*, May 1899.
45. Turner, "Negro Should Not Enter the Army."
46. Turner, "Negro Should Not Enter the Army."
47. Turner, "Negro Should Not Enter the Army."
48. Turner, "Negro Should Not Enter the Army."
49. Turner, "Negro Should Not Enter the Army."
50. Turner, "Negro Should Not Enter the Army."
51. Henry McNeal Turner, "Shoot the Fool Negroes," *Voice of Missions*, October 1899.
52. Turner, "Shoot the Fool Negroes."
53. Turner, "Shoot the Fool Negroes."
54. Redkey (comp. and ed.), *Respect Black*, 186.
55. Redkey (comp. and ed.), *Respect Black*, 186.
56. Redkey (comp. and ed.), *Respect Black*, 186–87.
57. Craig R. Smith, "The Anti-War Rhetoric of Daniel Webster," *Quarterly Journal of Speech*, vol. 85, no. 1 (Feb. 1999): 13.
58. Turner, "Cuba and the Negro."
59. Marks, *Black Press*, 110, 122, 123.

Chapter 4: "McKinley, the God of Fool Negroes": Turner and the Presidential Election of 1900

1. "A Sample of Georgia Justice," *St. Johnsbury Caledonian* (Vt.), Jan. 10, 1900. *Chronicling America: Historic American Newspapers*, Lib. of Congress. http://chroniclingamerica.loc.gov/lccn/sn84023253/1900-01-10/ed-1/seq-2/.
2. "Honoring the Old Roman," *Colored American* (Washington, DC), Jan. 20, 1900. *Chronicling America: Historic American Newspapers*, Lib. of Congress. http://chroniclingamerica.loc.gov/lccn/sn83027091/1900-01-20/ed-1/seq-1/.
3. Henry McNeal Turner, *Celebration of the First Anniversary of Freedom* (Augusta: G.U.L. of Georgia, 1866), 14.
4. For more on Turner's role in the Colored Conventions Movement, see "Further Silence upon Our Part Would Be an Outrage: Bishop Henry McNeal Turner and the Colored Convention Movement," in *Colored Conventions in the Nineteenth Century and the Digital Age*, edited by Gabrielle Foreman (Duke University Press, Forthcoming).

Notes

5. Howard Bell, *A Survey of the Negro Convention Movement:1830–1861* (New York: Arno Press, 1969), 13–14.

6. *Proceedings of the Freedmen's Convention of Georgia*, 4–5, http://coloredconventions.org/items/show/524.

7. *Proceedings of the Council of the Georgia Equal Rights Association Assembled at Augusta, GA, April 4th 1866* (Augusta:1866), 4–5, http://coloredconventions.org/items/show/1193; *Proceedings of the Convention of the Equal Rights and Educational Association of Georgia* (Augusta: 1866), 2–3.

8. Andre E. Johnson, *An African American Pastor before and during the American Civil War*, Vol. 3: *The Literary Archive of Henry McNeal Turner: American Reconstruction, 1866-1880* (New York: Edwin Mellen Press, 2013), 25.

9. "Affairs in South Carolina," *New York Times*, May 5, 1867.

10. Johnson (ed.), *African American Pastor*, Vol. 3, 151.

11. Johnson (ed.), *African American Pastor*, Vol. 3, 151.

12. Johnson (ed.), *African American Pastor*, Vol. 3, 41.

13. Johnson (ed.), *African American Pastor*, Vol. 3, 44–45.

14. Paul Laurence Sanford, "The Negro in the Political Reconstruction of Georgia, 1866–1872" (master's thesis, Atlanta University, 1947), 18.

15. A full treatment of Turner as a state representative during Reconstruction is much needed but is beyond my scope here. While there are no published works detailing his elected public career, there are three unpublished works that deserve mention for those wanting more information on Turner's role as a state representative. Ethel Maude Christler, "Participation of Negroes in the Government of Georgia, 1867–1870" (1932), ETD Collection for AUC Robert W. Woodruff Library, Paper EP15599; Paul Laurence Sanford, "The Negro in the Political Reconstruction of Georgia, 1866–1872" (1947), ETD Collection for AUC Robert W. Woodruff Library, Paper 2110; Elbert Martin, "The Life of Henry McNeal Turner: 1834–1870" (master's thesis, Florida State University, 1975).

16. Henry McNeal Turner, "On the Eligibility of Colored Members, in Participation of Negroes in the Government of Georgia: 1867–1870" (master's thesis, Atlanta University, 1932), 96, emphasis original.

17. Johnson (ed.), *African American Pastor*, Vol. 3, 166.

18. Sanford, "Negro in the Political Reconstruction of Georgia," 40.

19. Johnson (ed.), *African American Pastor*, Vol. 3, 199–200.

20. Johnson (ed.), *African American Pastor*, Vol. 3, 200.

21. Johnson (ed.), *African American Pastor*, Vol. 3, 171.

22. "Call for a Southern States Convention," *Semi-weekly Louisianian*, Oct. 8, 1871, http://chroniclingamerica.loc.gov/lccn/sn83016631/1871-10-08/ed-1/seq-3/.

23. Henry McNeal Turner, "Speech of Mr. Turner," *Official Proceedings of the Republican Convention: 1868, 1872, 1876, 1880* (Minneapolis: Johnson, 1903), 296.

24. Turner, "Speech of Mr. Turner," 296–97.

25. Johnson (ed.), *African American Pastor*, Vol. 3, 111.

26. Johnson (ed.), *African American Pastor*, Vol. 3, 111–12.

27. Andre E. Johnson (ed.), *An African American Pastor before and during the American Civil War*, Vol. 4: *The Literary Archive of Henry McNeal Turner, 1880–1892* (New York: Edwin Mellen Press, 2015), 2.

28. Johnson (ed.), *African American Pastor*, Vol. 4, 76–77.

29. Johnson (ed.), *African American Pastor*, Vol. 5, 129–30.

30. Johnson (ed.), *African American Pastor*, Vol. 5, 164.

31. Johnson (ed.), *African American Pastor*, Vol. 5, 167–70.

32. Andre E. Johnson (ed.), *An African American Pastor before and after the American Civil War*, Vol. 6: *The Literary Archive of Henry McNeal Turner, 1893–1900* (New York: Edwin Mellen Press, 2018).

33. The *Times* erroneously printed that Turner's editorial came from the "Missioners Voice." During this time, Turner was the editor of the *Voice of Missions* newspaper that served as an organ for the AME Church.

34. The *Times* published the name of the victim as "Jointry," but it should have read "Joiner."

35. "Negroes Get Guns," *New York Times*, March 17, 1897, http://query.nytimes.com/gst/abstract.html?res=9F02E7DF163DE433A25754C1A9659C94669ED7CF&legacy=true.

36. *Roanoke Times* (Va.), March 23, 1897. *Chronicling America: Historic American Newspapers*. Lib. of Congress. http://chroniclingamerica.loc.gov/lccn/sn95079490/1897-03-23/ed-1/seq-2/.

37. *Abbeville Press and Banner* (SC), March 24, 1897. *Chronicling America: Historic American Newspapers*. Lib. of Congress. http://chroniclingamerica.loc.gov/lccn/sn84026853/1897-03-24/ed-1/seq-4/; *Semi-weekly Messenger* (Wilmington, NC), March 26, 1897. *Chronicling America: Historic American Newspapers*. Lib. of Congress. http://chroniclingamerica.loc.gov/lccn/sn91068367/1897-03-26/ed-1/seq-2/.

38. *Broad Ax* (Salt Lake City, Utah), March 27, 1897. *Chronicling America: Historic American Newspapers*, Lib. of Congress. http://chroniclingamerica.loc.gov/lccn/sn84024055/1897-03-27/ed-1/seq-1/.

39. *Roanoke Times* (Va.), March 24, 1897. *Chronicling America: Historic American Newspapers*, Lib. of Congress. http://chroniclingamerica.loc.gov/lccn/sn95079490/1897-03-24/ed-1/seq-1/.

40. *Chipley Banner* (Fla.), June 16, 1900. *Chronicling America: Historic American Newspapers*, Lib. of Congress. http://chroniclingamerica.loc.gov/lccn/sn95047263/1900-06-16/ed-1/seq-1/.

41. *Chipley Banner*, June 16, 1900.

42. *Sun* (New York [NY], Aug. 19, 1900. *Chronicling America: Historic American Newspapers*, Lib. of Congress. http://chroniclingamerica.loc.gov/lccn/sn83030272/1900-08-19/ed-1/seq-11/; *Bamberg Herald* (SC), Aug. 23, 1900. *Chronicling America: Historic American Newspapers*, Lib. of Congress. http://chroniclingamerica.loc.gov/lccn/sn86063790/1900-08-23/ed-1/seq-4/; *Colored American* (Washington, DC), Aug. 25, 1900. *Chronicling America: Historic American Newspapers*, Lib. of Congress. http://chroniclingamerica.loc.gov/lccn/sn83027091/1900-08-25/ed-1/seq-9/; see also Stephen Ward Angell, *Bishop Henry McNeal Turner and African American Religion in the South* (Knoxville: University of Tennessee Press, 1992), 217.

43. Henry McNeal Turner, "We Are for Bryan," *Voice of Missions*, July 1900.

44. "Bishop Turner for Bryan," *New York Times*, Sept. 11, 1900.

45. "Bishop H. M. Turner," *Cleveland Gazette*, Sept. 29, 1900, http://dbs.ohiohistory.org/africanam/html/page83db.html?ID=19386.

46. "Bishop H. M. Turner," *Cleveland Gazette*, September 29, 1900.

47. "Bishop H. M. Turner," *Cleveland Gazette*, September 29, 1900.

48. "Bishop Turner Bitter," *Cleveland Gazette*, October 27, 1900, http://dbs.ohiohistory.org/africanam/html/page6b3e.html?ID=19402.

49. *Seattle Republican* (Wash.), Sept. 28, 1900, http://chroniclingamerica.loc.gov/lccn/sn84025811/1900-09-28/ed-1/seq-1/.

50. *Seattle Republican* (Wash.), Sept. 28, 1900.

51. "Political Pot Pie," *Seattle Republican* (Wash.), Oct. 5, 1900. *Chronicling America: Historic American Newspapers*, Lib. of Congress. http://chroniclingamerica.loc.gov/lccn/sn84025811/1900-10-05/ed-1/seq-3/.

52. *Colored American* (Washington, DC), Oct. 6, 1900, *Chronicling America: Historic American Newspapers*, Lib. of Congress. http://chroniclingamerica.loc.gov/lccn/sn83027091/1900-10-06/ed-1/seq-2/; *Colored American* (Washington, DC), Oct. 13, 1900, *Chronicling America: Historic American Newspapers*, Lib. of Congress. http://chroniclingamerica.loc.gov/lccn/sn83027091/1900-10-13/ed-1/seq-2/; *Colored American*, Oct. 13, 1900. *Chronicling America: Historic American Newspapers*, Lib. of Congress. http://chroniclingamerica.loc.gov/lccn/sn83027091/1900-10-13/ed-1/seq-13/.

53. "Negro Pastor for McKinley," *New York Times*, October 1, 1900.

54. "Negroes at Cooper Union," *New York Times*, October 4, 1900, http://query.nytimes.com/gst/abstract.html?res=9A06E2DA173FE433A25757C0A9669D946197D6CF&legacy=true.

55. "Bryan Not Our Friend," *Iowa State Bystander* (Iowa), Nov. 2, 1900. *Chronicling America: Historic American Newspapers*, Lib. of Congress. http://chroniclingamerica.loc.gov/lccn/sn83025186/1900-11-02/ed-1/seq-8/.

56. Henry McNeal Turner, "McKinley's Policy Denounced," *Voice of Missions*, October 1900.

57. Turner, "McKinley's Policy Denounced."

58. Turner, "McKinley's Policy Denounced."

59. Sam Hose was an African American man lynched in Atlanta on April 23, 1899.

60. Turner, "McKinley's Policy Denounced."

61. Turner, "McKinley's Policy Denounced."

62. Turner, "McKinley's Policy Denounced."

63. Henry McNeal Turner, "Turner Is a Democrat," *Voice of Missions*, October 1900.

64. Turner, "Turner Is a Democrat."

65. Turner, "Turner Is a Democrat."

66. Turner, "Turner Is a Democrat."

67. Henry McNeal Turner, "He Is a Democratic Bishop," *Voice of Missions*, November 1900.

68. Henry McNeal Turner, "Negro Office Holders," *Voice of Missions*, November 1900.

69. Henry McNeal Turner, "Fool Negroes Crazy about President McKinley," *Voice of Missions*, December 1900.

70. Turner, "Fool Negroes Crazy about President McKinley."

71. Turner, "Fool Negroes Crazy about President McKinley."

72. Turner, "Fool Negroes Crazy about President McKinley."

73. Turner, "Fool Negroes Crazy about President McKinley."

74. Henry McNeal Turner, "McKinley, the God of Fool Negroes, Re-Elected," *Voice of Missions*, December 1900.

75. Turner, "McKinley, the God of Fool Negroes, Re-Elected."

76. Turner, "McKinley, the God of Fool Negroes, Re-Elected."

77. Turner, "McKinley, the God of Fool Negroes, Re-Elected."

78. Henry McNeal Turner, "The *Voice of Missions* Will Be Turned into Other Hands," *Voice of Missions*, December 1900.

79. Patrick J. Kelly, "The Election of 1896 and the Restructuring of Civil War Memory," *Civil War History*, vol. 49, no. 3 (2003): 254–80, 255.

80. "Bishop Turner All Right," *Colored American*, Nov. 24, 1900.

81. Turner, "*Voice of Missions* Will Be Turned into Other Hands."

Chapter 5: "The Salvation of the Negro": Turner and the Rhetoric of Emigration

1. Henry McNeal Turner, "The Resignation of Bishop Turner," *Christian Recorder*, Jan. 3, 1901.
2. Turner, " Resignation of Bishop Turner."
3. Henry McNeal Turner, "Bishop Turner Opposes Fifth Year Term in the AME Church," *Christian Recorder*, Sept. 22, 1898. The Henry McNeal Turner Project, http://www.thehenrymcnealturnerproject.org/2018/03/bishop-turner-opposes-fifth-year-term.html.
4. Henry McNeal Turner, "Contemplations," *Christian Recorder*, June 11, 1885. The Henry McNeal Turner Project, http://www.thehenrymcnealturnerproject.org/2017/08/contemplations-june-11-1885.html.
5. Henry McNeal Turner, "Plain Words on Plain Topics," *Christian Recorder*, July 1, 1886. The Henry McNeal Turner Project., http://www.thehenrymcnealturnerproject.org/2018/07/plain-words-on-plain-topics-july-1-1886.html.
6. Henry McNeal Turner, "Success under Disadvantages," *Christian Recorder*, Sept. 2, 1886. The Henry McNeal Turner Project, http://www.thehenrymcnealturnerproject.org/2018/07/success-under-disadvantages-christian.html.
7. "Senior bishop" is awarded to the most senior bishop who currently serves on the Board of Bishops. Turner became senior bishop in 1895.
8. Henry McNeal Turner, *Voice of the People*, February 1901.
9. Turner, *Voice of the People*, February 1901.
10. Turner, *Voice of the People*, February 1901.
11. Edwin S. Redkey (comp. and ed.), *Black Exodus: Black Nationalist and Back-to-Africa Movements, 1890–1910* (New Haven: Yale University Press), 252–62.
12. Falechiondro Karcheik Sims-Alvarado, "The African-American Emigration Movement in Georgia during Reconstruction" (dissertation, Georgia State University, 2011), 29, 25, http://scholarworks.gsu.edu/history_diss/.
13. Sims-Alvarado, "African-American Emigration Movement," 39.
14. Sims-Alvarado, "African-American Emigration Movement," 40.
15. Sims-Alvarado, "African-American Emigration Movement," 40–41.
16. Howard H. Bell, "The Negro Emigration Movement, 1849–1854: A Phase of Negro Nationalism." *Phylon Quarterly*, vol. 20, no. 2 (1959): 132–42, 133–35; "To Stay or to Go? The National Emigration Convention of 1954," Colored Conventions: Bringing Nineteenth-Century Black Organizing to Digital Life, http://coloredconventions.org/exhibits/show/conventions-black-press.
17. Robert M. Kahn, The Political Ideology of Martin Delany, *Journal of Black Studies*, vol. 14, no. 4 (1984): 415–40, 416.
18. "To Stay or to Go? The National Emigration Convention of 1954."
19. *Proceedings of the National Emigration Convention of Colored People* (Pittsburgh: A. A. Anderson, 1854), 33–70.
20. Martin Robinson Delany, *The Condition, Elevation, Emigration and Destiny of the Colored People of the United States*. 1852, https://www.gutenberg.org/files/17154/17154-h/17154-h.htm.
21. Kahn, *Political Ideology of Martin Delany*, 430.
22. Sims-Alvarado, "African American Emigration Movement in Georgia," 66.
23. Andre E. Johnson (ed.), *An African American Pastor before and during the American Civil War*, Vol 3: *The Literary Archive of Henry McNeal Turner: American Reconstruction, 1866–1880* (New York: Edwin Mellen Press, 2013), 26.
24. Johnson (ed.), *African American Pastor*, Vol. 6, 44.

25. Andre E. Johnson (ed.), *An African American Pastor before and during the American Civil War*, Vol. 4: *The Literary Archive of Henry McNeal Turner, 1880–1892* (New York: Edwin Mellen Press, 2017), 34.

26. Andre E. Johnson (ed.), *An African American Pastor before and during the American Civil War*, Vol. 1: *The Literary Archive of Henry Mc Neal Turner, 1859–1865* (New York: Edwin Mellen Press, 2010), 13, 139.

27. For more on this meeting, see Kate Masur, "The African American Delegation to Abraham Lincoln: A Reappraisal," *Civil War History*, vol. 56, no. 2 (2010): 117–44.

28. Edwin Redkey (comp. and ed.), *Respect Black: The Writings and Speeches of Henry McNeal Turner* (New York: Arno Press, 1971), 13.

29. Redkey (comp. and ed.), *Respect Black*, 13.

30. Andre Johnson (ed.), *An African American Pastor before and during the American Civil War*, Vol. 3: *The Literary Archive of Henry McNeal Turner: American Reconstruction, 1866–1880* (New York: Edwin Mellen Press, 2013), 68–69.

31. Henry McNeal Turner, *The Negro in All Ages: A Lecture Delivered in the Second Baptist Church of Savannah, Georgia* (D. G. Patton, 1873), 28.

32. Turner, *Negro in All Ages*, 29.

33. Johnson (ed.), *African American Pastor*, Vol. 3, 177–78.

34. Johnson (ed.), *African American Pastor*, Vol. 3, 179.

35. Johnson (ed.), *African American Pastor*, Vol. 3, 99.

36. Johnson (ed.), *African American Pastor*, Vol. 3, 99.

37. Johnson (ed.), *African American Pastor*, Vol. 3, 105.

38. Julius Bailey, *Race Patriotism: Protest and Print Culture in the A.M.E. Church* (Knoxville: University of Tennessee Press, 2012), 88.

39. Bailey, *Race Patriotism*, 84.

40. Andre E. Johnson, *The Forgotten Prophet: Bishop Henry McNeal Turner and the African American Prophetic Tradition* (Lanham, MD: Lexington Books, 2012), 73.

41. Johnson, *Forgotten Prophet*, 73.

42. Johnson (ed.), *African American Pastor*, Vol. 4, 9.

43. Johnson (ed.), *African American Pastor*, Vol. 4, 11.

44. Johnson (ed.), *African American Pastor*, Vol. 4, 13.

45. Johnson (ed.), *African American Pastor*, Vol. 4, 14.

46. Johnson (ed.), *African American Pastor*, Vol. 4, 19.

47. Johnson (ed.), *African American Pastor*, Vol. 4, 20.

48. Johnson (ed.), *African American Pastor*, Vol. 4, 20.

49. Johnson (ed.), *African American Pastor*, Vol. 4, 20.

50. Johnson (ed.), *African American Pastor*, Vol. 4, 20–21.

51. Johnson (ed.), *African American Pastor*, Vol. 4, 21.

52. Johnson (ed.), *African American Pastor*, Vol. 4, 33.

53. Johnson (ed.), *African American Pastor*, Vol. 4, 42.

54. Johnson (ed.), *African American Pastor*, Vol. 4, 183.

55. Johnson (ed.), *African American Pastor*, Vol. 4, 183.

56. Redkey (comp. and ed.), *Black Exodus*, 43.

57. Stephen Ward Angell, *Bishop Henry McNeal Turner and African American Religion in the South* (Knoxville: University of Tennessee Press, 1992), 218; Henry McNeal Turner, *African Letters* (Nashville: AME Publishing House, 1893), 58, https://docsouth.unc.edu/church/turneral/turner.html.

58. Turner, *African Letters*, 15.

59. Turner, *African Letters*, 33.
60. Turner, *African Letters*, 43–44.
61. Turner, *African Letters*, 52–54.
62. Turner, *Respect Black*, 136.
63. Henry McNeal Turner, "A Colored National Convention," *Voice of Missions*, Aug. 1, 1893.
64. Johnson, *Forgotten Prophet*, 80.
65. Henry McNeal Turner, Negro Convention Speech, *Voice of Missions*, December 1893.
66. Johnson, *Forgotten Prophet*, 91.
67. Johnson, *Forgotten Prophet*, 91.
68. *Voice of Missions*, January 1894.
69. Redkey (comp. and ed.), *Black Exodus* 262–63; "New Emigration Convention," *Voice of the People*, November 1901.
70. "New Emigration Convention."
71. Redkey (comp. and ed.), *Black Exodus*, 263.
72. Redkey (comp. and ed.), *Black Exodus*, 264; "Another Colonization Scheme," *Alexandria Gazette* (Va.), Jan. 7, 1902. *Chronicling America: Historic American Newspapers*, Lib. of Congress. http://chroniclingamerica.loc.gov/lccn/sn85025007/1902-01-07/ed-1/seq-1/.
73. Henry McNeal Turner, "On Negro Colonization," *Colored American* (Washington, DC), Nov. 23, 1901. *Chronicling America: Historic American Newspapers*, Lib. of Congress. http://chroniclingamerica.loc.gov/lccn/sn83027091/1901-11-23/ed-1/seq-11/.
74. On October 16, 1901, President Theodore Roosevelt invited his advisor Booker T. Washington to dinner at the White House, setting off a wave of condemnation and outrage. While previous presidents had invited African Americans to the White House, never had any president invited them to dinner, thus breaking social equality norms. For example, the two Memphis, Tennessee, papers published scathing and racist indictments against the invitation. In the *Commercial Appeal*, one editorial read, "This is a white man's country. It will continue to be such as long as clean blood flows through the veins of white people. . . . If some course-fibred men cannot understand them it is no concern of the Southern people. Sufficient answer to them is that race supremacy precludes social equality." The *Scimitar* offered the following editorial: "The most damnable outrage which has ever been perpetrated by any citizen of the United States was committed yesterday by the President when he Invited a nigger to dine with him at the White House. . . . Had the guest of the President on the occasion mentioned been a black Republican of Hayti, no doubt there might have been some excuse because of diplomatic reasons, but the fact Is that he went out of his way and extended a special Invitation to a nigger to sit down at table with him a nigger whose only claim to distinction is that by comparison with the balance of his race he has been considered somewhat superior." For more reactions on the fallout from the dinner, see "Roosevelt Dined Booker Washington," in the *St. Louis Republic* (Mo.), Oct. 18, 1901. *Chronicling America: Historic American Newspapers*. Lib. of Congress. http://chroniclingamerica.loc.gov/lccn/sn84020274/1901-10-18/ed-1/seq-1/. For a more in-depth history of the event, see Clarence Lusane, *The Black History of the White House* (San Francisco: City Lights, 2011); and Deborah Davis, *Booker T. Washington, Theodore Roosevelt, and the White House Dinner That Shocked a Nation* (New York: Atria Books, 2012).
75. "The Negro Point of View," *Washington Times* (DC), Nov. 3 1901. *Chronicling America: Historic American Newspapers*. Lib. of Congress. http://chroniclingamerica.loc.gov/lccn/sn87062245/1901-11-03/ed-1/seq-13/.

76. Henry McNeal Turner, "Bishop Turner Replies to Rev. R. Seymour," *Voice of Missions*, December 1901.

77. Henry McNeal Turner, "Says It Is a Misrepresentation," *Atlanta Constitution*, Jan. 14, 1902, p. 6.

78. "Colored Emigration and Commercial Convention," *Star of Zion*, Feb. 20, 1902.

79. "Let Them Go," *Hattiesburg Daily Progress* (Miss.), May 30, 1902. *Chronicling America: Historic American Newspapers*, Lib. of Congress. http://chroniclingamerica.loc.gov/lccn/sn87065165/1902-05-30/ed-1/seq-2/.

80. *Seattle Republican* (Wash.), June 20, 1902. *Chronicling America: Historic American Newspapers*, Lib. of Congress. http://chroniclingamerica.loc.gov/lccn/sn84025811/1902-06-20/ed-1/seq-1/.

81. *Waterbury Democrat* (Conn.), May 1, 1902. *Chronicling America: Historic American Newspapers*, Lib. of Congress. http://chroniclingamerica.loc.gov/lccn/sn93053725/1902-05-01/ed-1/seq-2/.

82. A. Benjamin Cooper, "Colored Emigration and Commercial Convention," *Southern Christian Recorder*, March 20, 1902.

83. Henry McNeal Turner, "Our Ship Stock Increases," *Voice of the People*, April 1901; Redkey (comp. and ed.), *Black Exodus*, 264–65; Robin W. Winks, *Blacks in Canada: A History*, 2nd ed. (Montreal: MQUP, 1997), 301; "Negroes Want to Leave," *Goldsboro Weekly Argus* (NC), June 5, 1902. *Chronicling America: Historic American Newspapers*, Lib. of Congress. http://chroniclingamerica.loc.gov/lccn/sn84020751/1902-06-05/ed-1/seq-6/.

84. Henry McNeal Turner, "A Characteristic Letter from Bishop Turner," *Hartford Courant*, September 5, 1902.

85. Henry McNeal Turner, "For Negro Emigration," *Voice of the People*, January 1903.

86. Turner, "For Negro Emigration."

87. Turner, "For Negro Emigration."

88. Turner, "For Negro Emigration."

89. "Colored National Convention," *Voice of the People*, March 1903.

90. Redkey (comp. and ed.), *Black Exodus*, 271.

91. Henry McNeal Turner, "Ships, Ships, African Ships!" *Voice of the People*, September 1903.

92. Turner, "Ships, Ships, African Ships!"

93. Henry McNeal Turner, "Colored National Emigration and Commercial Association," *Voice of the People*," January 1904.

94. Redkey (comp. and ed.), *Black Exodus*, 276.

95. Melbourne Stenson Cummings, "The Rhetoric of Bishop Henry McNeal Turner Leading Advocate in the African Emigration Movement: 1866–1907" (dissertation, University of California, Los Angeles, 1972), 111, 116.

96. Tunde Adeleke, *UnAfrican Americans: Nineteenth-Century Black Nationalists and the Civilizing Mission* (Lanham, MD: Lexington Books, 1998), 101, 104.

97. Adeleke, *UnAfrican Americans*, 106.

98. For an overview of Black identity studies and race, see Anthony Moran, "Identity, Race, and Ethnicity," in *Routledge Handbook of Identity Studies*, edited by Anthony Elliott (New York: Routledge, 2011).

99. Cummings, "Rhetoric of Bishop Henry McNeal," 13.

100. Moran, "Identity, Race, and Ethnicity," 2011.

101. Masur, " "African American Delegation," 117–44, 137.

102. Johnson (ed.), *African American Pastor*, Vol. 1, 139.

103. Masur, "African American Delegation," 144.

104. James H. Cone, *Black Theology, Black Power* (Maryknoll, NY: Orbis Books, 1969).

105. Henry McNeal Turner, "Will It Be Possible for the Negro to Attain, in This Country, unto the American Civilization?," in *Twentieth Century Negro Literature, Or: A Cyclopedia of Thought on the Vital Topics Relating to the American Negro*, edited by D. W. Culp, 45 (Naperville, IL: J. L. Nichols, 1902).

Chapter 6: "Hell Is an Improvement So Far As the Negro Is Concerned": Turner and the Damning of America

1. Quarto-Centennial of H. M. Turner as Bishop in the A.M.E. Church: Celebrated in St. Paul A.M.E. Church, Saint Louis, Missouri. A.M.E. Sunday School Union, Nashville, 1905, 5, http://hdl.handle.net/2027/emu.010002588729.

2. Quarto-Centennial of H. M. Turner as Bishop in the A.M.E. Church, 14.

3. Quarto-Centennial of H. M. Turner as Bishop in the A.M.E. Church, 15–16.

4. Andre E. Johnson (ed.), *An African American Pastor before and during the American Civil War*, Vol. 1: *The Literary Archive of Henry McNeal Turner, 1859–1865* (New York: Edwin Mellen Press, 2010), 30.

5. Johnson (ed.), *African American Pastor*, Vol. 1, 54.

6. Johnson (ed.), *African American Pastor*, Vol. 1, 147.

7. Andre E. Johnson (ed.), *An African American Pastor before and during the American Civil War*, Vol 2: *The Literary Archive of Henry McNeal Turner, 1863–1865* (New York: Edwin Mellen Press, 2012), 90.

8. Johnson (ed.), *African American Pastor*, Vol. 2, 147–48.

9. Andre E. Johnson (ed.), *An African American Pastor before and during the American Civil War*, Vol 3: (New York: Edwin Mellen Press, 2013), 14–15.

10. Johnson (ed.), *African American Pastor*, Vol. 3, 203.

11. Johnson (ed.), *African American Pastor*, Vol. 3, 204.

12. Johnson (ed.), *African American Pastor*, Vol. 3, 207.

13. Johnson (ed.), *African American Pastor*, Vol. 3, 209.

14. Johnson (ed.), *African American Pastor*, Vol. 3, 210.

15. Johnson (ed.), *African American Pastor*, Vol. 3, 224.

16. Johnson (ed.), *African American Pastor*, Vol. 3, 224.

17. Andre E. Johnson, *An African American Pastor before and during the American Civil War* Vol. 4: *The Literary Archive of Henry McNeal Turner, 1880–1892* (New York: Edwin Mellen Press, 2015)

18. Johnson (ed.), *African American Pastor*, Vol. 4, 18.

19. Johnson (ed.), *African American Pastor*, Vol. 3, 142.

20. Johnson (ed.), *African American Pastor*, Vol. 4, 33–34.

21. Johnson (ed.), *African American Pastor*, Vol. 4, 37.

22. Johnson (ed.), *African American Pastor*, Vol. 4, 38.

23. Johnson (ed.), *African American Pastor*, Vol. 4, 148.

24. Andre E. Johnson (ed.), *An African American Pastor before and after the American Civil War*, Vol. 6: *The Literary Archive of Henry McNeal Turner, 1893–1900* (New York: Edwin Mellen Press, 2016), 80.

25. Johnson (ed.), *African American Pastor*, Vol. 6, 129.

26. Johnson (ed.), *African American Pastor*, Vol. 6, 131.
27. Johnson (ed.), *African American Pastor*, Vol. 6, 90.
28. Johnson (ed.), *African American Pastor*, Vol. 6, 98–99.
29. Johnson (ed.), *African American Pastor*, Vol. 6, 109.
30. Johnson (ed.), *African American Pastor*, Vol. 6, 42.
31. Johnson (ed.), *African American Pastor*, Vol. 6, 43.
32. Johnson (ed.), *African American Pastor*, Vol. 6, 46.
33. Johnson (ed.), *African American Pastor*, Vol. 6, 75, 87.
34. "Not the Negro's Home, *Washington Post*, May 7, 1904, p. 7; *St. Louis Republic* (Mo.), May 19, 1904. *Chronicling America: Historic American Newspapers*, Lib. of Congress. http://chroniclingamerica.loc.gov/lccn/sn84020274/1904-05-19/ed-1/seq-16/.
35. *Iowa State Bystander* (Des Moines, Iowa), Jan. 26, 1906. *Chronicling America: Historic American Newspapers*. Lib. of Congress. http://chroniclingamerica.loc.gov/lccn/sn83025186/1906-01-26/ed-1/seq-1/.
36. David Fort Godshalk, *Veiled Visions: The 1906 Atlanta Race Riot and the Reshaping of American Race Relations* (Chapel Hill: University of North Carolina Press, 2005), 69–70.
37. Georgia Equal Rights Convention address, Feb. 14, 1906, http://credo.library.umass.edu/cgi-bin/pdf.cgi?id=scua:mums312-b002-i289.
38. "A Contemptible Rag," *New York Times*, February 16, 1906.
39. *Salt Lake Herald* (Utah), Feb. 16, 1906. *Chronicling America: Historic American Newspapers*. Lib. of Congress. http://chroniclingamerica.loc.gov/lccn/sn85058130/1906-02-16/ed-1/seq-3/.
40. *Wenatchee Daily World*. (Wenatchee, Wash.), Feb. 16, 1906. *Chronicling America: Historic American Newspapers*. Lib. of Congress. http://chroniclingamerica.loc.gov/lccn/sn86072041/1906-02-16/ed-1/seq-1/.
41. *Cairo Bulletin*. (Cairo, Ill.), Feb. 16, 1906. *Chronicling America: Historic American Newspapers*. Lib. of Congress. http://chroniclingamerica.loc.gov/lccn/sn93055779/1906-02-16/ed-1/seq-1/.
42. *Lancaster News*. (Lancaster, SC), Feb. 21, 1906. *Chronicling America: Historic American Newspapers*. Lib. of Congress. http://chroniclingamerica.loc.gov/lccn/sn83007465/1906-02-21/ed-1/seq-6/.
43. *Weekly True Democrat* (Tallahassee, Fla.), Feb. 23, 1906. *Chronicling America: Historic American Newspapers*. Lib. of Congress. http://chroniclingamerica.loc.gov/lccn/sn95047417/1906-02-23/ed-1/seq-2/.
44. *Bamberg Herald* (Bamberg, SC), Feb. 22, 1906. *Chronicling America: Historic American Newspapers*. Lib. of Congress. http://chroniclingamerica.loc.gov/lccn/sn86063790/1906-02-22/ed-1/seq-3/.
45. Henry McNeal Turner, "Turner Denies He Cursed the Flag " *Atlanta Constitution*, February 24, 1906.
46. Turner, "Turner Denies He Cursed the Flag "
47. Turner, "Turner Denies He Cursed the Flag "
48. Turner, "Turner Denies He Cursed the Flag "
49. Turner, "Turner Denies He Cursed the Flag "
50. Turner, "Turner Denies He Cursed the Flag "
51. *Appeal* (Saint Paul, Minn.), March 3, 1906. *Chronicling America: Historic American Newspapers*. Lib. of Congress. http://chroniclingamerica.loc.gov/lccn/sn83016810/1906-03-03/ed-1/seq-2/.

52. *Richmond Planet.* (Richmond, Va.), March 3, 1906. *Chronicling America: Historic American Newspapers,* Lib. of Congress. http://chroniclingamerica.loc.gov/lccn/sn84025841/1906-03-03/ed-1/seq-4/.

53. *Montana Plaindealer.* (Helena), March 16, 1906. *Chronicling America: Historic American Newspapers,* Lib. of Congress. http://chroniclingamerica.loc.gov/lccn/sn84036199/1906-03-16/ed-1/seq-1/.

54. *Times Dispatch* (Richmond, Va.), March 11, 1906. *Chronicling America: Historic American Newspapers,* Lib. of Congress. http://chroniclingamerica.loc.gov/lccn/sn85038615/1906-03-11/ed-1/seq-18/.

55. Stephen Ward Angell, *Bishop Henry McNeal Turner and African American Religion in the South* (Knoxville: University of Tennessee Press, 1992): 244–45; *Montana Plaindealer* (Helena, Mont.), May 18, 1906. *Chronicling America: Historic American Newspapers.* Lib. of Congress. http://chroniclingamerica.loc.gov/lccn/sn84036199/1906-05-18/ed-1/seq-1/; Edwin Redkey (comp. and ed.), *Respect Black: The Speeches and Writings of Henry McNeal Turner* (New York: Arno Press, 1971), 198–99.

56. Turner, "Selfish Politicians Making Labor Scare by Anti-Negro Crusade," *Atlanta Constitution,* June 9, 1906, p. 8.

57. Angell, *Bishop Henry McNeal Turner,* 245; see also Godshalk, *Veiled Visions,* especially chapter 4.

58. Harvey K. Newman and Glenda Crunk, "Religious Leaders in the Aftermath of Atlanta's 1906 Race Riot," *Georgia Historical Quarterly,* vol. 92, no. 4 (2008): 460–85, 463.

59. "Turner Says Atlanta Riots Prove We Should Emigrate," *New York Age,* November 15, 1906.

60. "Bishop H. M. Turner Made Bitter Attack," *Macon Telegraph,* April 16, 1907; "Bishop Turner Challenges Tillman," *Topeka Plaindealer,* April 19, 1907; "Bishop Turner Challenges Tillman," *Cleveland Gazette,* April 20, 1907; "Bishop Turner Denounces Ben Tillman," *Chicago Broad Ax,* April 27, 1907.

61. "The Flag Attacked by Colored Bishop," *New York Times,* June 30, 1907.

62. "The Flag Attacked by Colored Bishop."

63. "Bishop Turner and the Flag," *New York Age,* July 11, 1907, p. 8.

64. "Bishop Turner Makes Address," *Atlanta Constitution,* November 15, 1907.

65. "Bishop Turner Makes Address,"

66. "Bishop Turner Makes Address."

67. Andre E. Johnson and Anthony J. Stone, "The Most Dangerous Negro in America": Rhetoric, Race and the Prophetic Pessimism of Martin Luther King Jr,. *Journal of Communication and Religion,* vol. 21, no. 1, 8–22, 10.

68. Johnson and Stone, "Most Dangerous Negro in America," 10.

69. See Henry McNeal Turner. *Celebration of the First Anniversary of Freedom.* Augusta: G.U.L. of Georgia, 1866.

70. See Henry McNeal Turner, "God Is a Negro," *Voice of Missions,* February 1898.

Conclusion: Reclaiming the Pessimistic Prophecy of Bishop Henry McNeal Turner

1. "Negro to Go South Again," Black Bishop Asserts, *Chicago Tribune,* October 14, 1913.

2. Stephen Ward Angell, *Bishop Henry McNeal Turner and African American Religion* (Knoxville: University of Tennessee Press, 1992), 248.

3. Mungo M. Ponton, *Life and Times of Bishop H. M. Turner* (Atlanta: A. B. Caldwell, 1917), 139.

4. Reverdy C. Ransom, "Bishop Henry McNeal Turner," The Henry McNeal Turner Collection, box 1, folder 2. Manuscript Division, Moorland-Spingarn Research Center, Howard University.

5. Henry Lincoln Johnson, "Bishop Turner Dead," *Atlanta Independent*, May 15, 1915.

6. Edwin Redkey (comp. and ed.), *Respect Black: The Speeches and Writings of Henry McNeal Turner* (New York: Arno Press, 1971), vii–ix.

7. Gary Dorrien, *The New Abolition: W. E. B. Du Bois and the Black Social Gospel* (New Haven: Yale University Press, 2015), 81.

8. J. Minton Batten, "Henry McNeal Turner, Negro Bishop Extraordinary," *Church History*, vol. 7, no. 3 (1938): 231–46, 232, 245.

9. Evelyn Brooks Higginbotham, *Righteous Discontent: The Women's Movement in the Black Baptist Church, 1880–1920* (Cambridge: Harvard University Press, 1993).

10. Andre E. Johnson and Anthony J. Stone Jr., "The Most Dangerous Negro in America: Rhetoric, Race and the Prophetic Pessimism of Martin Luther King Jr." *Journal of Communication and Religion*, vol. 41, no. 1 (2018):8–22.

INDEX

Abolition, 27, 122, 124, 160
Adeleke, Tunde, 143
Africa, trip to, 130–32, 144. *See also* Emigration
African Americans, 3–5, 7–8, 11–18, 20–21, 23, 25–28, 30–31, 33–34, 37–38, 41–43, 46–47, 50–51, 53, 55–57, 59–61, 63, 68–69, 71–86, 88–90, 92–98, 100, 102–13, 118–22, 124–29, 133–47, 150–59, 162, 164–69, 172, 174–76; prophetic tradition, 10–12, 15; religion, 48; rhetoric, 20; soldiers, 73, 79, 84
African Methodist Episcopal Church (AME), 5, 8, 12–13, 35, 47–48, 53, 57, 68, 70, 72, 81–82, 87, 94, 96–97, 99–101, 104, 108, 115, 117, 125, 130–31, 135, 137, 139, 146, 149–50, 157, 159, 166, 172, 175
African Methodist Episcopal Church Zion (AMEZ), 4
Agitative rhetoric, 19
Agyekum, Kofi, 19
Allen, Bishop Richard, 12
Amendments, 26–31, 33–34, 36, 41–42, 67, 89, 94–95, 106, 120–21; Fifteenth, 26, 30–31, 94; Fourteenth, 28–30, 33–34, 36, 95; Platt, 67; Teller, 67; Thirteenth, 27, 89, 120–21
American Colonization Society (ACS), 118–24, 126, 143–44
American exceptionalism, divine mission of America, 13, 50
Angell, Stephen Ward, 47–48, 131, 163
Anti-Black rhetoric, 165; degradation, 24, 35, 55, 70, 79, 98, 104, 108, 129, 133, 146, 157–59, 166–68; idleness, 165; murder, 6, 28, 35, 38, 40, 71, 82–83, 93, 99, 102, 139, 151, 154; shiftless, 165
Arnett, B. W., 116, 149
Astwood, H. C. C., 100, 104
Atlanta Civic League, 164
Azor, 126

Baptists, 57–58, 61–62, 74–75, 89, 160, 176; American Baptist Convention, 58; Black Baptists, 57, 61–62; National Baptist Convention, 57, 75
Batten, J. Minton, 173
Bercovitch, Sacvan, 10
Bibb, Mary, 120. *See also* Women
Bible, 6, 12, 49–50, 52–53, 55, 69, 99–100
Black abstraction, 24–25, 56
Black codes, 27; Jane Crow, 11; Jim Crow, 7, 11, 39, 41, 83, 103, 160, 167, 171–72
Black identity, 20, 145
Black press, 25, 74–75, 99
Black rhetorical theologian, 21, 45–65
Black self-esteem, 145; "believe he is somebody," 157; Black agency, 143, 175; Black pride, 145; self-determination, 145, 176; self-hatred, 168
Blackness, 17, 47, 55, 60, 157, 164; color, 5, 24, 30, 32, 54–58, 60–61, 78, 80–84, 89–90, 100, 122, 124, 130, 136, 138, 144, 156, 162, 166, 174
Blaine, James G., 95
Bradley, H. S., 41

Bradley, Joseph P., 33–34
Bruce, B. K., 129
Brummett, Barry, 9
Bryan, William Jennings (W. J.), 20–21, 86, 88, 101, 103–7
Burroughs, Nannie H., 75. *See also* Women
Burton, Orvil Vernon, 29–30

Campbell, Samuel, 131
Campbell, Tunis, 90–91
Carey, Mary Ann Shad, 120. *See also* Women
Christianity, 4, 8, 30, 32–34, 37, 45–51, 62, 68, 70, 72, 74, 77, 87, 91, 96–100, 113, 116–17, 119, 121, 124, 127, 131, 139, 146, 152–55, 163, 173
Citizens, 27, 37, 74–75, 77, 92, 96, 100, 102, 140; Black citizens, 27, 103; colored citizens, 57, 77, 92, 102, 161; of the United States, 27, 29–30, 42, 126, 162
Citizenship, 5, 27, 29–31, 34–37, 74, 89, 93, 102, 157, 172; right of, 30, 93, 102
Civil rights, 26–29, 31–36, 41–42, 73, 93, 98, 101, 112–13, 135, 157, 176
Civil Rights Acts, 26–29, 31–33, 35–36, 42, 157
Civil War, 8, 12, 21, 23, 27, 30, 49, 65, 68, 72–73, 76, 78, 81, 85, 89, 109, 112, 120, 145, 150–51, 167–68; Negro regiments, 69, 83; rhetoric, 68; Union cause, 8
Civility, 5
Civilization gap, 143
Clement, William, 100
Clergy: bishops, 20, 48, 54, 99, 104, 109, 111, 113, 115–17, 130, 149; deacons, 30, 109, 131; elders, 48, 54, 109, 116; ministers, 10, 35, 48, 52–55, 80–82, 85, 108, 116–17, 125, 127, 130, 150, 164–66
Coates, Ta-Nehisi, 17
Cole, Jean Lee, 72. *See also* Women
Colenso, John William, 49
Colonization, 73, 84–85, 118–19, 121–23, 126, 128, 142–43
Colonization Society, 73, 118–19, 122–23, 126, 128, 142–43
Colored Co-Operative Civic League, 164
Colored Conventions Movement, 88–90
Colored Methodist Episcopal Church (CME), 4
Cone, James, 146, 174

Confederacy: sympathizer, 91; state rights, 35
Cook, Anthony, 167
Cook, William D., 104
Cooper, A. Benjamin, 139
Coppinger, William, 122
Creation, 21, 26, 55–56, 60, 67–86, 112, 128, 164; hierarchy in the cosmos, 60; origins of, 60
Cromley, Robert, 30
Crummell, Alexander, 120–21
Cuffe, Paul, 119
Culp, D. W., 3–4
Cummings, Melbourne, 142, 145. *See also* Women
Cunningham, David, 62
Cushing's Manual, 89

Darsey, James, 8
Davis, Jefferson, 69, 166
Davis, Rev. Robert, 116–17
Delany, Martin R., 120, 142
Democratic Congress, 95
Democrats/Democratic Party, 25, 40, 86, 94–95, 97–98, 101–3, 105–11, 113, 125, 161, 175
"Devil is white," 156
Doctrine, 46–49, 52, 54–55, 62–63
Donald, Bernice, 28–29. *See also* Women
Dorrien, Gary, 173
Douglass, Frederick, 18, 20, 57, 120, 122–23
Dred Scott decision, 35–36
Du Bois, W. E. B., 11, 20, 145–46, 160, 173, 176

Emancipation, 4, 12–13, 20, 27, 50, 65, 69, 85–87, 89, 112, 121, 145, 152, 168
Emancipation Proclamation, 27, 69, 152, 168
Embry, James C., 47
Emigration: African, 111, 117–18, 121, 123, 125, 134; Colored National Emigration Association, 134–35; National Emigration Convention, 120; proto-emigration, 118
Equality, 5, 13, 25, 32–33, 40, 85, 88, 95, 153, 159, 169, 172
Ethics of slavery, 49

Filipinos, 68, 81, 83–85
Flag, 21, 75, 77, 81–83, 95, 137, 160–66, 169; American, 160, 166

Index

Franklin, John Hope, 173
Frazier, E. Franklin, 173
Freedmen's Bureau, 30, 153
Freedmen's Convention, 89
Freedom, 8–9, 11–13, 25, 27, 30, 32, 36–38, 50, 64, 69, 71, 81, 85, 89, 95, 102, 106–9, 121, 133, 143, 145, 152–53, 168
Freedom's Prophet, 12

Gaines, W. J., 100, 117, 149
Garfield, James, 98, 155
Garnet, Henry Highland, 120
Garvey, Marcus, 142, 176
Genesis, 49, 60
Georgia Equal Rights Convention (GERC), 160
Gibson, John, 38
God: Black, 58; "God is a Negro," 21, 47–48, 57–61, 63–64, 146; God-talk, 47, 59, 61; male, 29, 60; rhetorically constructed, 24, 64; white, 58, 60, 130
Government: Congress, 8, 27–33, 36, 40, 42, 76, 84, 88, 90, 93, 95, 97, 102, 107, 111, 125, 134, 138–39, 141, 153, 165: conservative, 4, 33, 35, 88, 91–92, 94–95, 125; General Assembly, 94; House of Representatives, 13, 92, 153; legislature, 8, 13, 29, 88, 90, 92–93, 107, 112, 125, 137, 140, 166
Grant, Abram, 115–16
Grant, Ulysses S., 33, 37, 98
Greer, Hannah, 131
Griffith, A. D. (Adolphus), 61

Hancock, Winfield S., 155
Harlan, John M., 25, 34, 36, 38–40, 99
Heard, William H., 6–7, 14, 18, 135, 139, 142
Hegemonic tradition/interpretation, 16, 47
Hendricks, Thomas H., 95
Hermeneutical framework, 64
Hermeneutics, 47
Higginbotham, Evelyn Brooks, 176. *See also* Women
Higginbotham, F. Michael, 27
Holsey, L. H., 4–5
Hood, J. W., 4
Howard-Pitney, David, 10
Hughes, Sarah A., 53. *See also* Women

Humans/humanity, 5, 7, 16–17, 25, 36–37, 46, 50, 55, 57–59, 69, 81, 84, 102, 107, 123, 134, 146, 150–51, 156–57, 167, 176; humanity of Africans, 55

Identity, 10, 15, 20, 64, 143, 145, 175
Immigration, 13
Inferiority, 13, 24, 43, 61, 84–85, 130, 135, 145, 156, 162–63; complex, 61, 145
Intermarriage, 155
International Migration Society, 118

Jeremiad, 9–12, 18, 69
Jesus Christ, 60, 62, 128
Johnson, Henry Lincoln, 173
Johnson, Henry Theodore (H. T.), 54–55

Kendi, Ibram X., 20
King, Martin Luther, Jr., 167, 176
Ku Klux Klan, night marauders, 31, 154

Lament/lamentation, 5, 7, 9, 14–16, 18, 20, 25, 33, 35, 37, 39, 40, 43, 48, 52, 58, 61, 79–80, 91, 97, 116, 129, 141, 144, 153, 155–56, 162, 166, 173–75; public lamentation, 18
Language: boisterous, 72; bombastic, 72, 166; grammar, 73, 176; hyperbole, 72, 164; syllables, 72
Lash, Kurt, 29
Liberia, 7, 118, 120–21, 126, 131–32, 138, 143
Liberian Colonization Society, 118
Liberty, 21, 29, 52, 67, 71, 74, 76, 82–84, 92, 109, 118, 126, 135, 152, 159, 162
Lincoln, Abraham, 8, 69, 95, 98, 112, 152, 168
Logan, Rayford, 173
Lomas, Charles W., 142
Lovinggood, R. S., 4
Lynching, 6, 18, 40, 57–58, 75, 79–81, 83–86, 99–101, 103, 105–7, 110–11, 128, 155–56, 160, 166, 172; disenfranchisement, 106, 164; hanging, 32–33, 52, 156; mob rule, 107

Malcolm X, 41, 157, 176
Mays, Benjamin, 43
McEdwards, Mary, 19. *See also* Women
McKinley, William, 21, 67–68, 81, 84, 86–87, 101–2, 104–13

McPherson, James M., 173
Memphis Massacre, 28–29
Methodist Church, 8
Methodist Polity, 47
Military
—British Army, 119
—Black Loyalists, 119
—Unites States Colored Troops: African Americans should support the war effort, 77; Colored Military, 76; fight the enlistment of colored men, 82; First Regiment, 8, 72; Scullionized Negroes, 83
Moore, Morris Marcellus, 115
Morehouse, Henry Lyman, 58

Nation of Islam, 157
National Negro Party, 100
Native Americans, 17, 29
Negroes: in America, 111; Negro hating, 23, 39, 98; Negro office holders, 108; Negro problem, 51; Negro question, 51, 124
New Israel, 9–11
Newspapers, 8, 25, 75, 81, 86, 99, 103, 108, 136, 138, 160–63, 165, 173; *Abbeville Press and Banner*, 99; *African Letters*, 131; *Albany News*, 56; *AME Church Review*, 157; *AME Journal Review*, 97; *AME Review*, 172; *Atlanta Constitution*, 50, 137, 157, 161; *Atlanta Independent*, 163, 173; *Atlanta Journal*, 105; *Baltimore American*, 156; *Bamberg Herald*, 161; *Brooklyn Defender*, 104; *Cairo Bulletin*, 161; *Chattanooga Times*, 38; *Chicago Daily Tribune*, 158, 171; *Christian Recorder*, 8, 30, 32–34, 45, 48–50, 70, 72, 91, 96–98, 113, 116–17, 121, 127, 131, 152–55, 173; *Cleveland Gazette*, 40, 74, 102; *Coffeyville American*, 75, 86; *Colored American*, 113, 136; *Colored Tribune*, 154; *Daily Capital Journal*, 61; *Galveston Daily News*, 56; *Gazette*, 102; *Grenada Sentinel*, 57; *Hartford Courant*, 138–39; *Hattiesburg Daily Progress*, 138; *Herald*, 86; *Independent*, 159, 163; *Indianapolis Freeman*, 26, 132; *Iowa State Bystander*, 75, 86, 105; *Lancaster News*, 161; *Louisiana Democrat*, 25; *Loyal Georgian*, 90; *Memphis Daily Appeal*, 34, 129; *Montana Plaindealer*, 163; *National Baptist Magazine*, 74; *New Orleans Christian Advocate*, 155; *New Orleans Daily Picayune*, 25; *New York Age*, 35; *New York Mail and Express*, 99; *New York Times*, 45, 53, 99, 101, 156, 160; *New York Tribune*, 140; *Omaha Daily Bee*, 57; *Recorder*, 45, 90–91, 94–95, 127–29, 156–57; *Richmond Planet*, 61, 163; *Richmond Times-Dispatch*, 163; *Roanoke Times*, 99; *Salt Lake City Broad Ax*, 86, 99; *Salt Lake Herald*, 161; *Savannah Colored Tribune*, 124–25; *Savannah Courier*, 56; *Savannah Morning News*, 41, 110; *Sea Coast Echo*, 56; *Seattle Republican*, 103, 138; *Southern Christian Recorder*, 139; *St. Joseph (Missouri) Radical*, 75; *St. Paul Appeal*, 163; *Tallahassee Weekly True Democrat*, 161; *Voice of Missions*, 39, 41, 47, 58, 64, 99, 101, 105, 108, 110–11, 117, 134, 136; *Voice of the People*, 113, 117, 135–36, 138; *Washington Bee*, 75–76; *Washington Post*, 121, 158; *Washington Times*, 136; *Wenatchee Daily World*, 161; *Wilmington Semi-weekly Messenger*, 99; *Wisconsin Weekly Advocate*, 75; *York Sun*, 45. See also Black press
Niagara Movement, 160

Oppression, 4, 14, 18, 26, 31, 49, 50, 56, 77, 79, 85, 86, 92, 118, 120, 134, 138, 162
Ordination, 8, 10, 53–54, 131, 150
Ottley, G. W., 121, 129, 155

Peacher, Eliza Ann, 8. See also Women
Persuasion, 47, 62–63, 69, 75, 143
Pessimism: Afro-pessimism, 16, 176; aggressive pessimism, 16
Pessimistic prophecy, 15, 18, 42, 171
Philippines, 67–68, 75, 80–81, 83–85, 174
Plessy v. Ferguson, 12, 21, 23–43, 45–46, 112
Political rights, 77, 83, 92–93, 100, 112, 122, 138
Politicians, 43, 89
Politics: of Reconstruction, 8, 13, 89, 96; white against Black, 109
Preaching, 7, 30, 48, 52–53; exhortation, 10, 52, 73, 76

Presidents, 8, 27, 33, 39, 67, 69, 72–73, 75–76, 81, 86, 88, 90, 93–94, 97–98, 101, 104–5, 108–9, 115–17, 122–25, 127, 135–37, 139, 142, 144, 152, 163, 165
Prophesying Daughters, 11. *See also* Women
Prophetic identities: pragmatic prophetic persona, 13; prophetic tradition, 8–12, 19
Providence (divine; of God), 49, 50, 88, 97, 149
Pulpit, 47, 52–53, 70, 104, 130
Puritans, 10–11
Purvis, Robert, 122

Qualls, Benjamin, 173

Race, 3–4, 7, 11–12, 17, 21, 23–25, 30, 32–33, 35, 37–38, 40–41, 51, 53, 57–59, 61, 64, 71–72, 75, 77, 79–82, 85, 88, 90, 96–100, 103, 105–9, 111–12, 117, 120, 124–25, 127–29, 135, 137–41, 145, 149, 151–52, 155–59, 161–67, 169, 171–75
Racism, 16–17, 30, 57, 61, 64, 85, 112, 120, 151, 155, 158, 163, 164, 168, 175
Railroads, 36–37, 45, 100
Ransom, Reverdy, 172
Reconstruction: post-Reconstruction, 95, 118; Reconstruction Acts, 29–30, 94; Reconstruction project, 31, 91
Redkey, Edwin, 130, 141
Reparations, 133–34
Republicans/Republican Party, 21, 30, 32–33, 41, 88, 92, 95–97, 99, 101–2, 104, 106–7, 109–13; national convention, 95; Union Republican Congressional Committee, 90
Revelation, 9, 12, 46, 49, 56
Revels, Willis H., 8
Rhetoric
—agitative, 19
—antiwar, 21, 68, 84–85
—apocalyptic, 9, 18
—Black, 165
—prophetic, 8–10, 12–15, 18, 113; celebratory prophecy, 15; disputation prophecy, 15; mission-oriented prophecy, 15, 133; prophetic disputation, 15
—rhetorical discourse, 146

—rhetorical history, 14, 21
—war, 68, 84
Roosevelt, Theodore, 136–37, 163–65

Sabbath Day, as Holy Day, 51, 71
Science, 7, 48, 51, 55–56, 128, 156; fossil records, 55; geology, 55–56
Segregation, 21, 24, 27, 46, 87, 164
"Separate but equal," 12, 24, 43, 112
Sermons, 8, 47, 52, 76, 162
Seward, William, 29
Seymour, R., 137
Shaffer, C. T., 115
Sims-Alvarado, Falechiondro Karcheik, 118–20
Slaveocentrism, 143
Slavery/slaves, 17, 27, 36, 38, 49–51, 69, 73, 87, 96, 109, 120, 140; divine, 9–13, 15, 46, 48–51, 53–54, 128, 133–34, 143, 171; extermination, 135, 140; Fugitive Slave Law, 120; and God, 49–50; providential, 50–51, 128, 171; reenslavement, 27, 140; transatlantic slave trade, 120
Smith, Charles (Charley), 38
Smith, Craig, 84
Smith, Hoke, 164
Spanish-American War, 74, 76, 78, 80; African Americans in, 72, 74, 81: Cuba/Cubans, 67, 74, 76–80, 82, 85, 135, 138, 159; "Spain knew no color," 78
Spiritualism, 54
Steward, Theophilus G., 47
Stone, Anthony J., 9, 167
Suffrage, 29–30, 89, 102, 112
Sumner, Charles, 32, 50
Supreme Court: justices, 5, 7, 13, 21, 24–25, 31, 33–34, 36–40, 49–50, 85, 92, 94–95, 97, 99, 122, 127, 134–35, 174 (*see also* Harlan, John M.); state court, 38

Tanner, Benjamin, 18, 47, 50, 127–28, 161
Terrill, Robert E., 41–42
Theology, 7, 20–21, 46–48, 52–53, 55, 62–63, 146, 174; Black, 21, 146, 174; Christian, 46, 48, 62; rhetorical, 21, 47, 55, 62–63; systematic, 47–48
Tilden, Samuel J., 95

Trinity: The Father, 20, 53, 62, 64; Holy Ghost (Holy Spirit; Spirit of God), 52–54, 132, 144; Jesus Christ, 60, 62, 128
Turner, Kathleen J., 15

US Constitution, 38, 100

Violence: anti-Black, 17, 164–65; race riot, 164
Voting and voters, 13, 29, 30, 32, 36–37, 58, 91–92, 95, 97, 101–2, 104, 106–10, 113, 119, 124, 164, 174–75; electoral vote, 72, 88–89, 95–96, 98–99; Federal Elections bill, 97; poll tax, 91; white man, 4–5, 25–26, 33, 50, 56, 58–62, 73, 81–83, 85, 96, 98, 107–9, 120, 124, 129–30, 137–38, 141, 154, 159–61, 163, 171

Wakefield, Samuel, 48
Washington, Booker T., 18, 86, 136–37, 160, 163
Wayman, Bishop A. W., 101, 159–60
Wayman, Harriet A., 101, 159. *See also* Women
West, Cornel, 16, 175
Wheeler, William, 95
White, G. Edward, 27
White, William J., 160
White nationalism, 147, 169
White people, 3, 5, 13, 17, 25, 32, 39, 43, 54, 57, 59, 61, 82, 121–22, 131, 136, 140, 144, 151, 155, 157–59, 162–65, 169
White superiority, 164
White supremacy, 17, 61, 132, 147, 174–75
Wilson, Kirt, 26–27
Women, 3, 11, 17, 29–30, 39, 53–54, 74–75, 79–81, 98, 107, 111, 135, 140, 153, 156, 174–76; divine call to ministry, 53
Woodson, Carter G., 173

X, Malcolm, 41, 157, 176

Zaresky, David, 14

ABOUT THE AUTHOR

Photo credit: University of Memphis

Andre E. Johnson is associate professor of rhetoric and media studies at the University of Memphis. He is director of the Henry McNeal Turner Project, a digital humanities project curating the writings of Bishop Henry McNeal Turner.

Printed in the United States
By Bookmasters